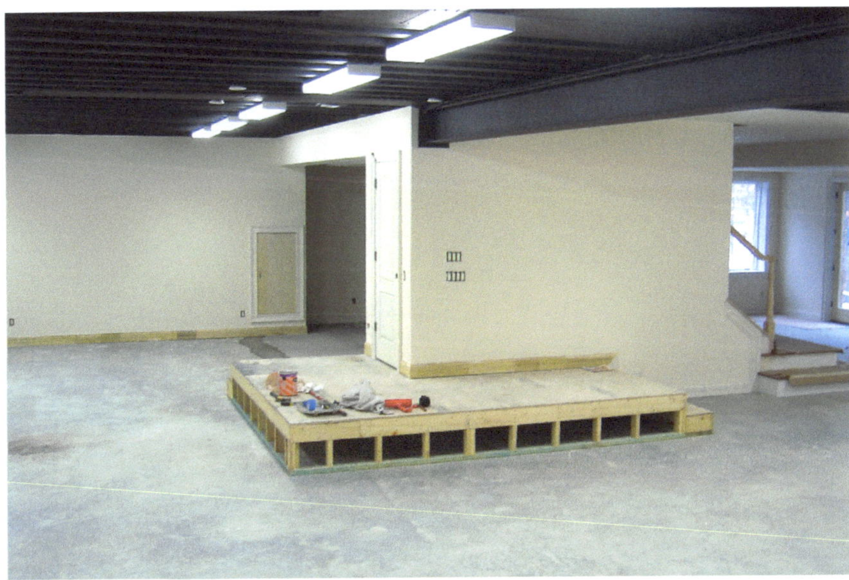

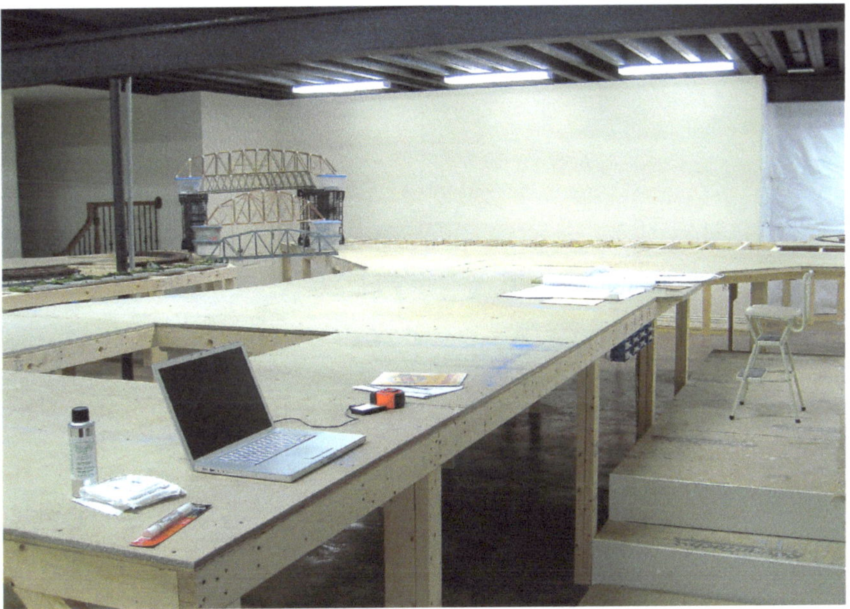

The Beginning...

The construction of the train layout in this book started in 2008 and was completed in 2015. This 2,000 square foot layout was built with two-by-fours, half-inch plywood, homasote, cork roadbed, GarGraves track, and Ross switches. The layout is wired to operate with the MTH Digital Command System or via conventional transformer control.

Photos show the elevated observation and control platform. The ceiling is painted black to hide the ceiling and house mechanicals. There are three lighting systems for the layout. I have fluorescent lights for general lighting and work, track lighting for dramatic evening and nighttime lighting and a third system of track lights focused on the walls for the sky lighting effects.

I built this layout to entertain me, my grandchildren, and my friends. I hope you enjoy this layout tour!

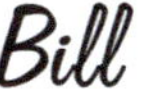
Bill

The Beginning...

The background sky was created with a can of white spray paint and New London Industries Cloud Stencils. An article about how to do this appeared in *O Gauge Railroading* magazine (ogaugerr.com) in Run 244, the August/September 2010 issue.

Four interconnecting track systems snake around the layout over many bridges and trestles. The maximum grade on the layout is 2%.

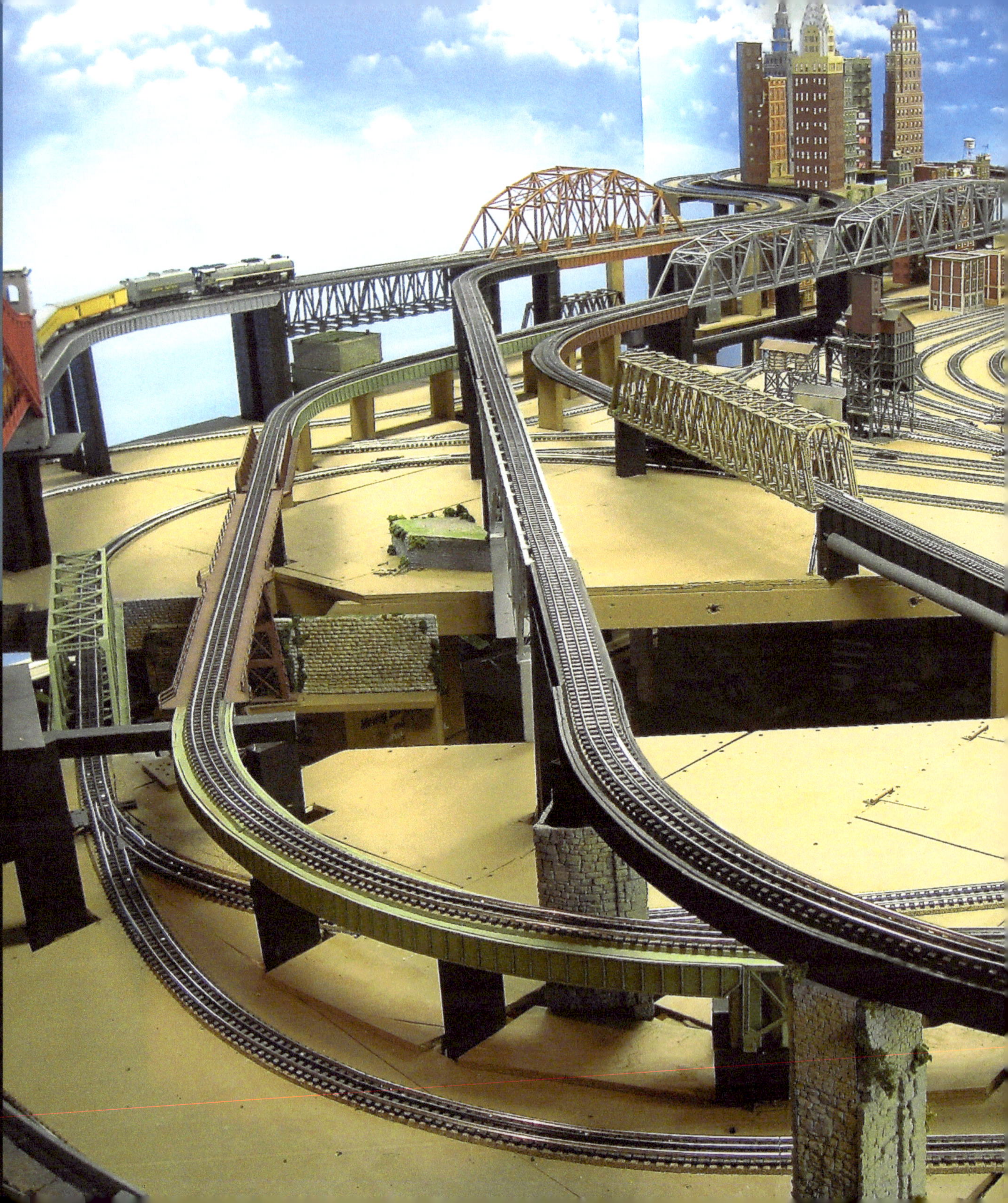

The Track Plan

Four main lines, two trolley lines and one elevated subway line make up the tracks which run around this layout. All the tracks pass through or under Tower City.

The upper photo at right shows the various tracks on multiple levels in a view of Tower City while it was under construction.

The bottom photo shows Tower City fully completed and ready for visitors to enjoy.

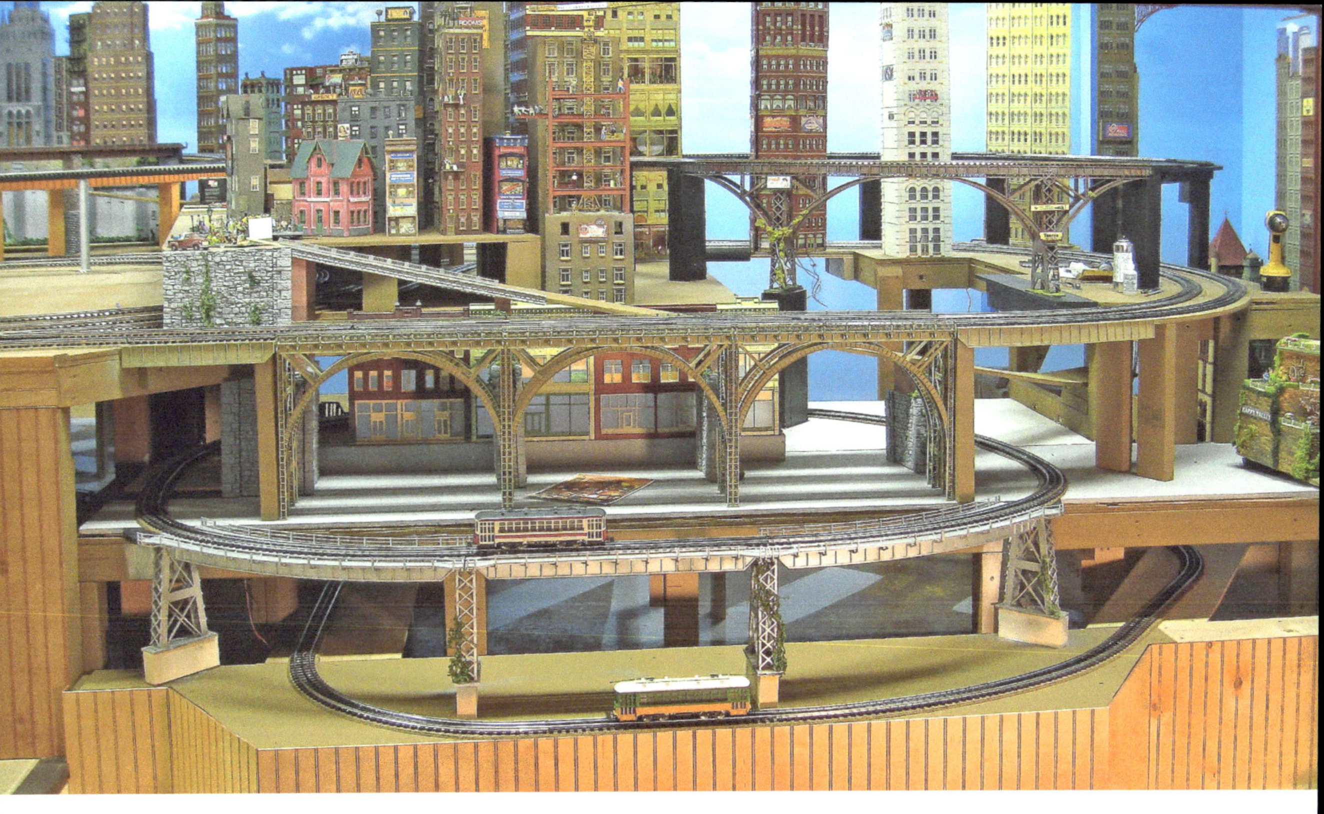

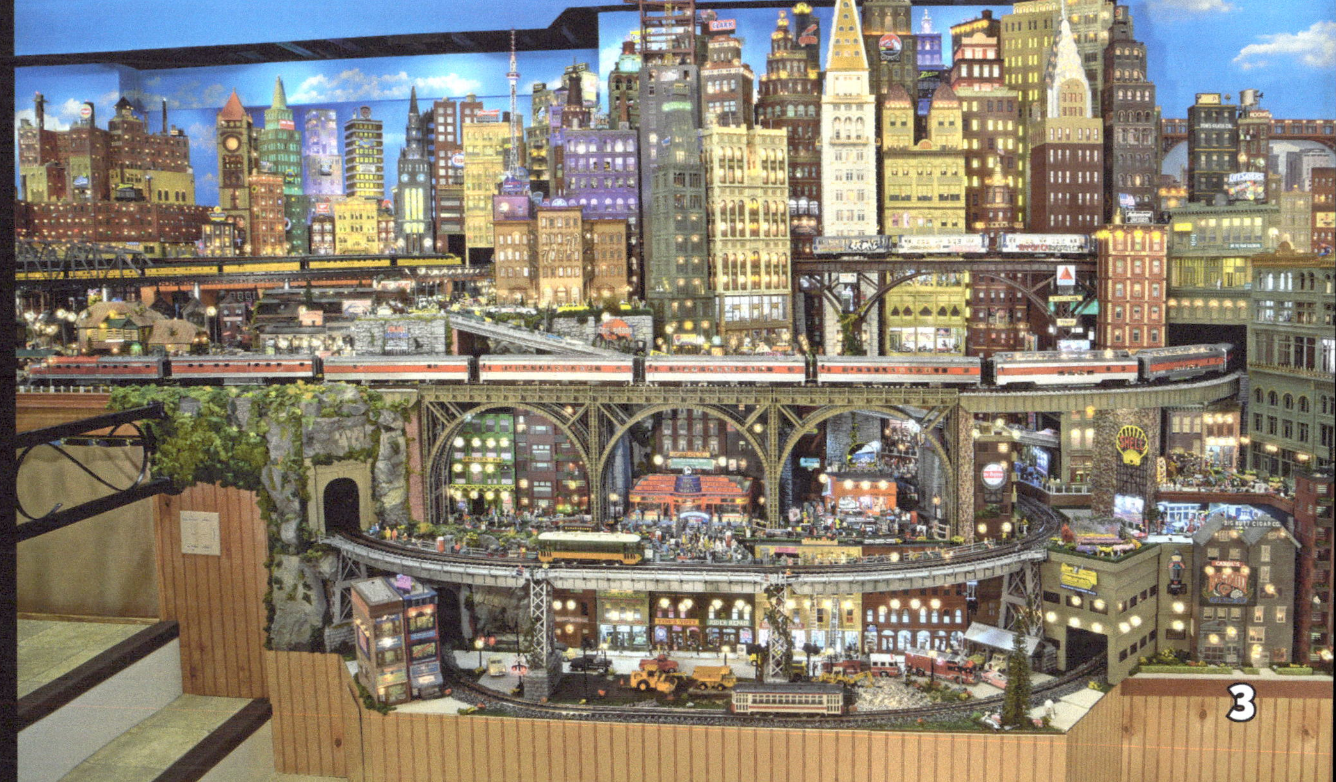

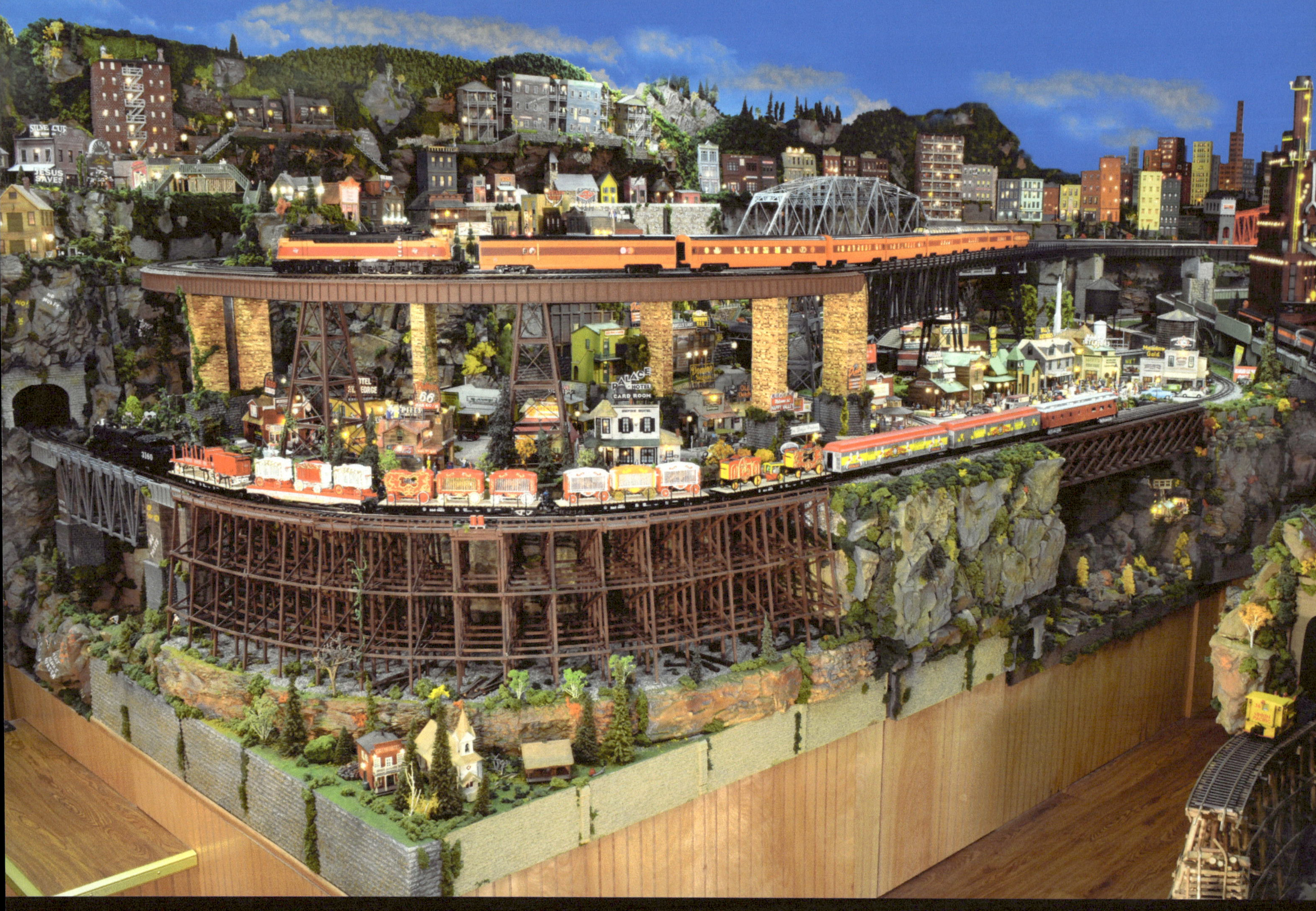

WELCOME TO MY TRAIN WORLD!

This 3-rail, O gauge display layout is filled with details, figures and scenes.
Trains travel over multiple bridges and trestles, while thousands of lights illuminate the layout.

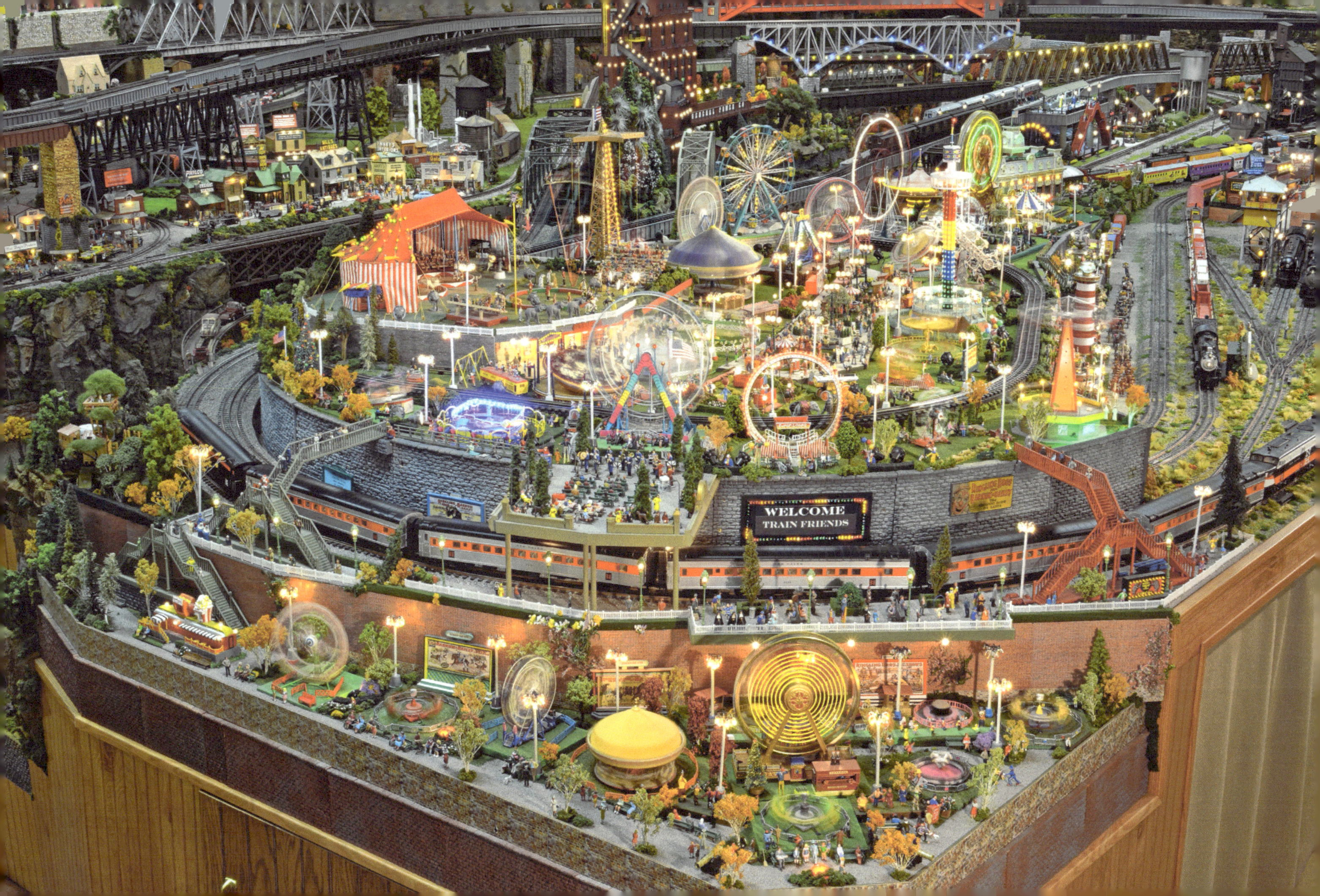

WELCOME
TRAIN FRIENDS

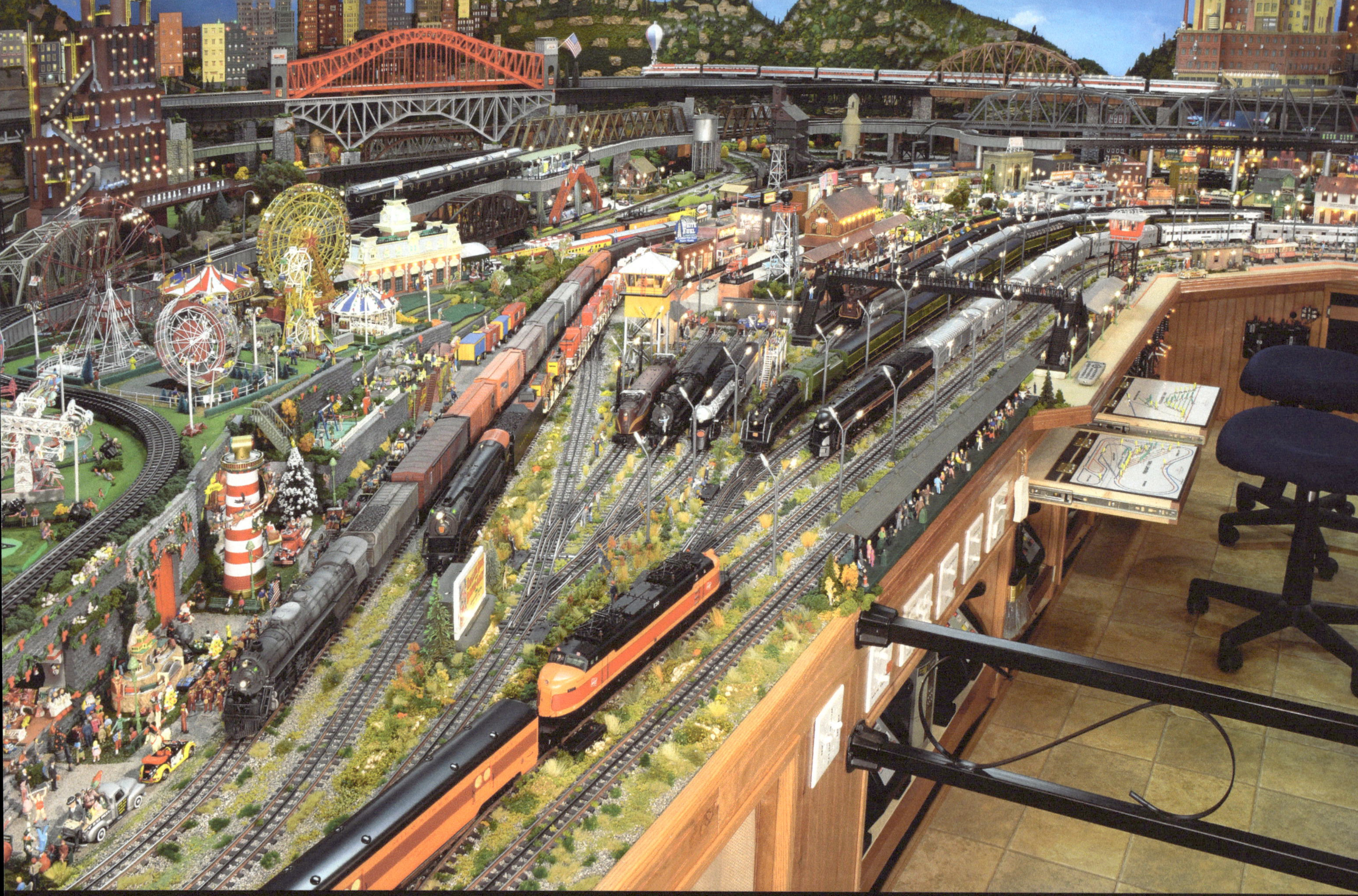

The 7-Track Passenger Yard and Engine Tracks

The elevated operating platform has pullout control panels for the track and switches. All the trains on the layout are easy to see from this elevated platform.

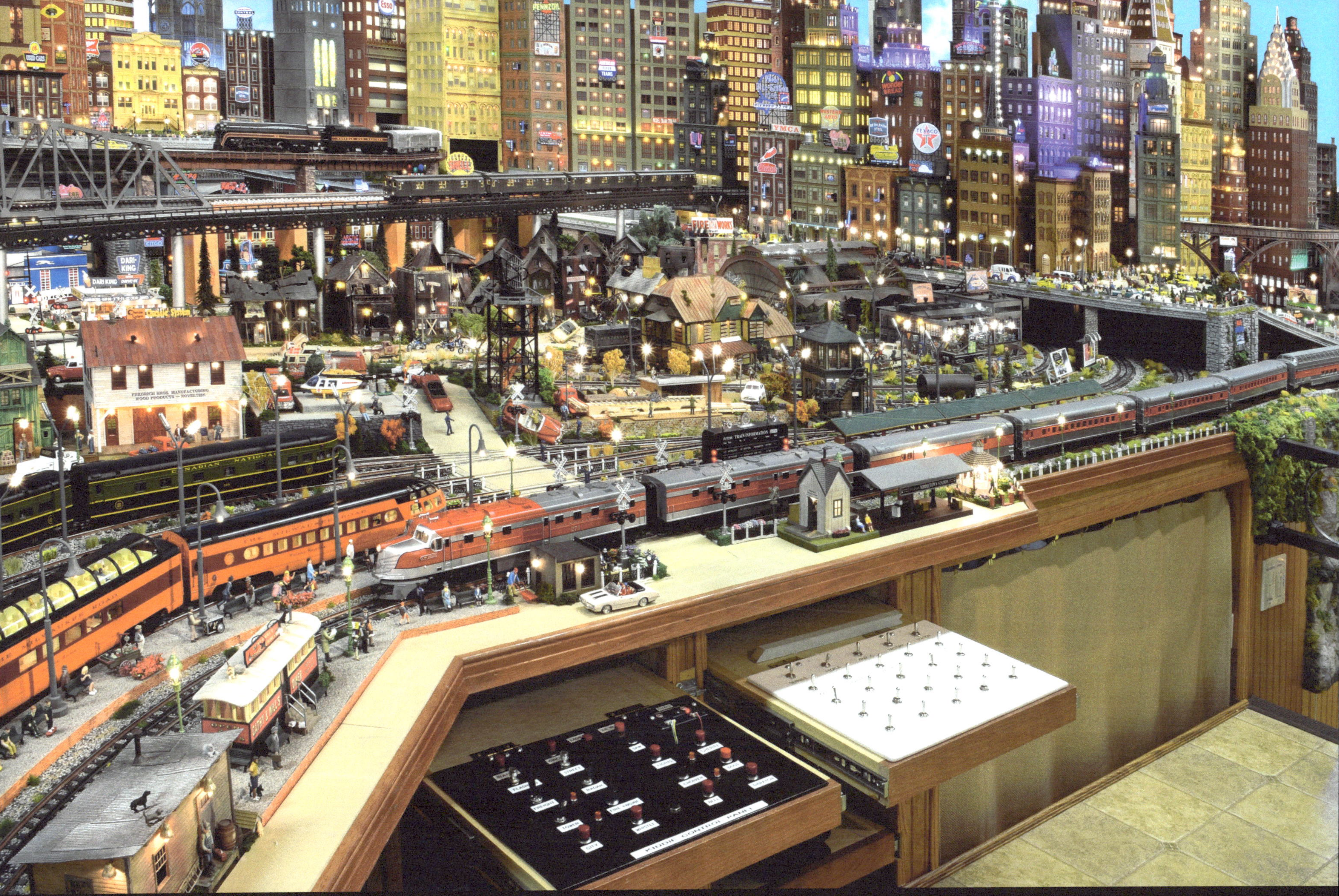

The View from the Right Side of the Operating Platform

These pull-out panels are for both children and adults to operate accessories and other layout features. In fact, that black panel with the red buttons is called the "Kiddie Panel." That's Tower City in the background!

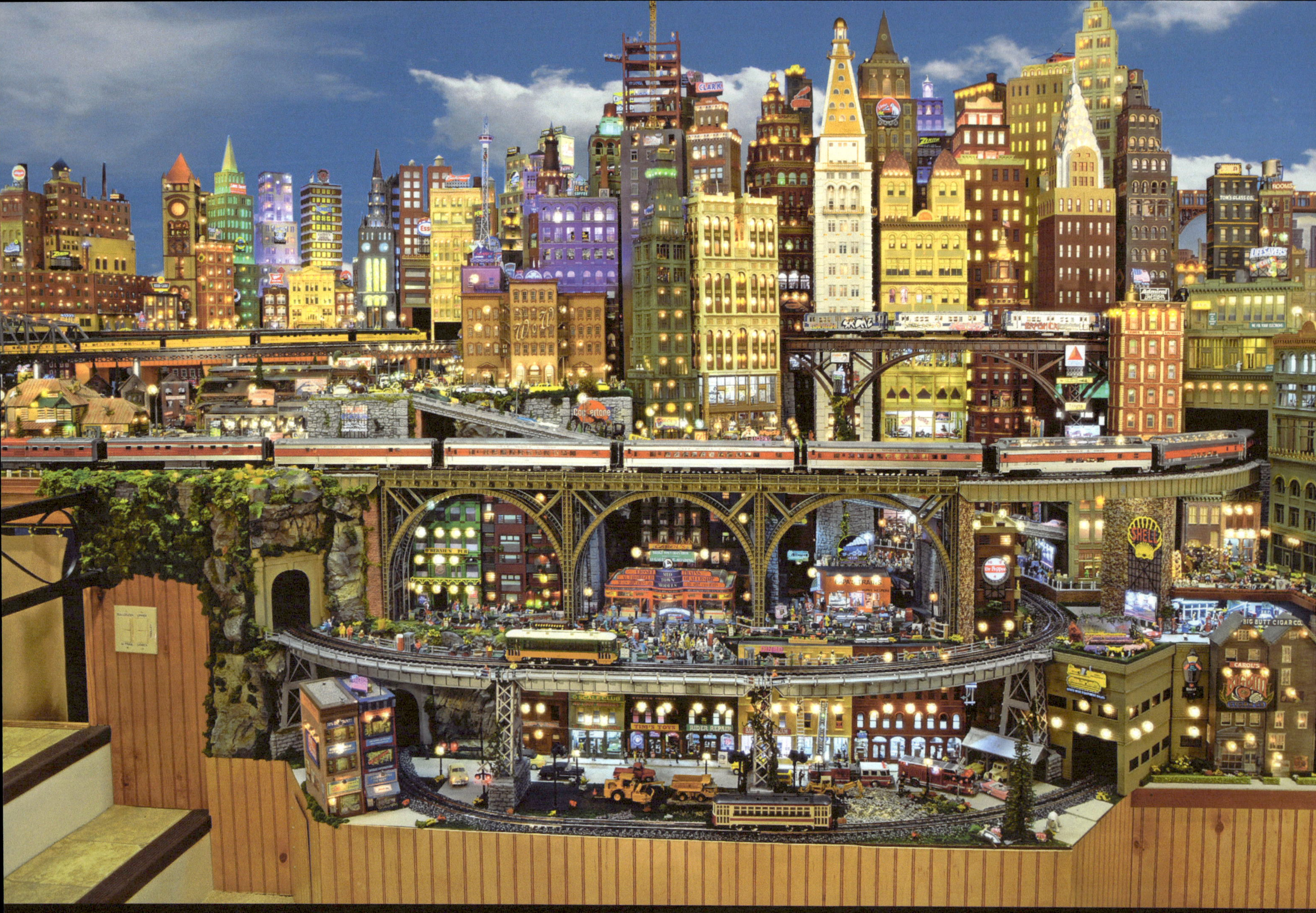

A Full View of Tower City

Tower City is 24 feet wide and 14 feet deep. The ceiling is 10 feet high, and some of the buildings almost touch the celling! All of these buildings are 1/4-inch scale.

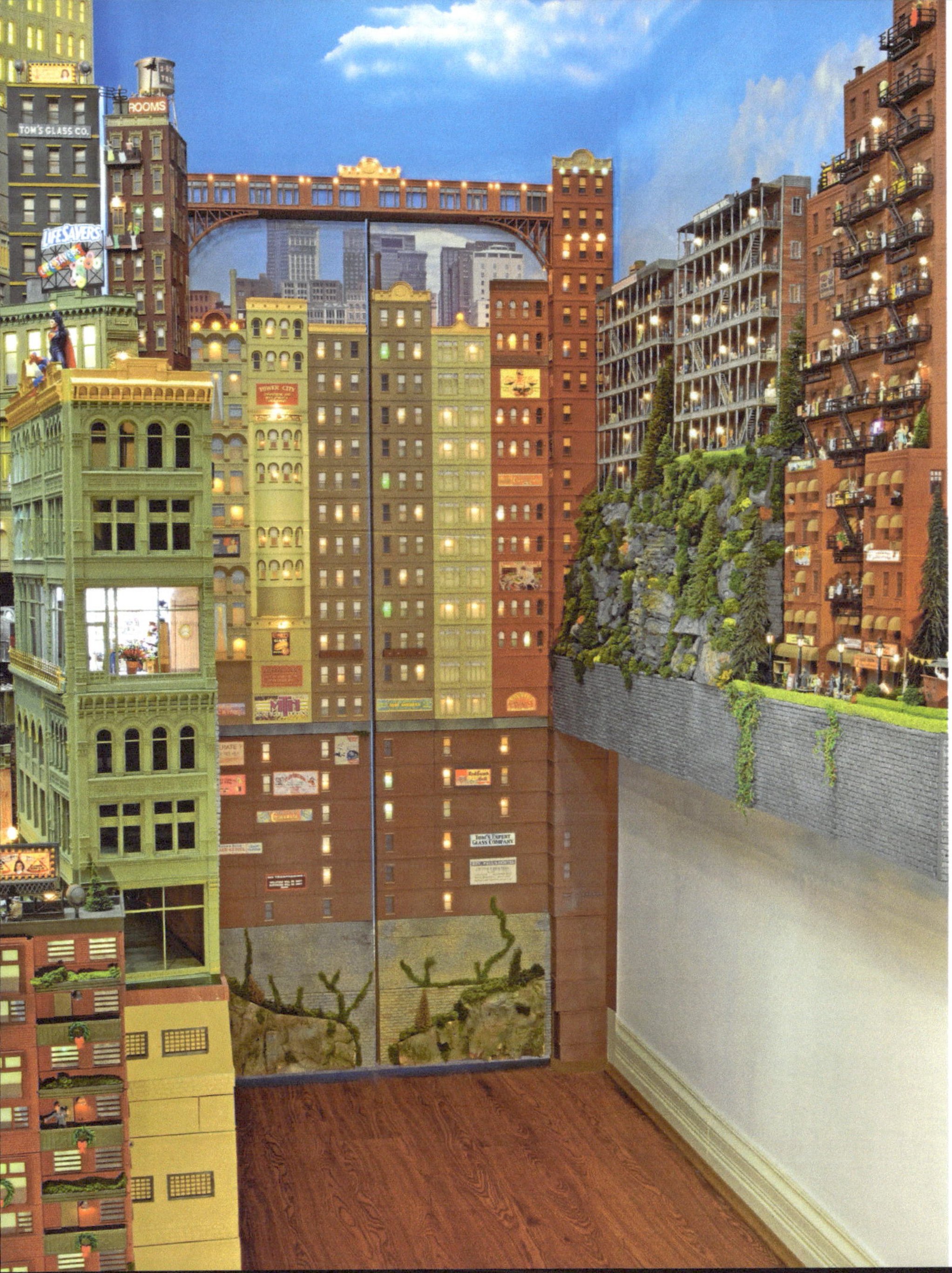

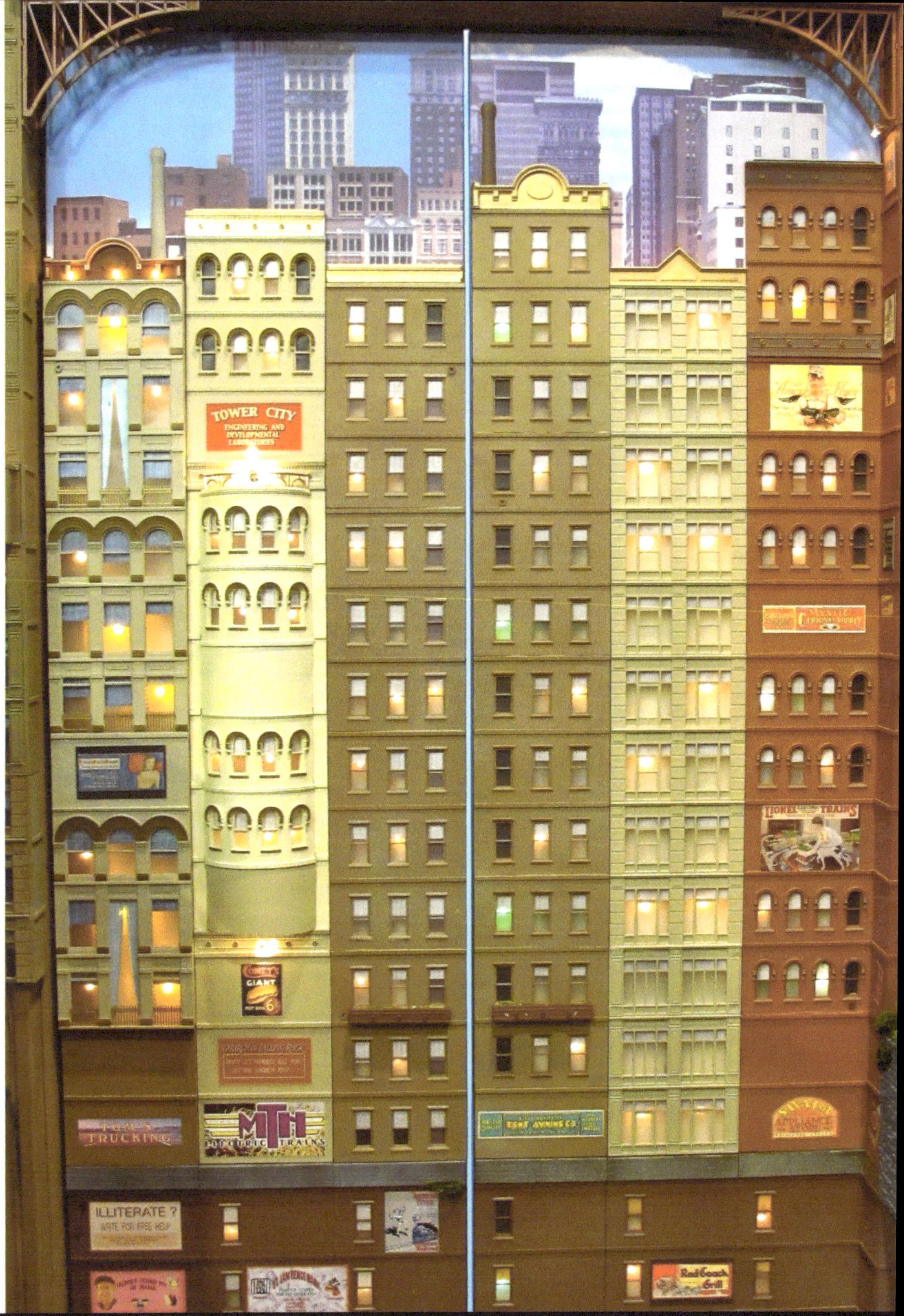

The City Doors

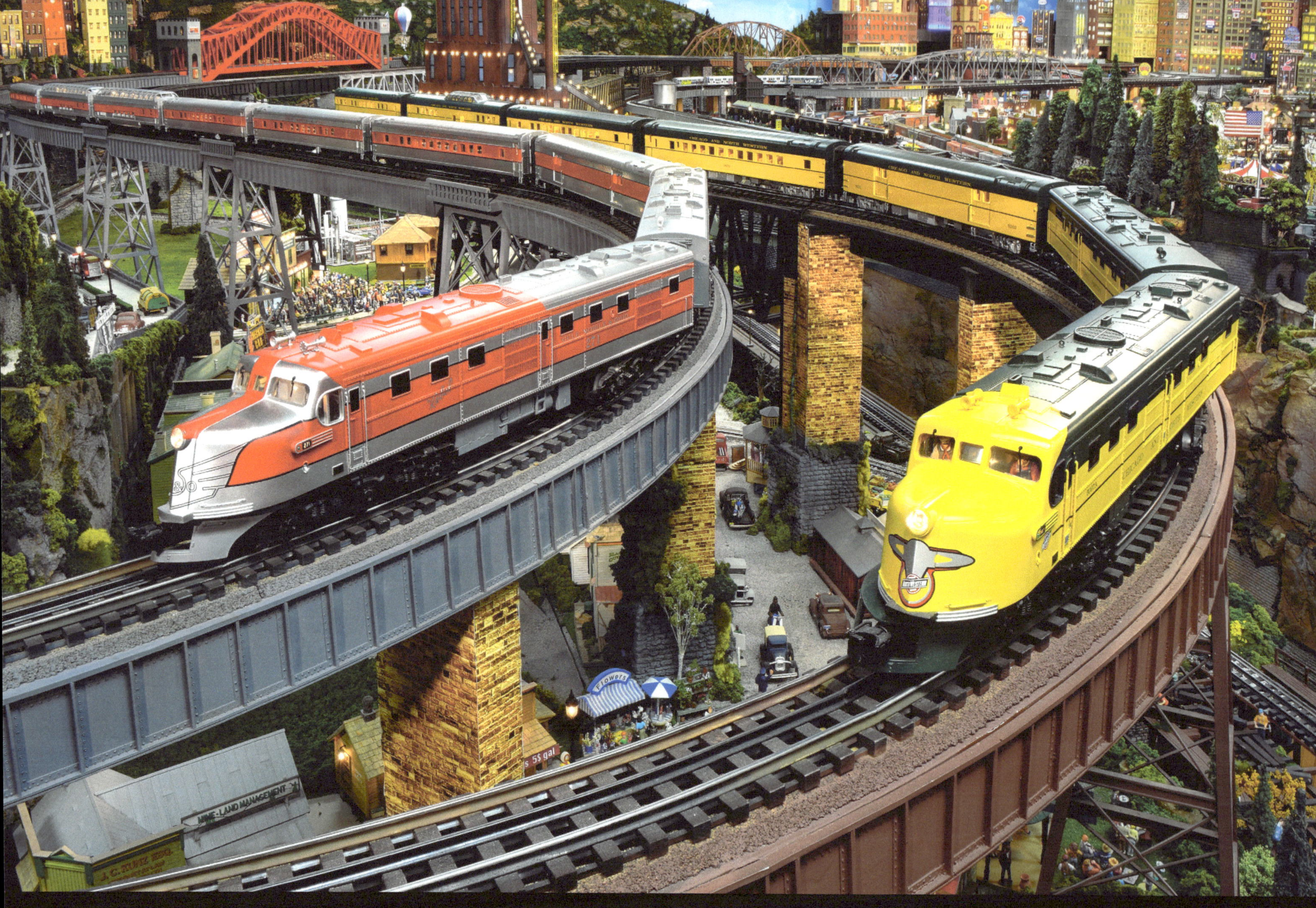

Elevated Tracks

The trains run over many elevated tracks and trestles. This makes the trains easy to run and enhances the visual experience for everyone who visits the layout...especially children!

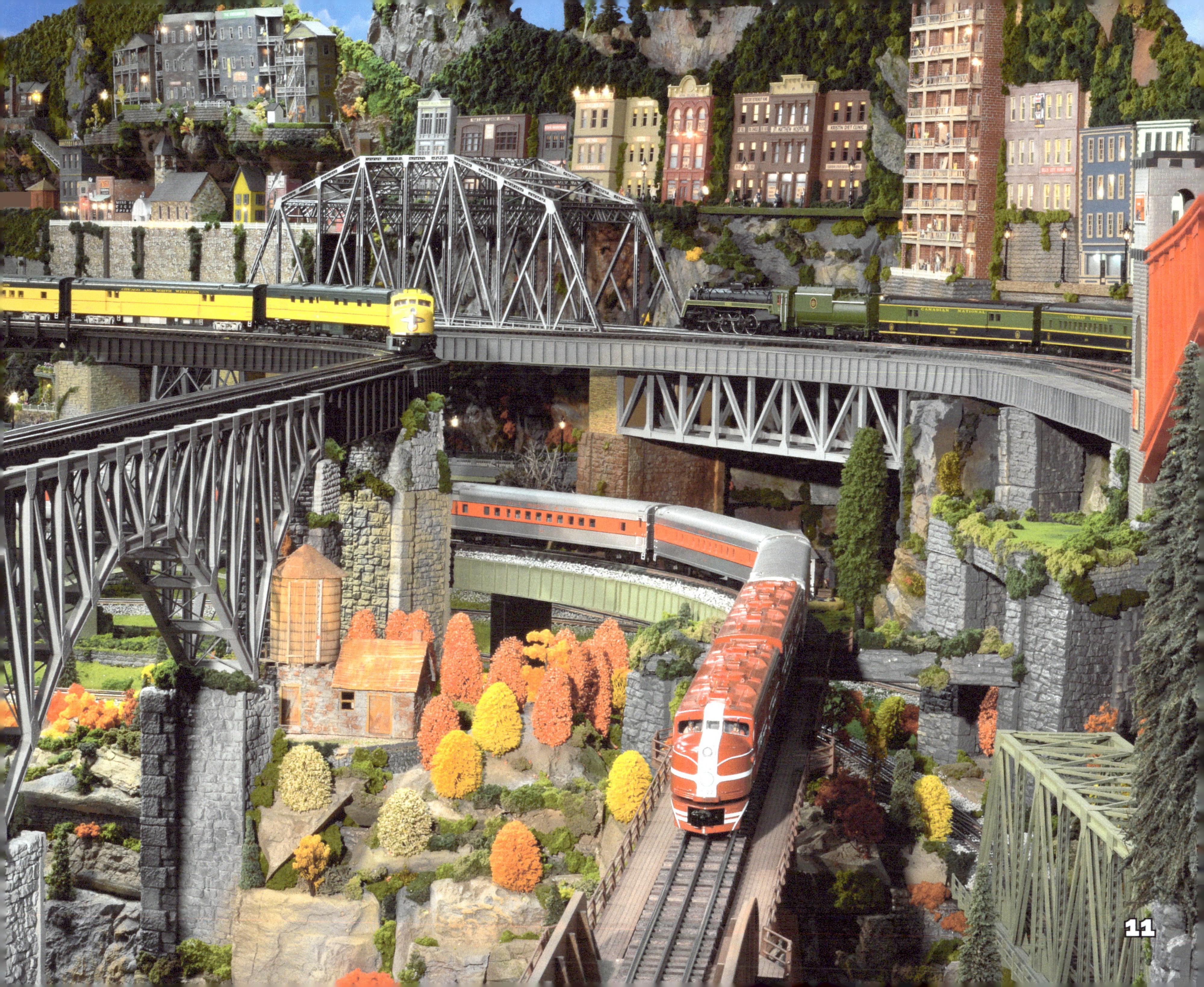

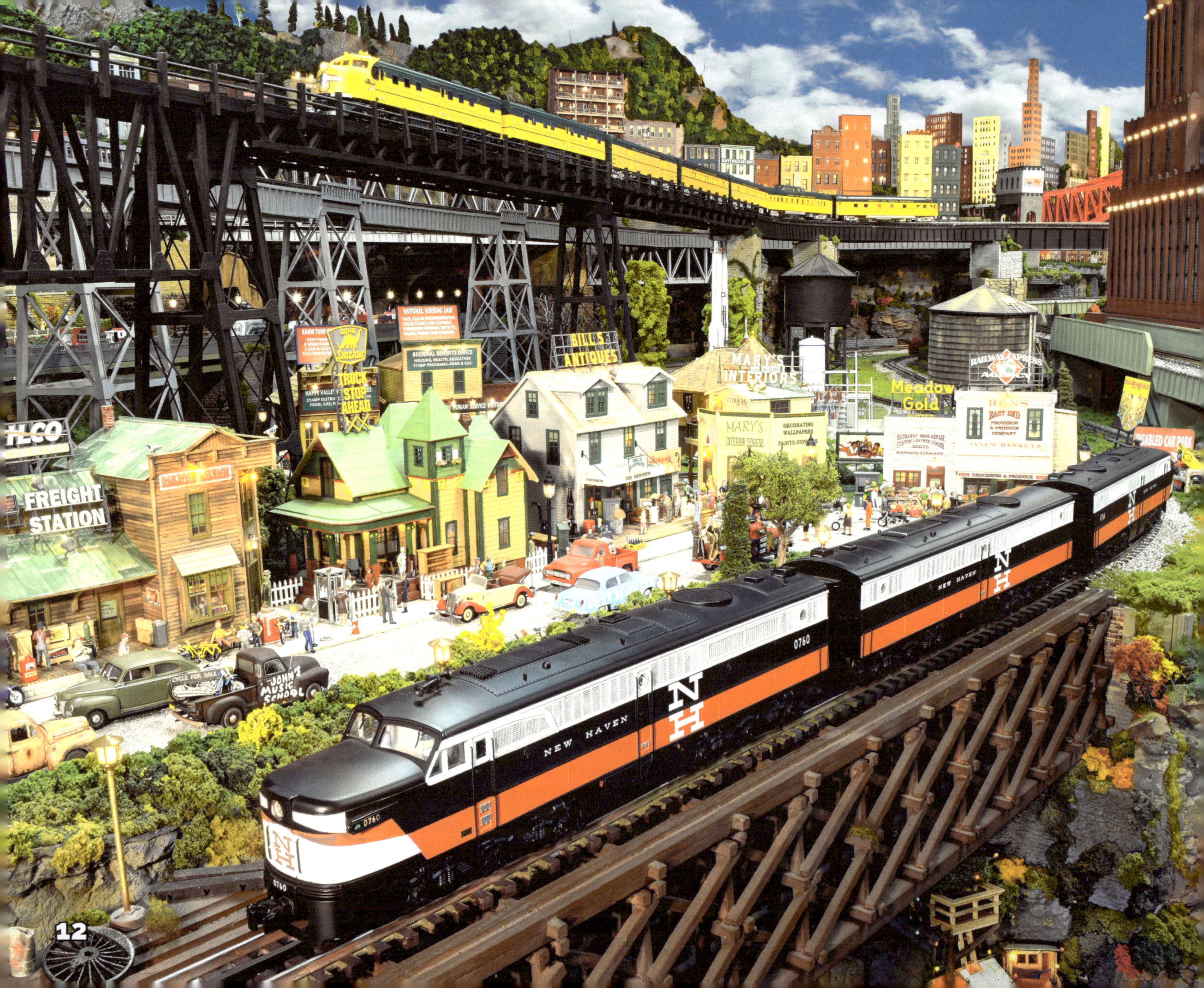

FREIGHT STATION
HCO
PARLOR & BILLIARDS
CYCLE FOR SALE
JOHN'S MUSIC SCHOOL
MARY'S INTERIOR DESIGNS
DECORATING
WALLPAPERS
PAINTS-SUPPLIES
BILL'S ANTIQUES
MARY'S INTERIORS
NATIONAL HOUSING LAW
REGIONAL BENEFITS OFFICE
TRUCK STOP AHEAD
Meadow Gold
RAILWAY EXPRESS
DISABLED CAR PARK
NEW HAVEN
0760
NH

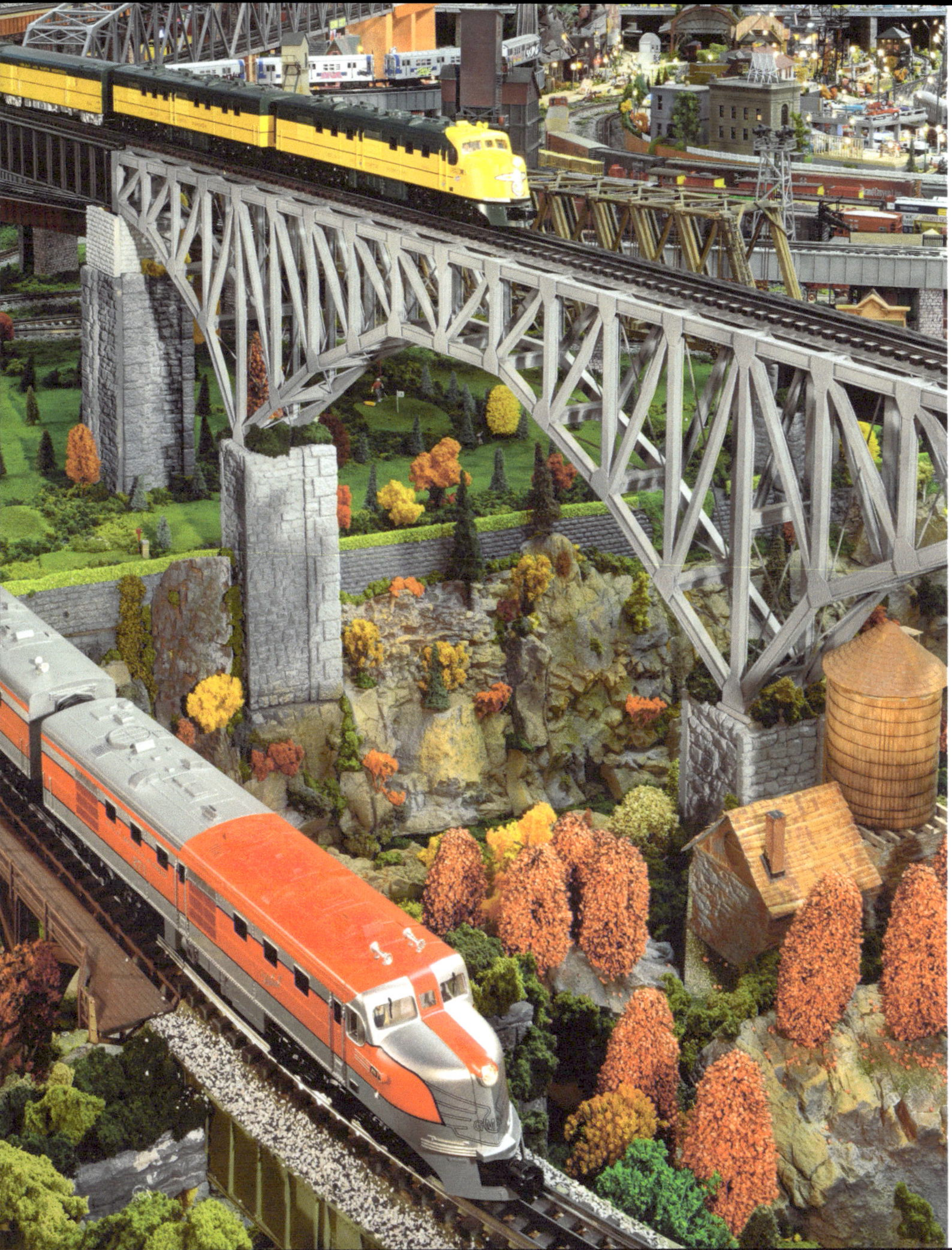

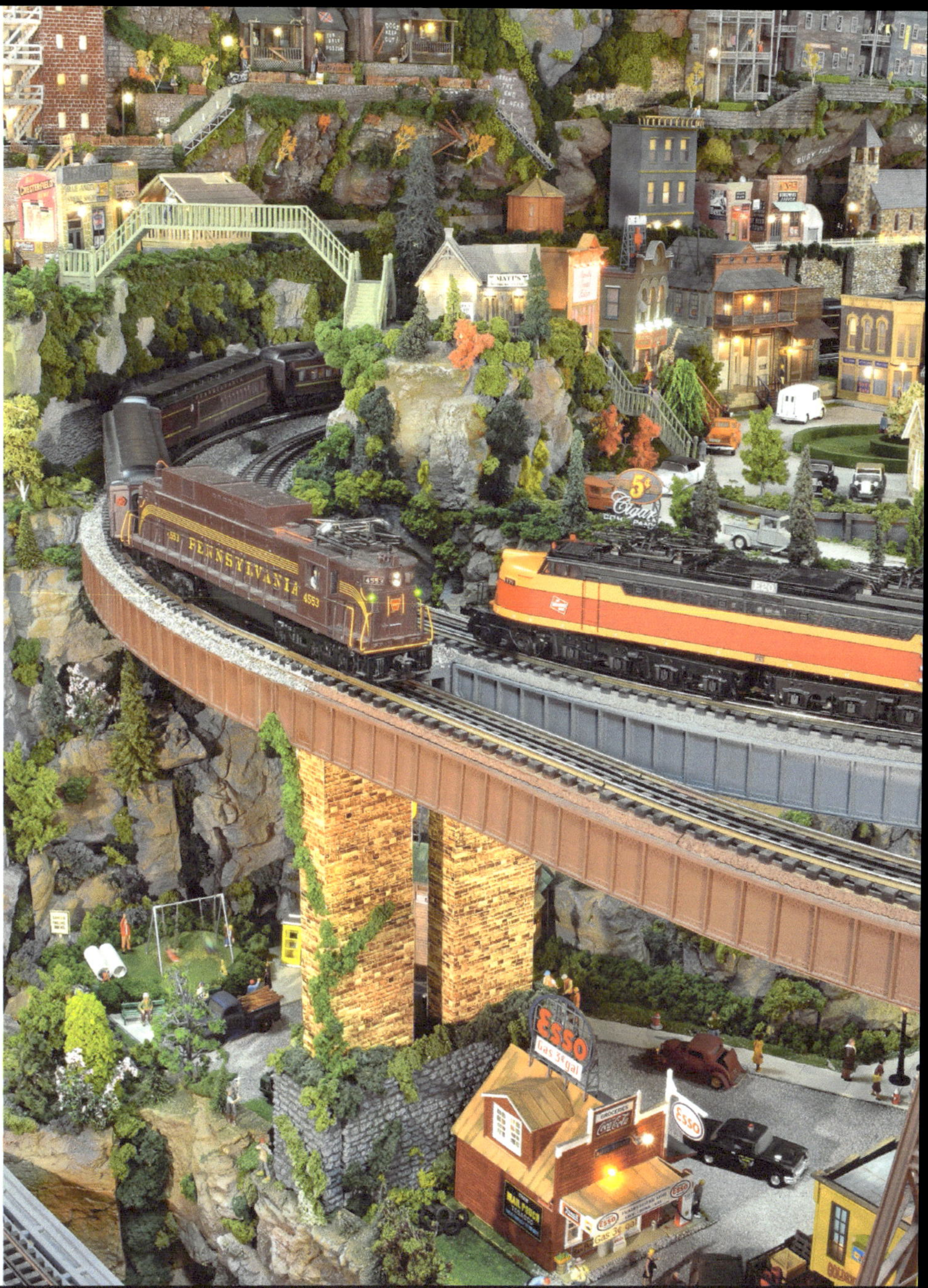

A Design Change Makes The Trains Visible!

On my first few layouts, mountains concealed too much of the track. The trains were not visible for most of their run around the railroad. On this layout, everyone can easily see the trains as they travel the main lines.

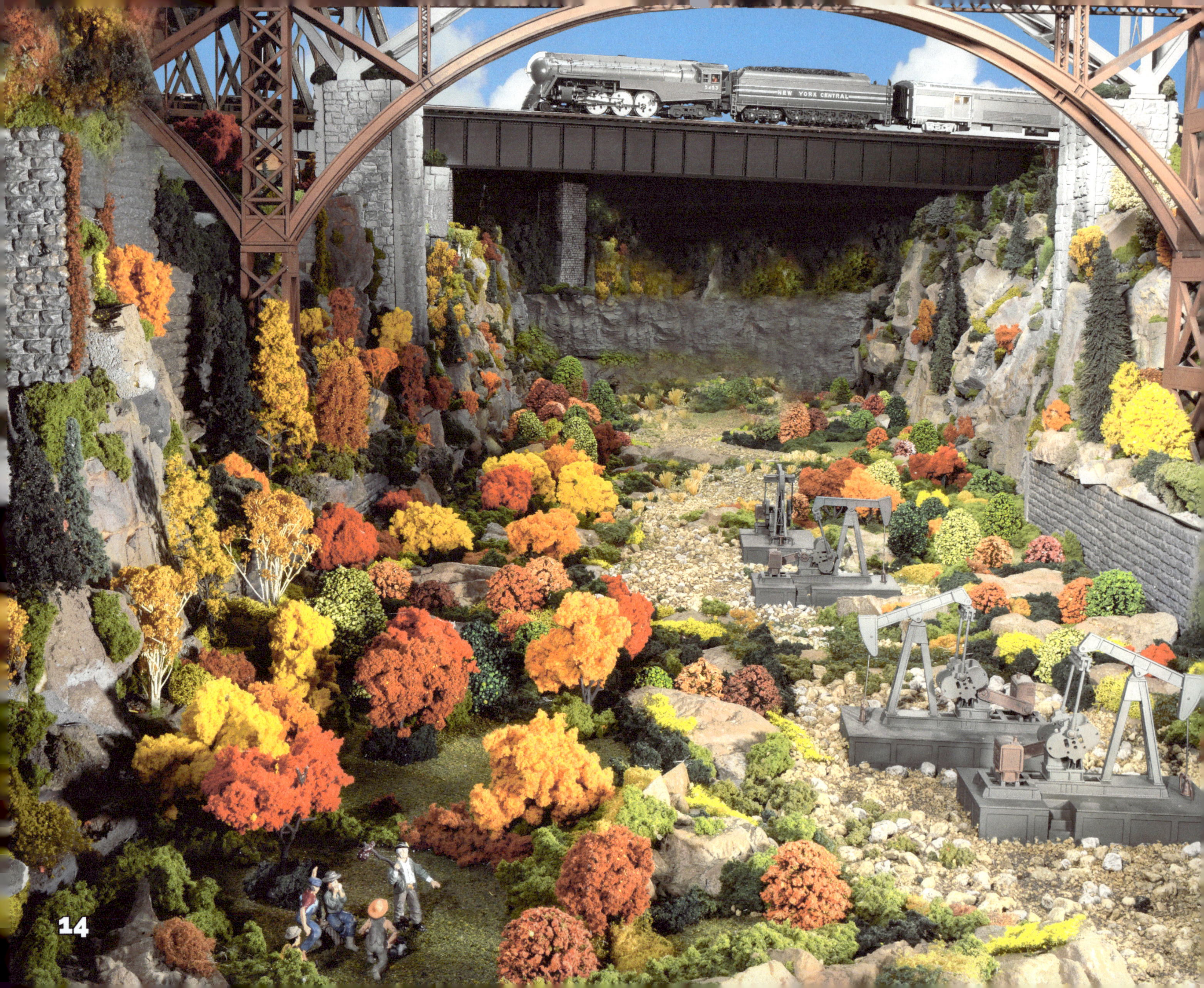
NEW YORK CENTRAL

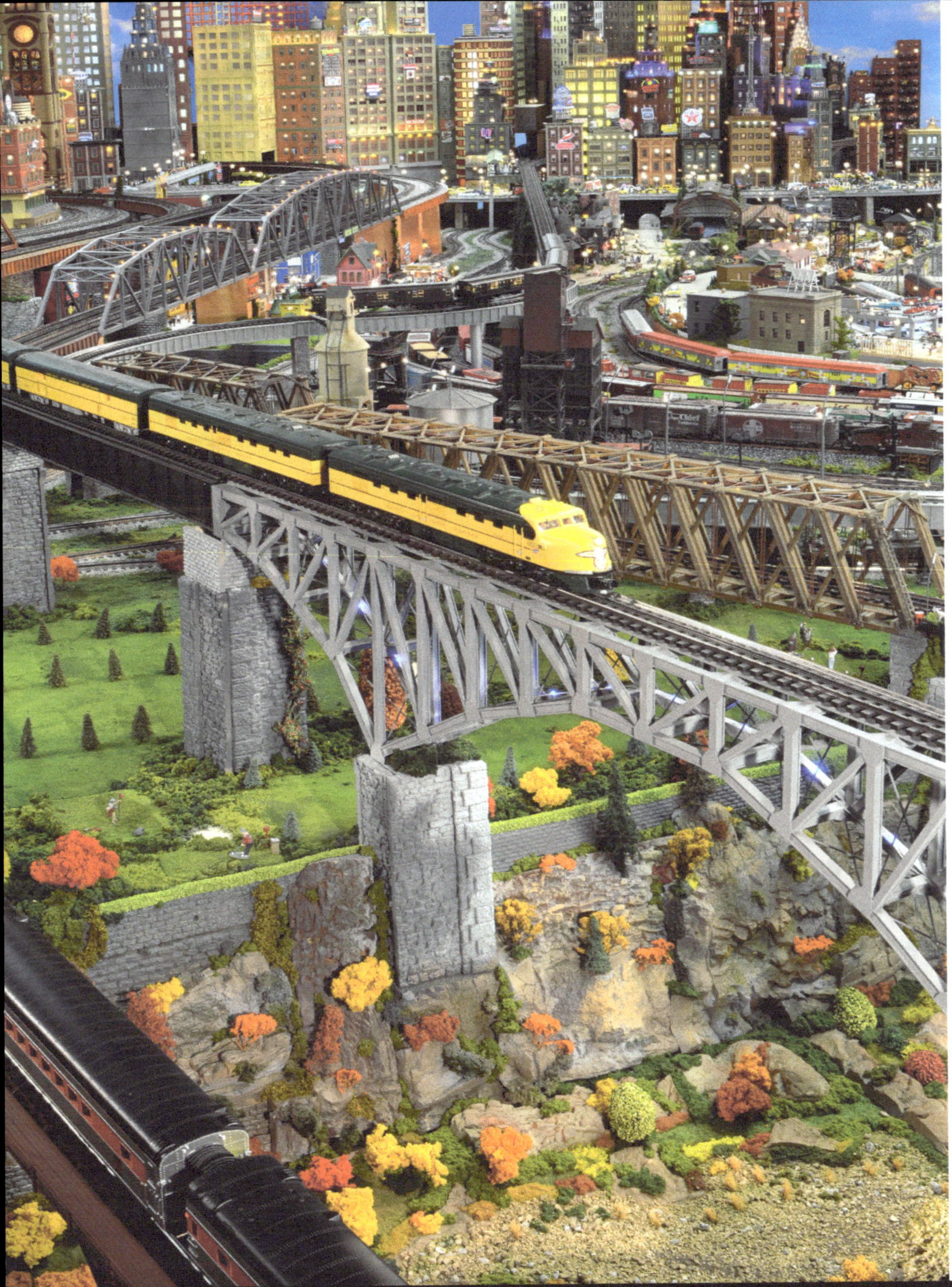

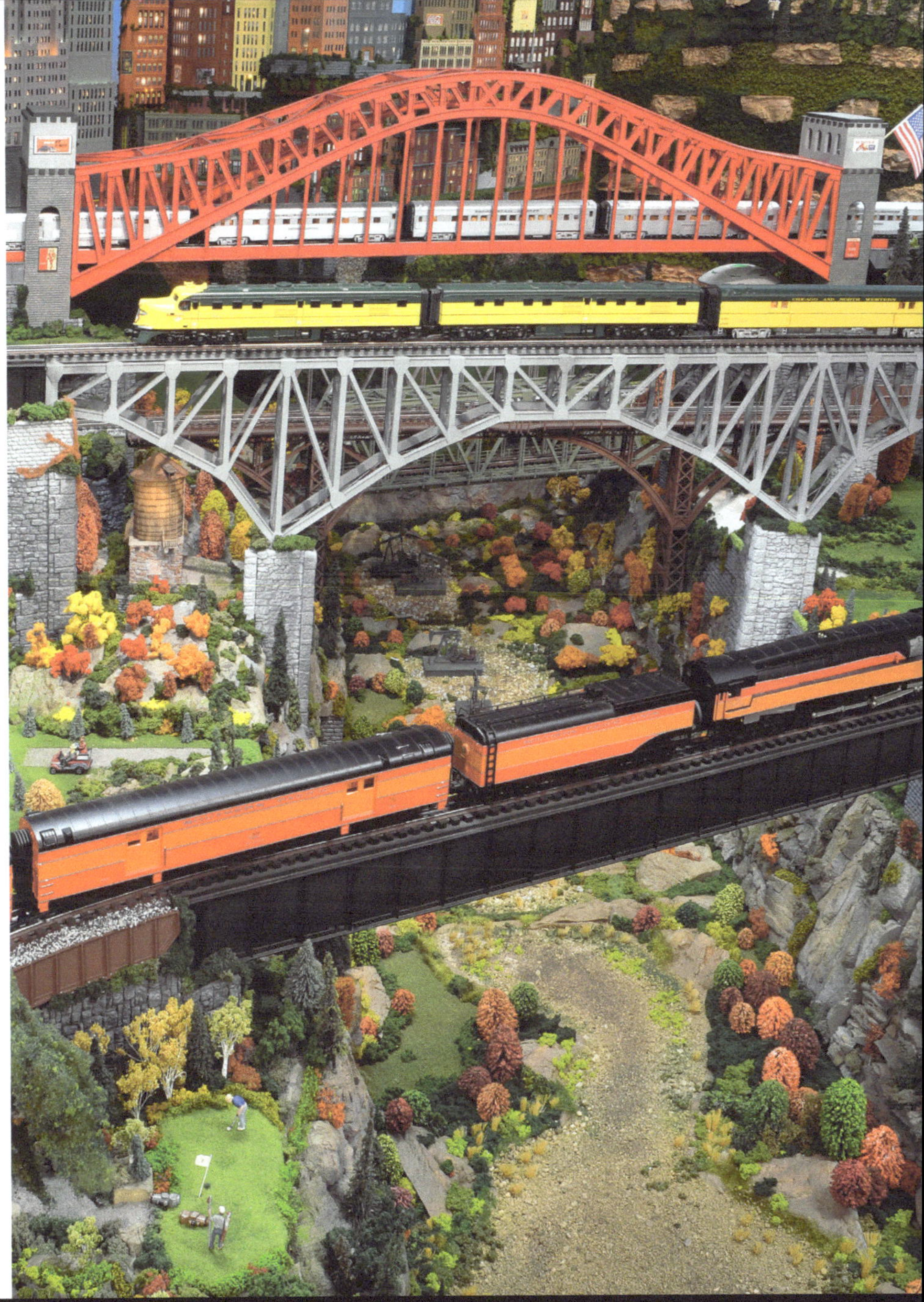

The Great Valley

Many of the bridges cross The Great Valley, which divides the front and rear halves of the layout.
The floor of the valley folds away to allow repair access. All of the scenery products used in the
construction of this valley are available from Scenic Express.

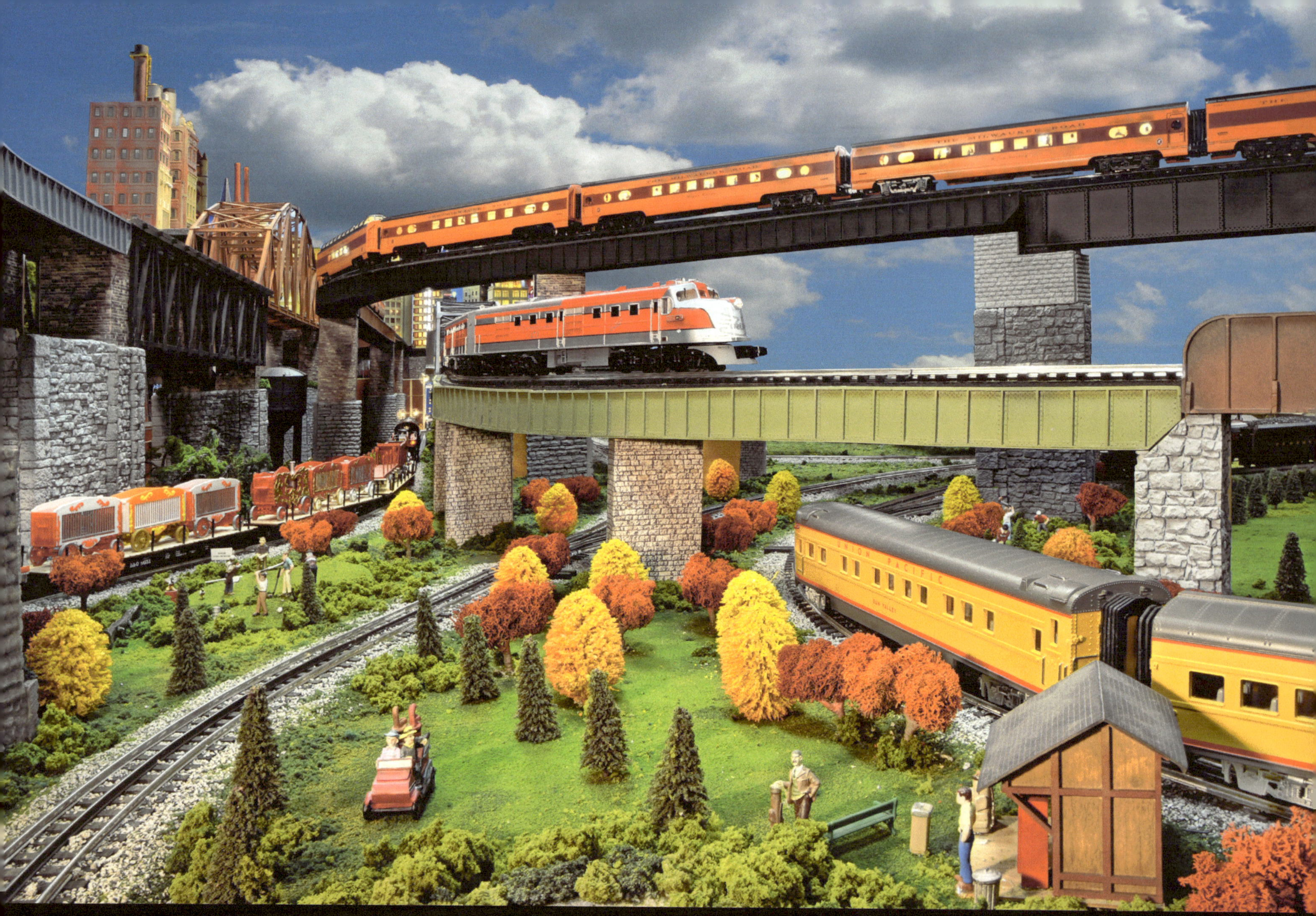

The Golf Course

I wanted to model a golf course so I could use the many 1/4" scale golfing figures which are available. The golf course fills a large green space on the layout. Golfers find many unusual obstacles on this course!

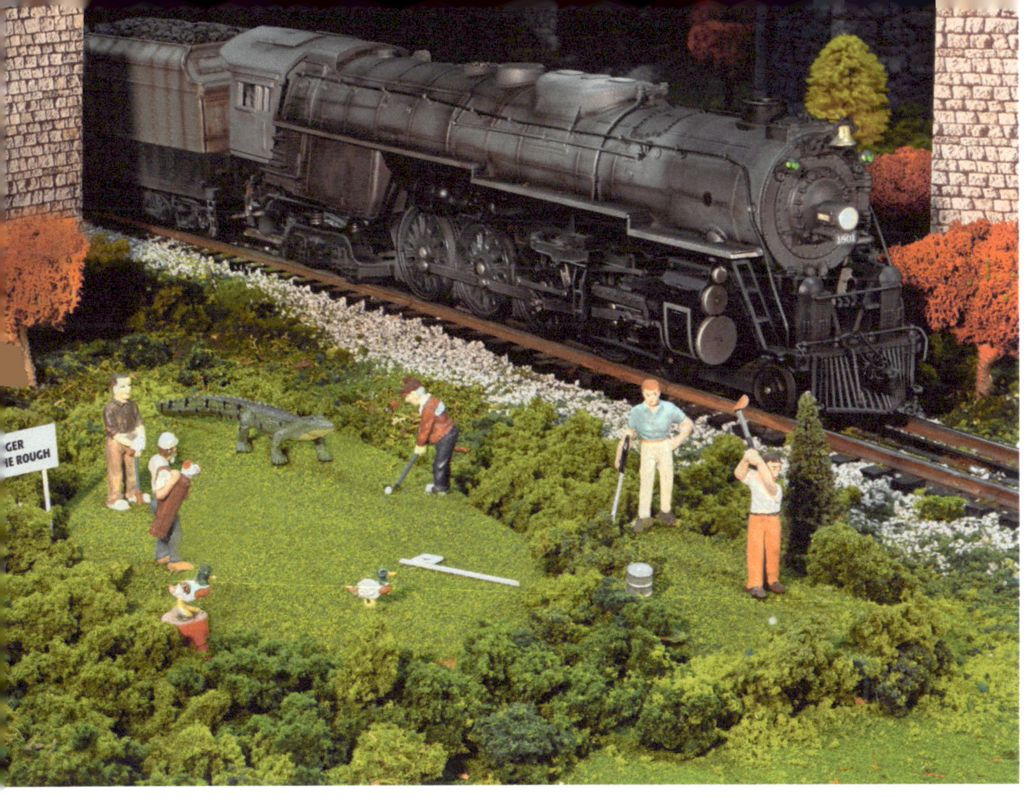
GER
HE ROUGH

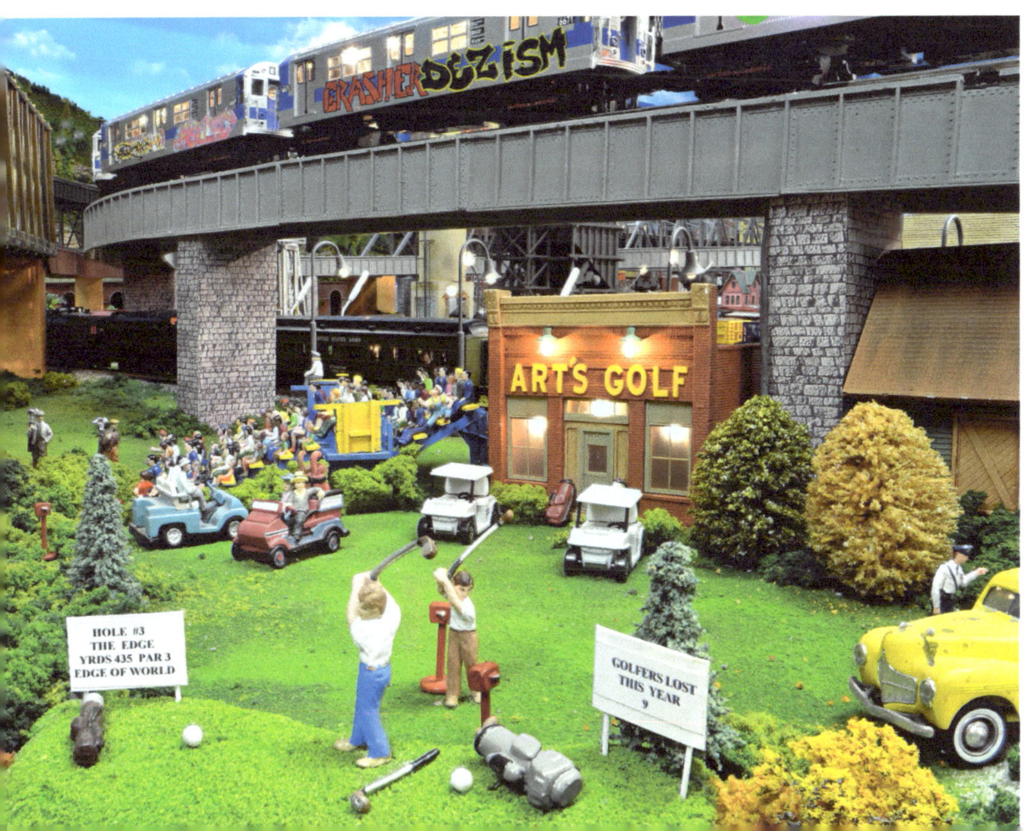
CRASHER
ART'S GOLF
HOLE #3
THE EDGE
YRDS 435 PAR 3
EDGE OF WORLD
GOLFERS LOST
THIS YEAR

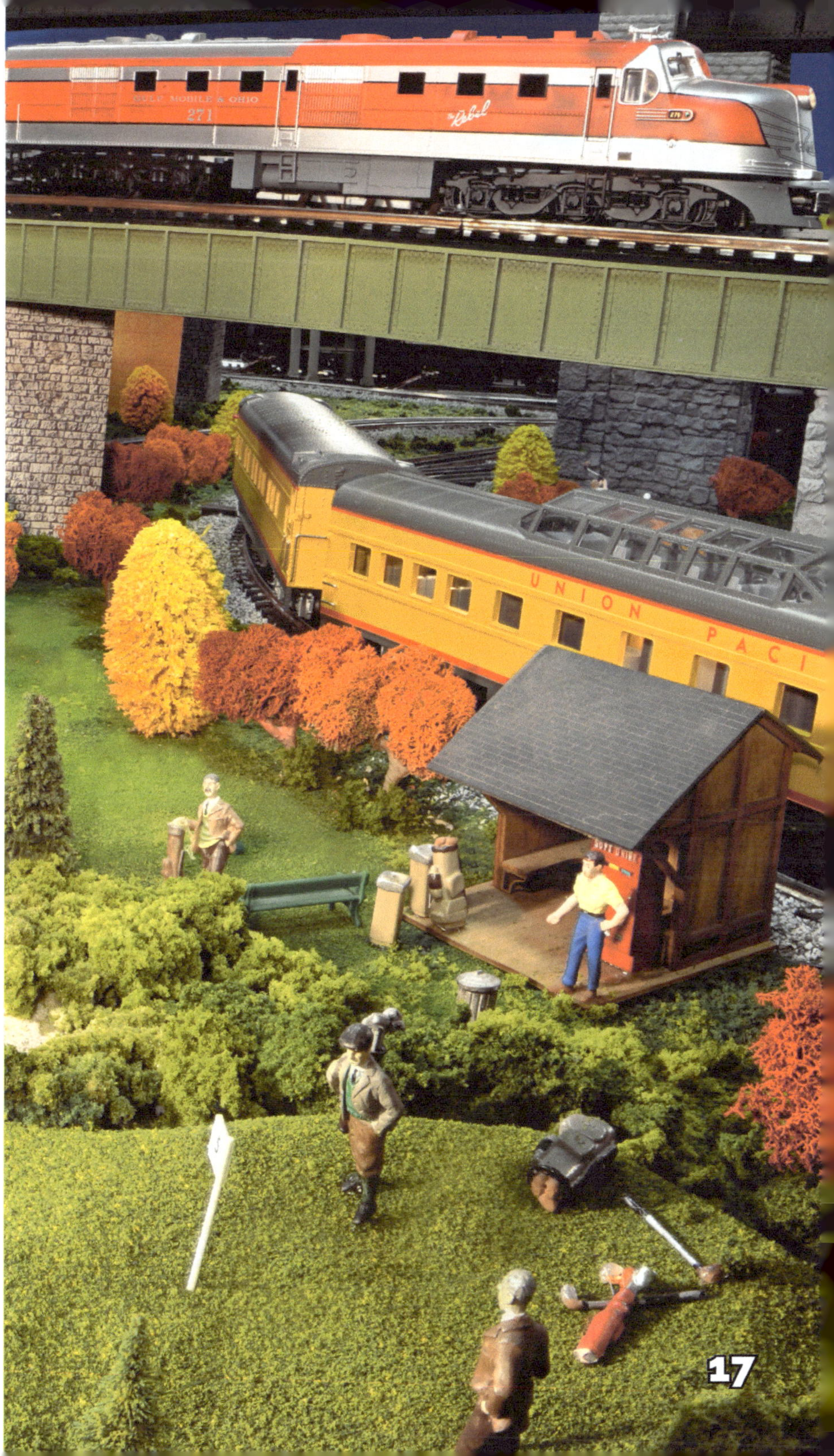

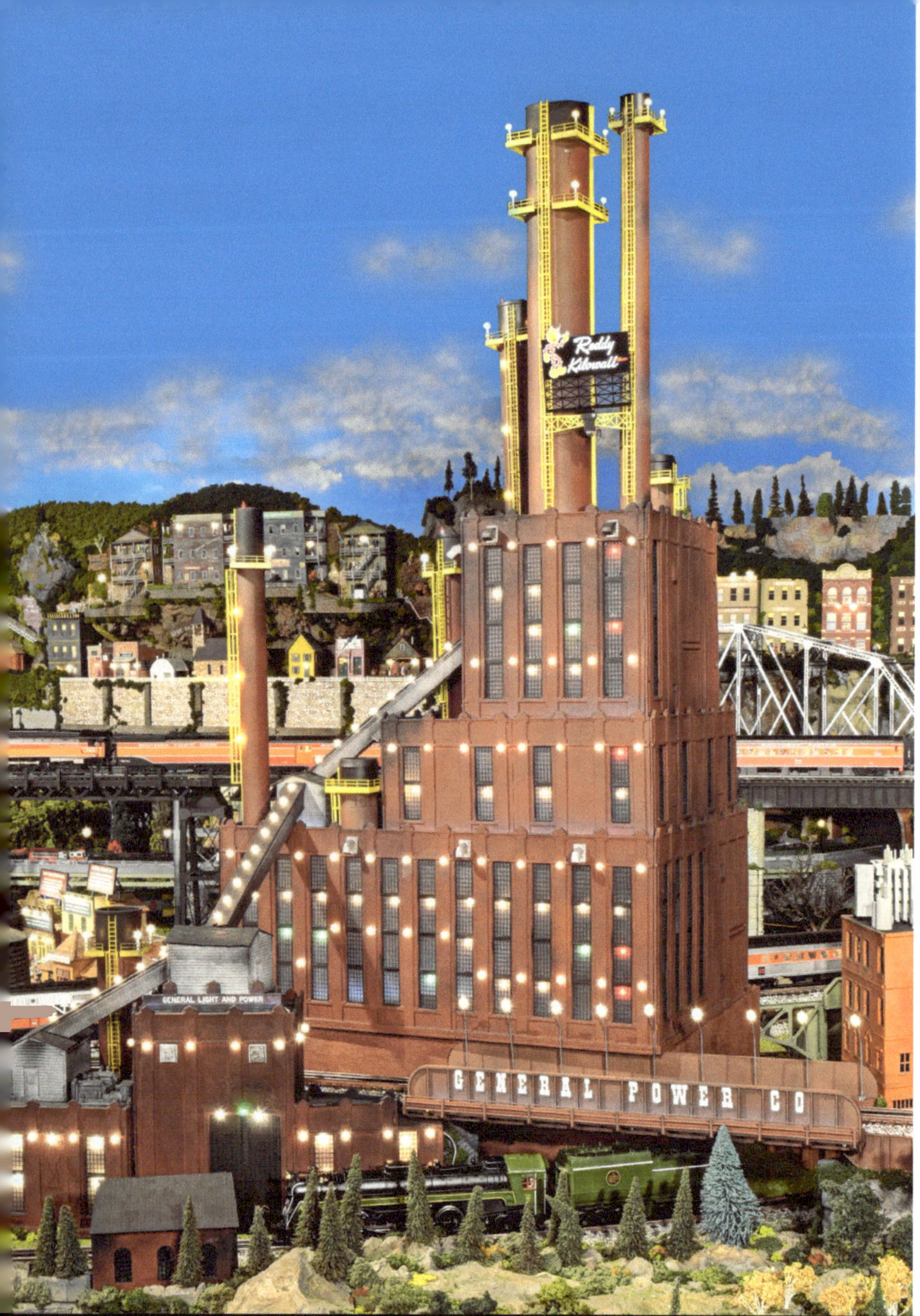

The Power Plant

The tall smoke stack of this power plant conceals a steel support pole for the house. There are over 400 lights in this power plant!

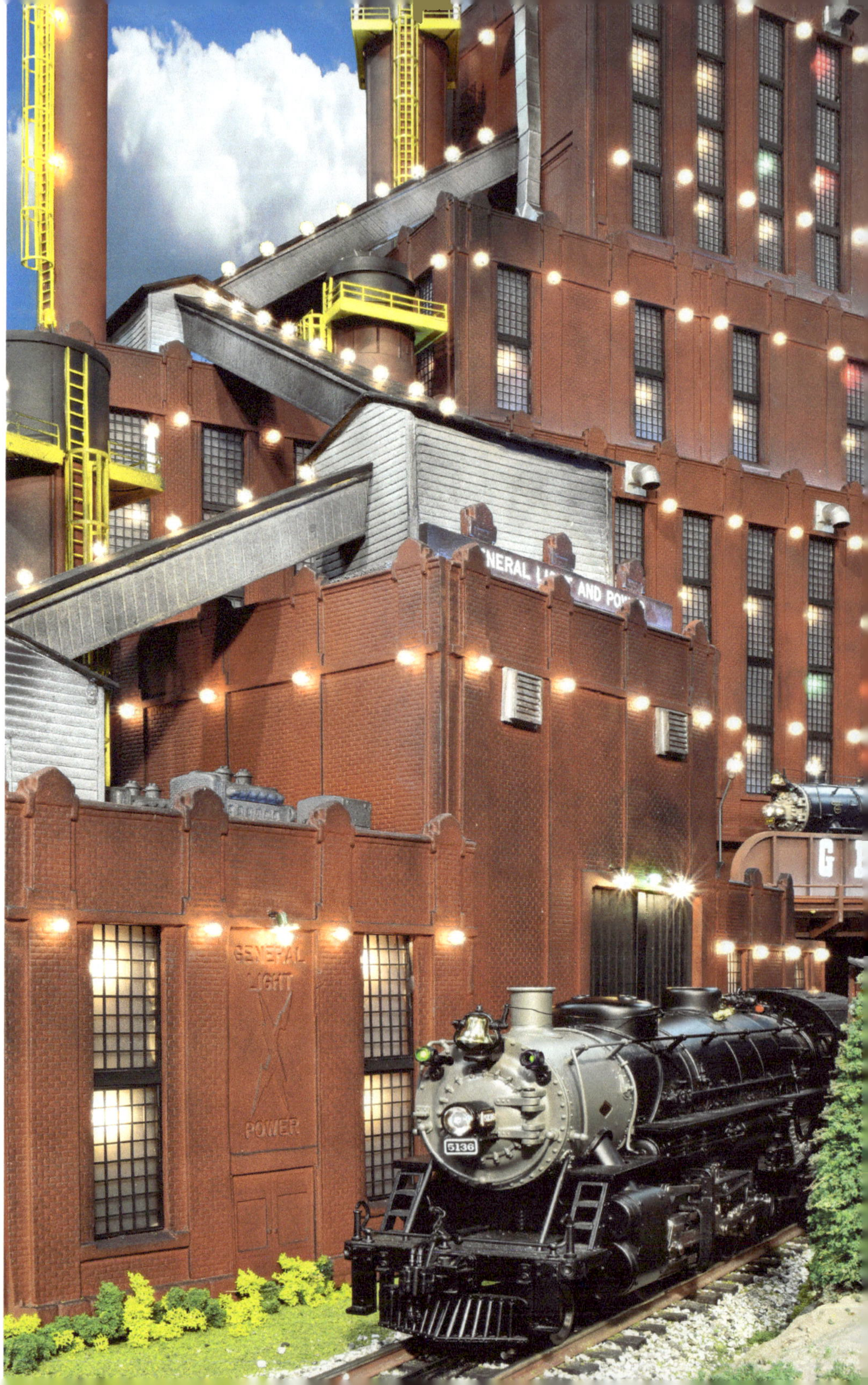

Tower City Industries

Tower City's largest factory is built on top of the rear walkway. Visitors can walk *through* the factory and view the building's electrical and lighting systems.

I installed a slow-blow fuse in each building because all the lights in these buildings draw a high amount of current.

The factory is home to both Korber Models and the famous "Middle Rail Company."

If you have operating problems on your model railroad, the "Middle Rail Company" can install a middle rail on your layout and cure all your operating problems!

All of the products which I used to build these industrial buildings came from Korber Models.

www.korbermodels.com

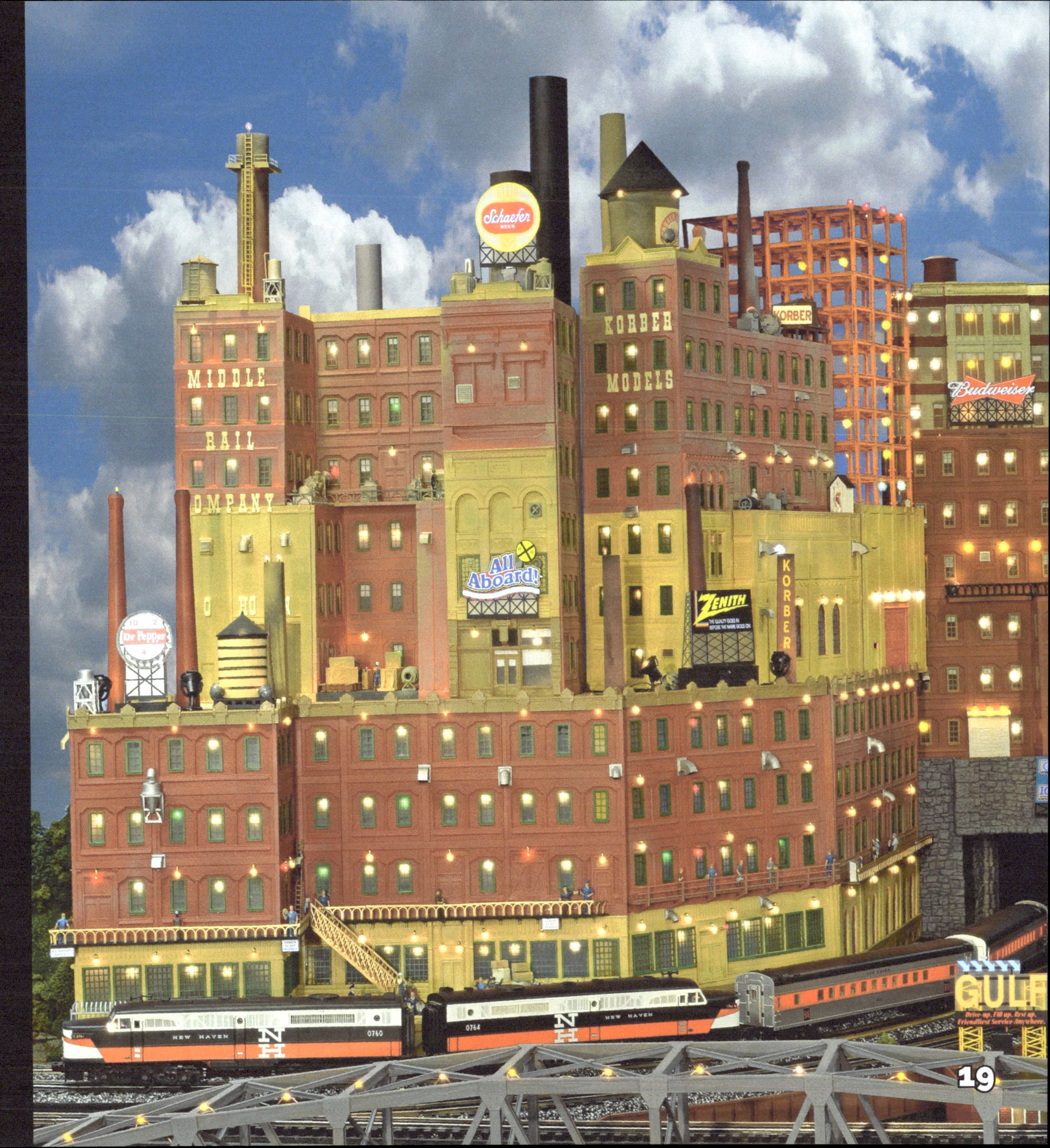

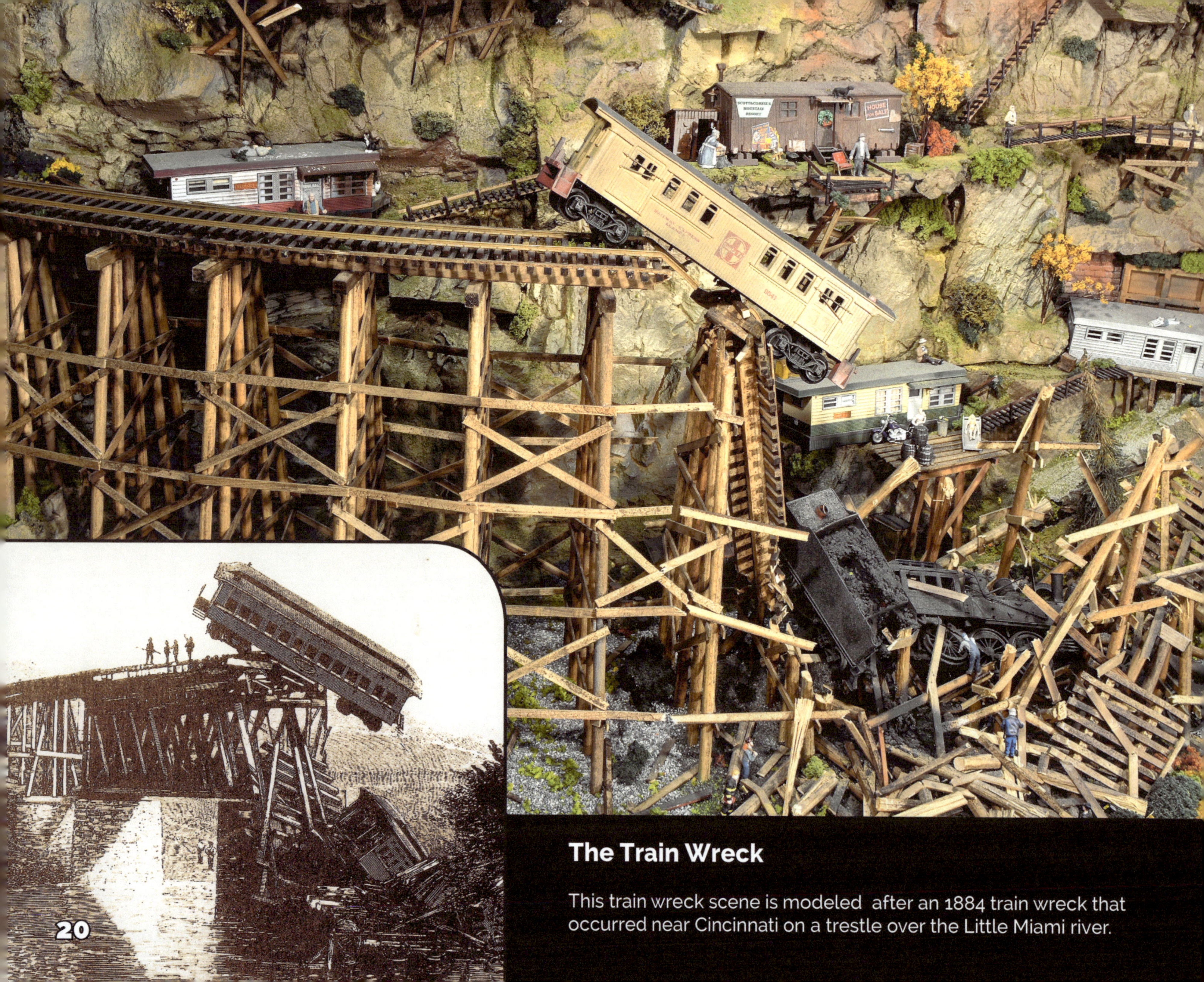

The Train Wreck

This train wreck scene is modeled after an 1884 train wreck that occurred near Cincinnati on a trestle over the Little Miami river.

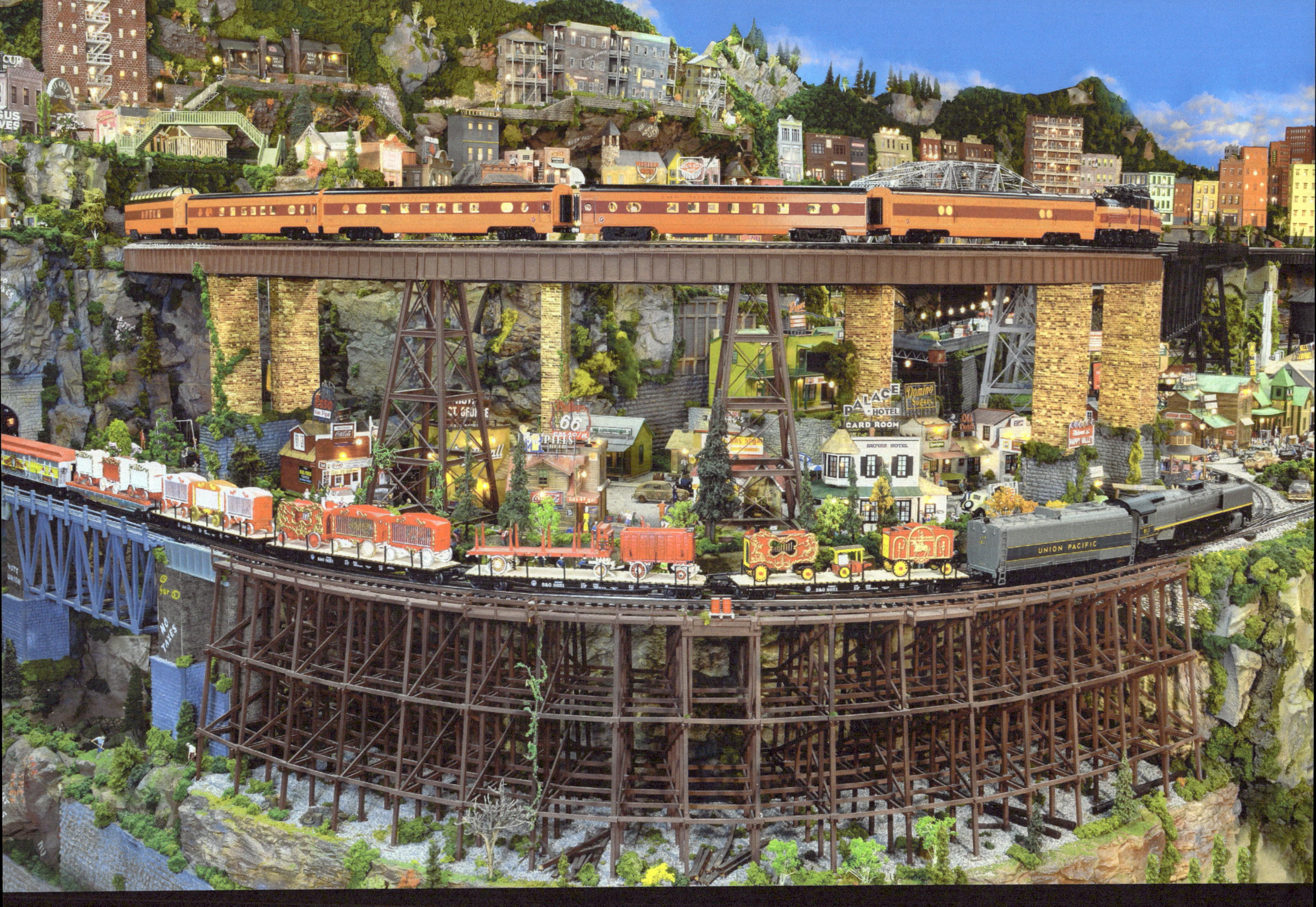

Happy Valley - Where Life is Perfect

The village of Happy Valley is set behind a large, curved wooden trestle.
This "place of perfection" is nestled at the base of the adjacent mountain range.

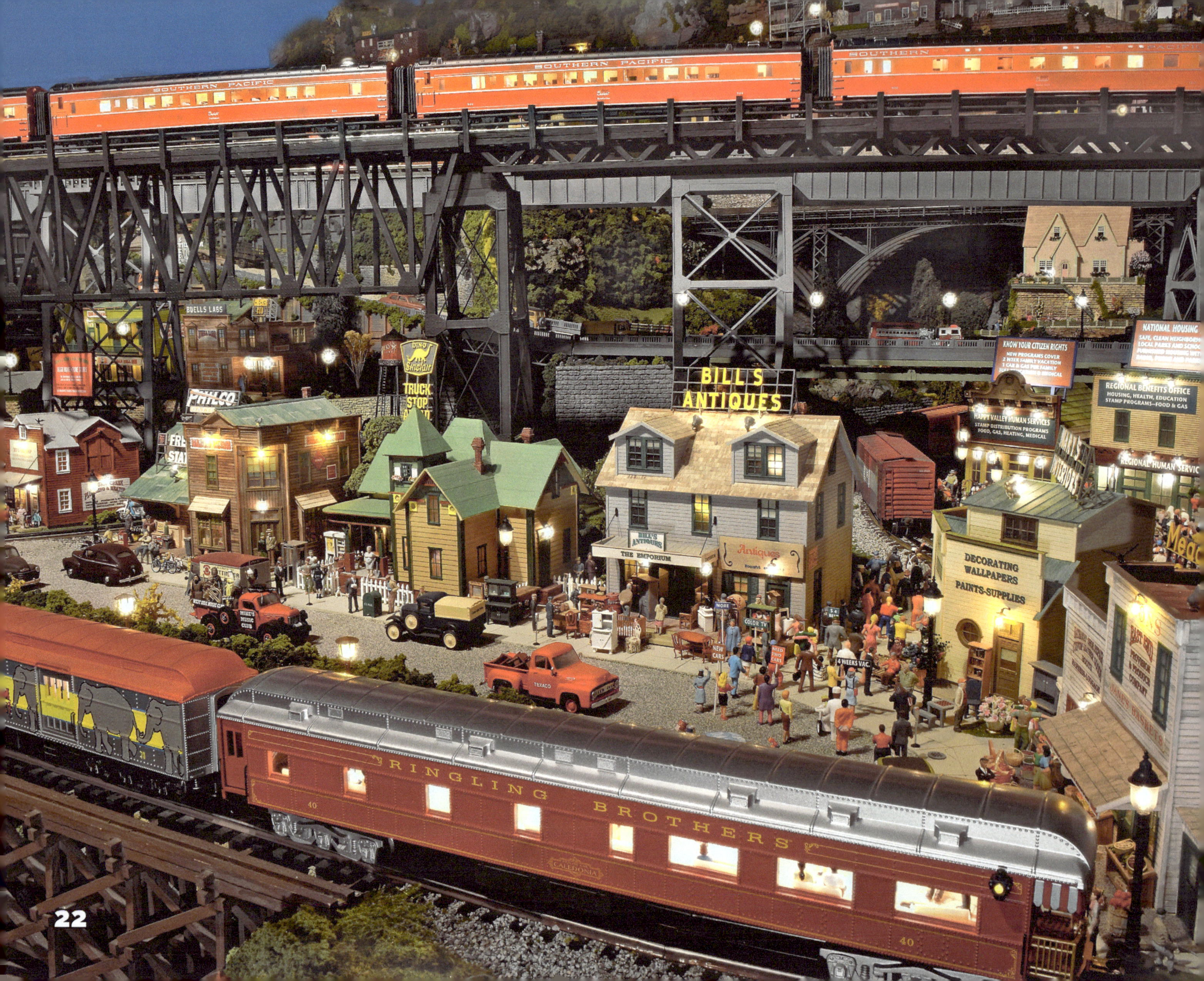

SOUTHERN PACIFIC
SOUTHERN PACIFIC
SOUTHERN
BUELLS LASS
PHILCO
Sinclair
DINO
TRUCK STOP AHEAD
BILL'S ANTIQUES
NATIONAL HOUSING
KNOW YOUR CITIZEN RIGHTS
REGIONAL BENEFITS OFFICE
HAPPY VALLEY HUMAN SERVICES
REGIONAL HUMAN SERVIC
BILL'S ANTIQUES
THE EMPORIUM
Antiques
DECORATING
WALLPAPERS
PAINTS-SUPPLIES
COLOR TV
MIKE'S MUSIC CLUB
TEXACO
RINGLING BROTHERS
CALEDONIA
40

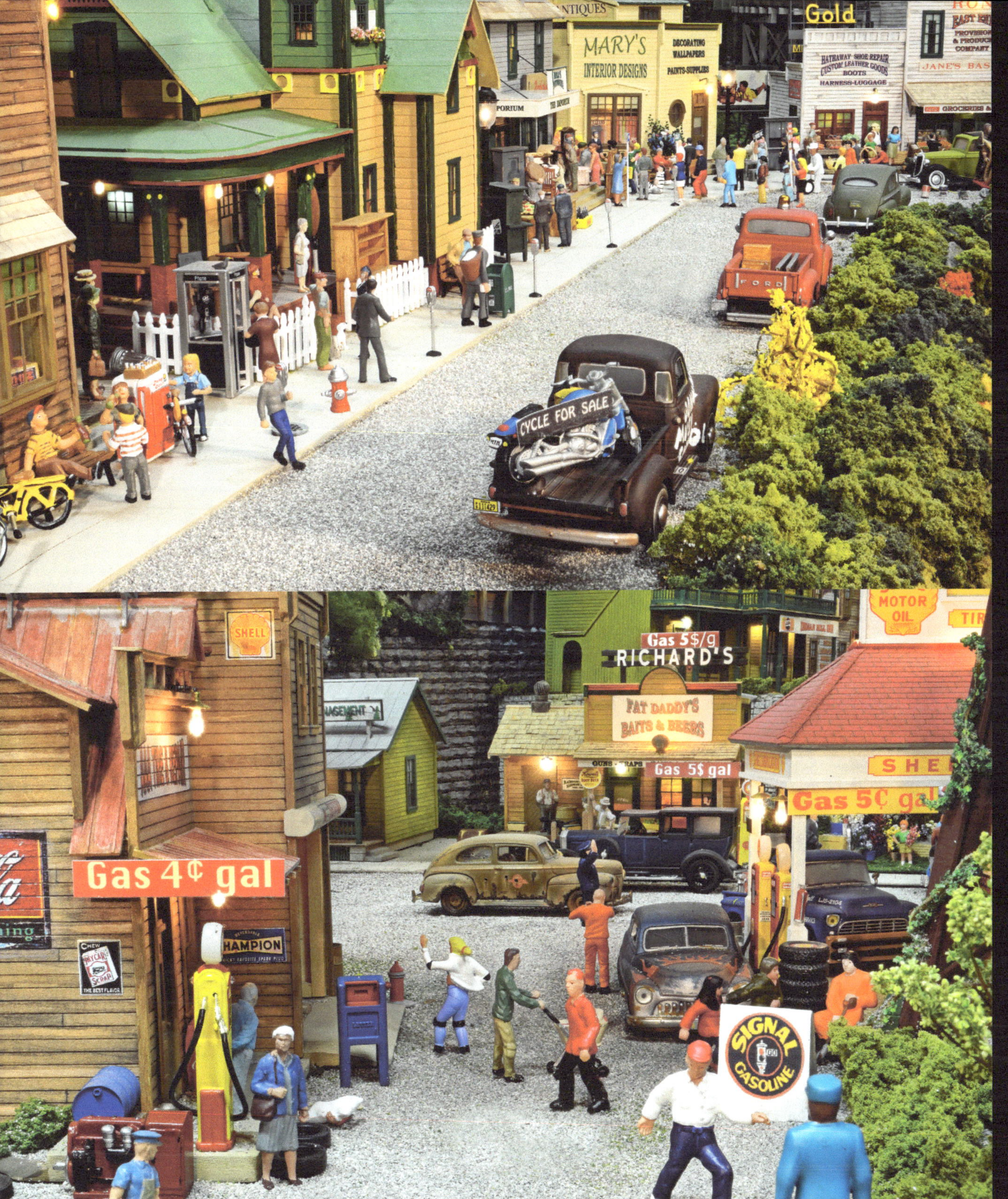

Peaceful Times

Ah...the good ol' days!

The streets are clean, all is in good repair and the stores in this small village are all busy.

A Gas Price War!

There's a gas price war going on! At one station the price is 5 cents per gallon, while across the alley a competing station has set his price at 4 cents per gallon.

On the other side of Main Street, greedy Richard has priced his gas at five DOLLARS per gallon! I'll bet he's not going to sell much gasoline today.

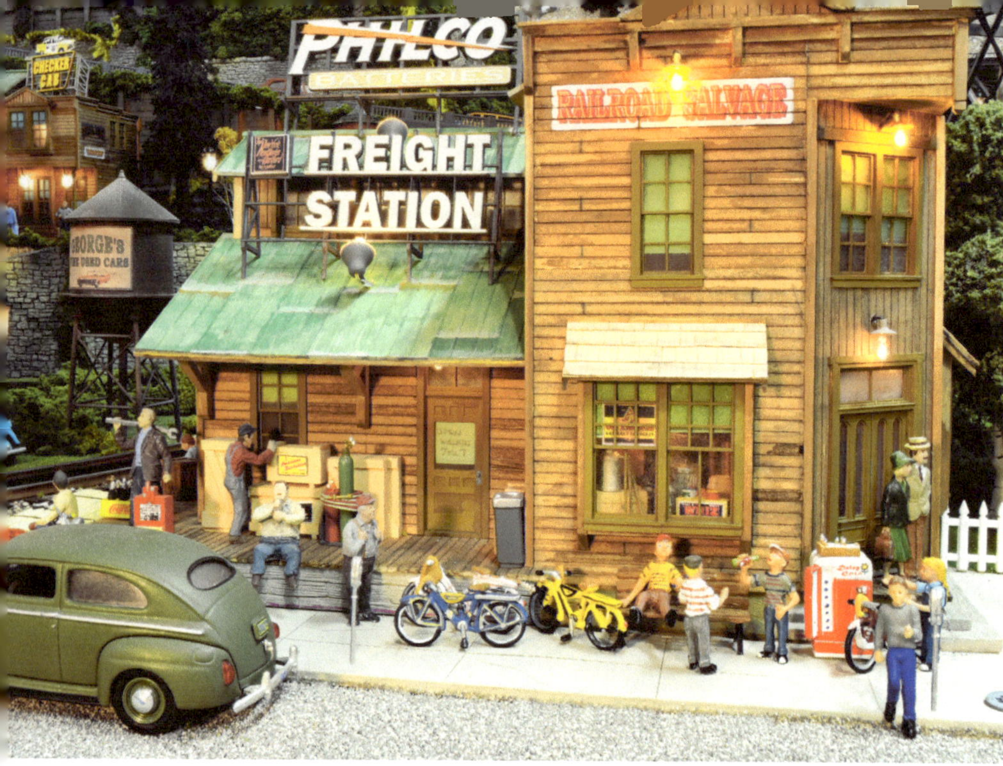

PHILCO
FREIGHT STATION
RAILROAD SALVAGE
GEORGE'S
CHECKER CAB

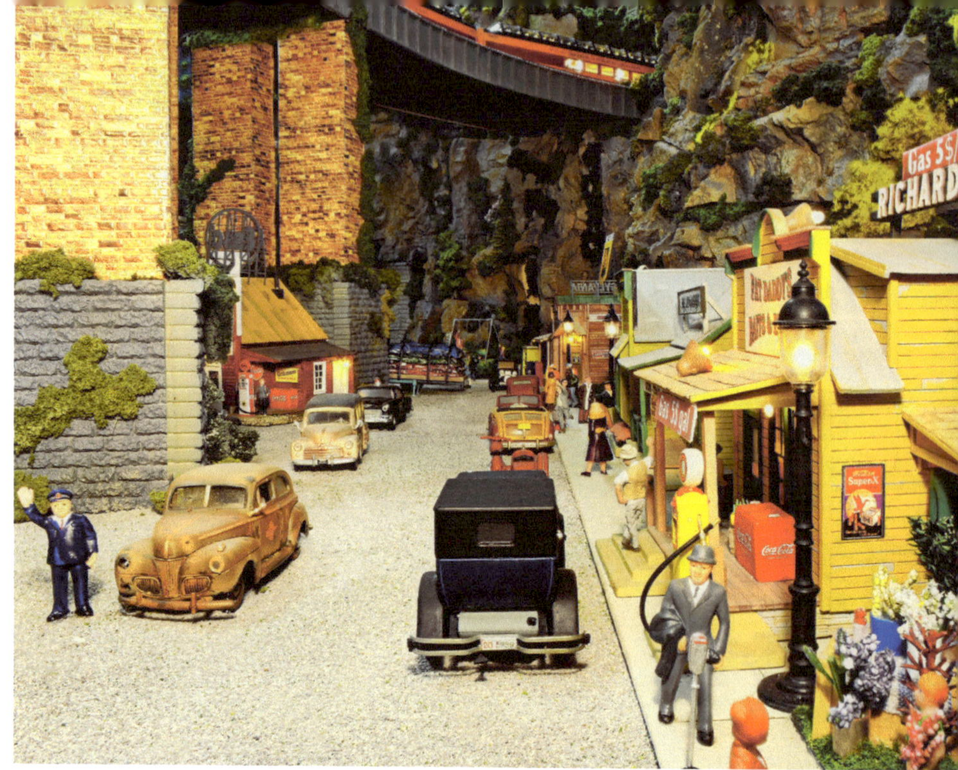

Gas 35
RICHARD

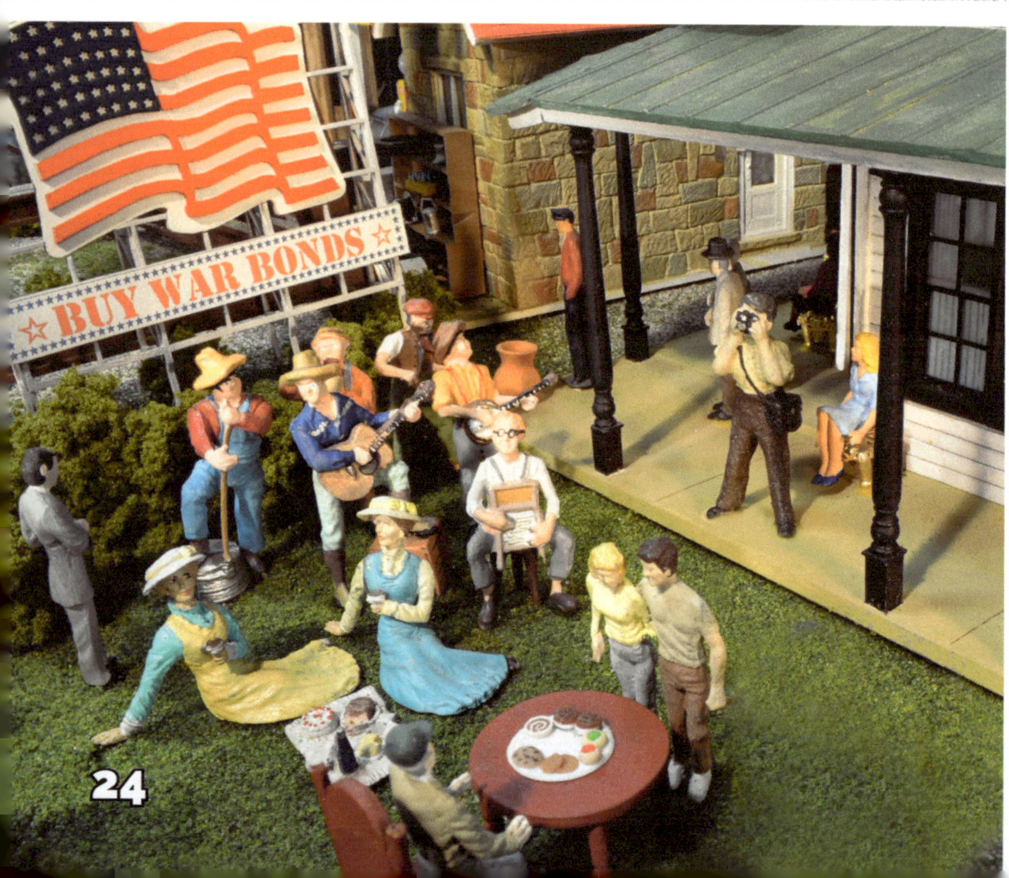

BUY WAR BONDS

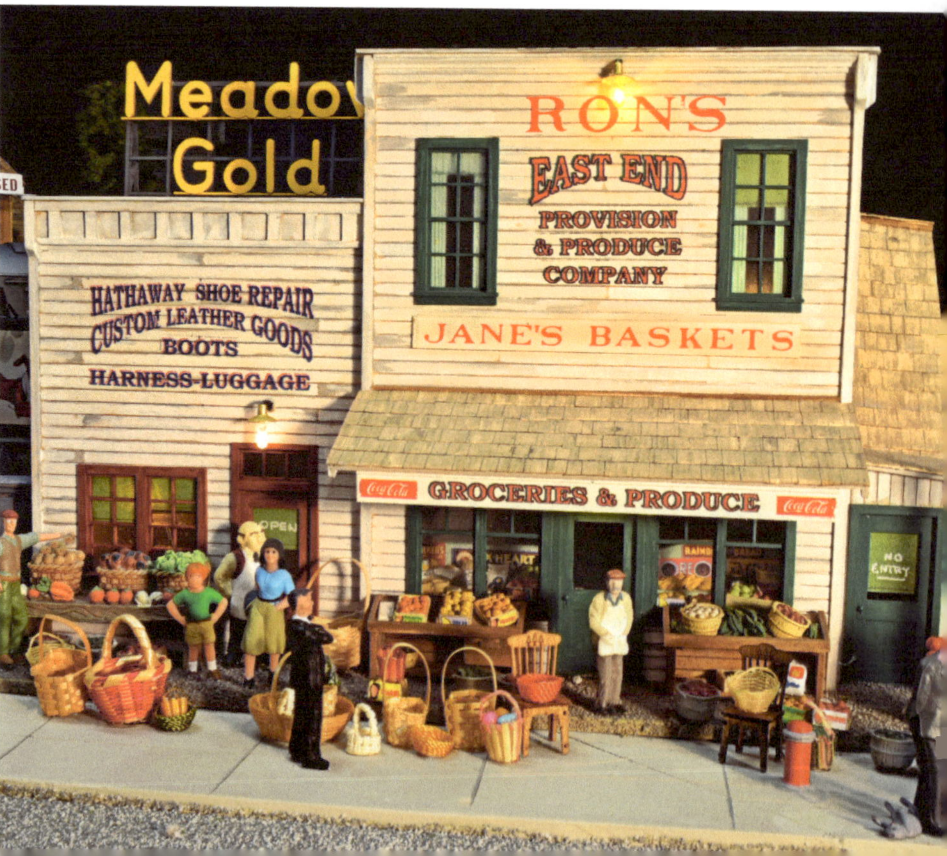

Meadow
Gold
RON'S
EAST END
PROVISION
& PRODUCE
COMPANY
HATHAWAY SHOE REPAIR
CUSTOM LEATHER GOODS
BOOTS
HARNESS-LUGGAGE
JANE'S BASKETS
GROCERIES & PRODUCE
OPEN
NO ENTRY

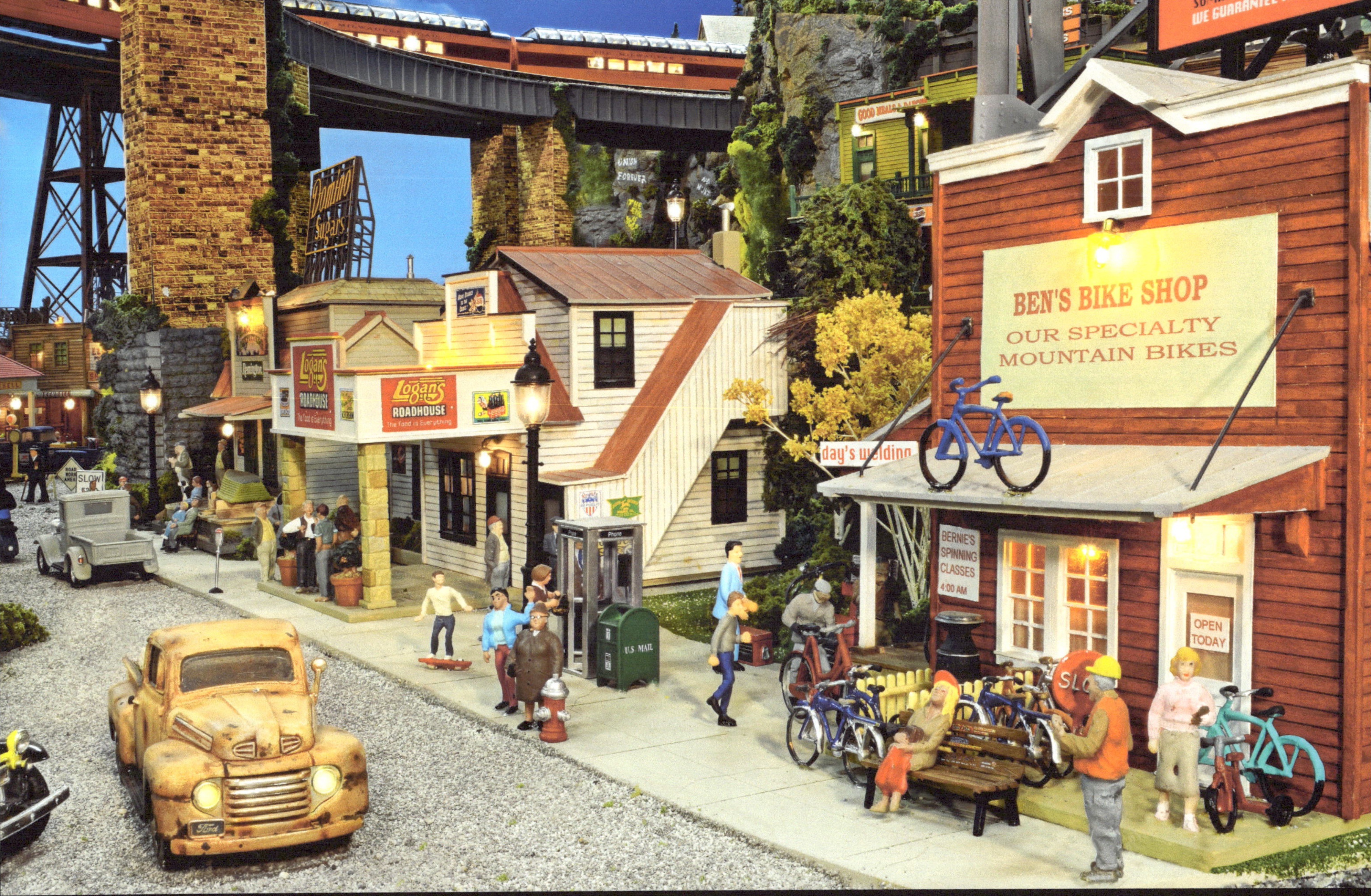

Happy Days in "Happy Valley"

I remember the day they installed the parking meters. Everyone complained! But when electricity and indoor plumbing arrived, all those complaints went away. Things are great now!

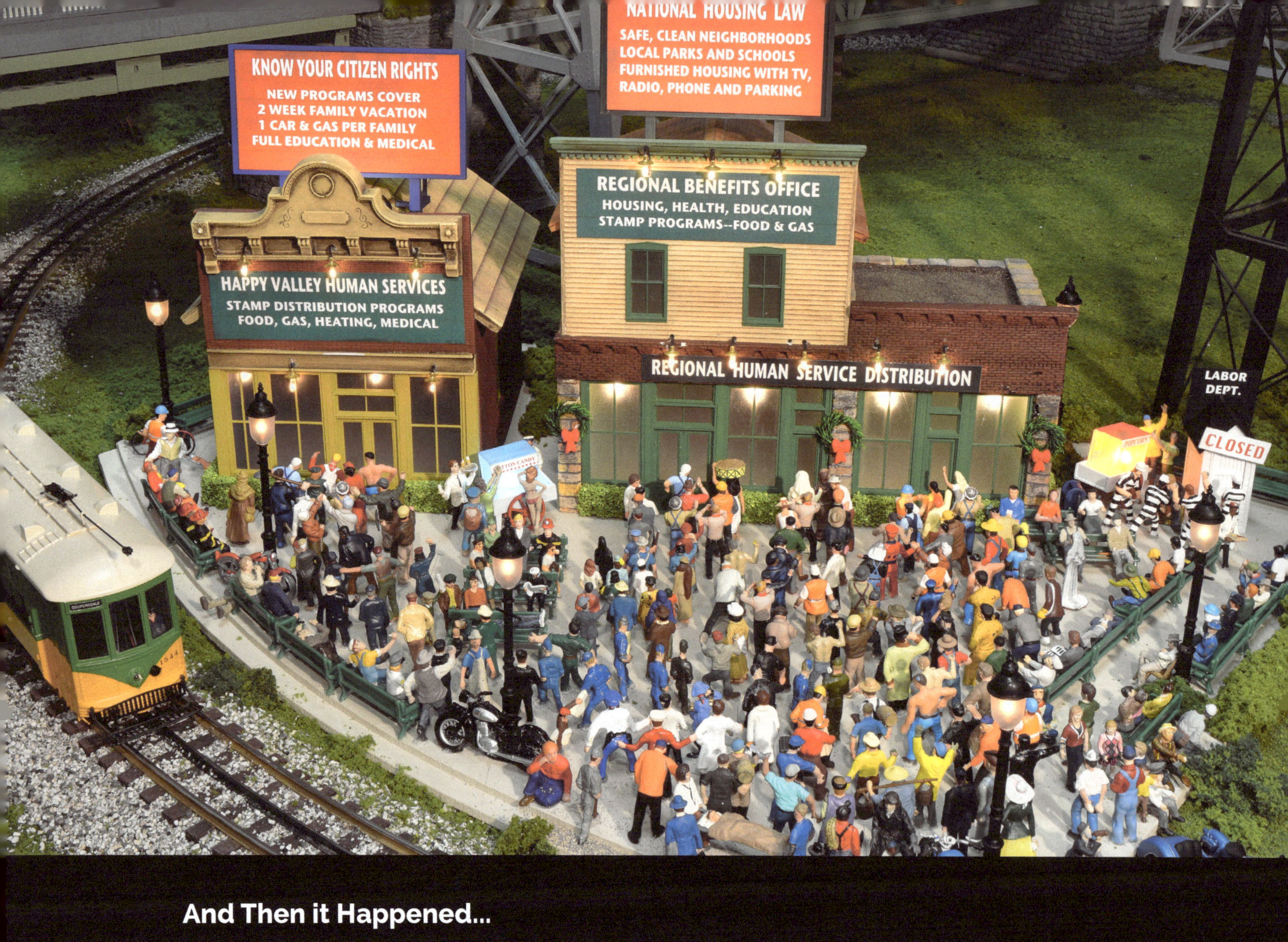

And Then it Happened...

When the Human Resource Center opened, everyone came to check it out. Now Happy Valley has protesters on Main Street! Why? Isn't life now even MORE perfect?

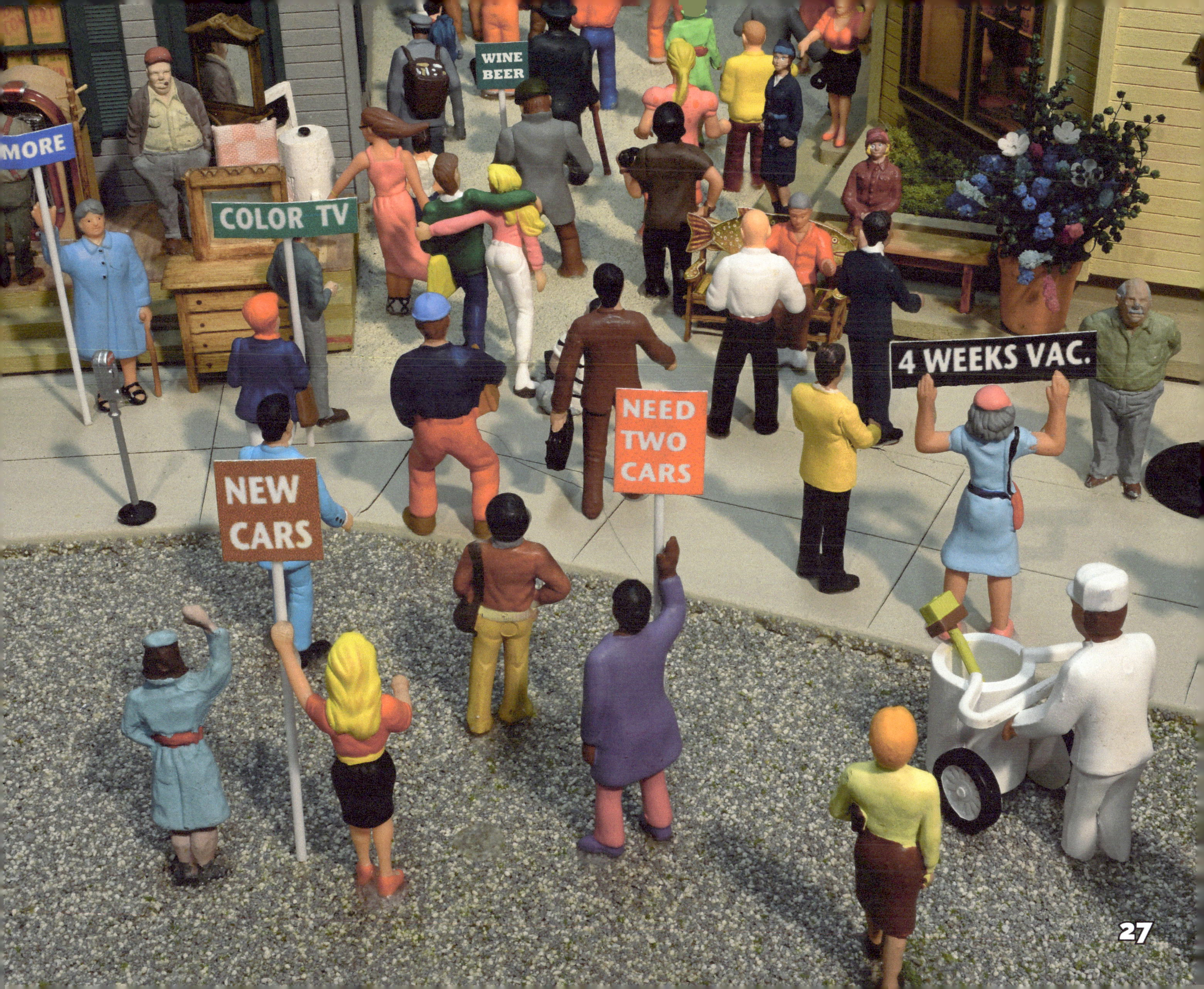

MORE
WINE
BEER
COLOR TV
4 WEEKS VAC.
NEED
TWO
CARS
NEW
CARS

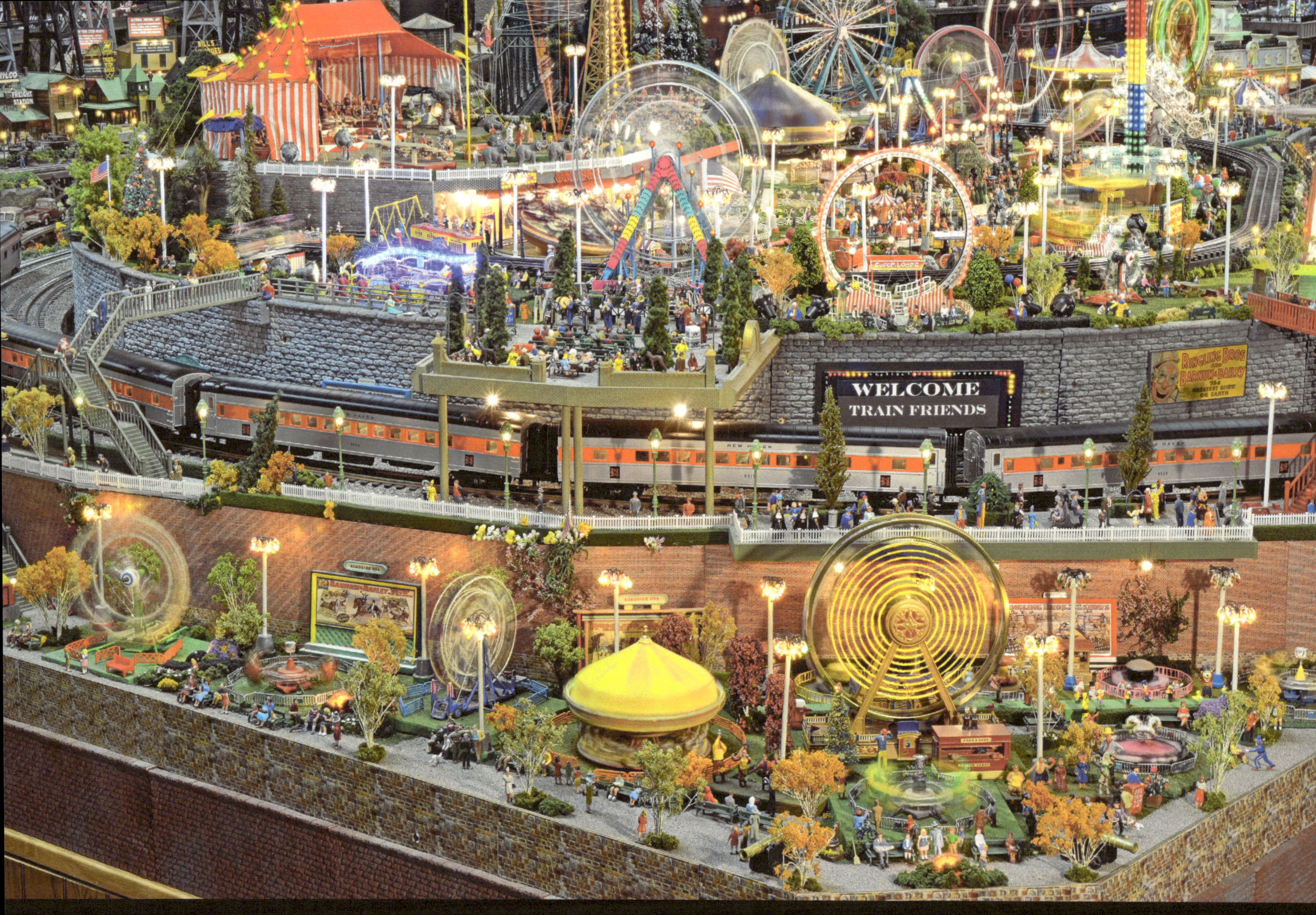

The Circus!

More than 50 animations, over 1,000 lights, circus sounds and pulsating calliope music make the circus come alive! Everybody loves going to the circus!

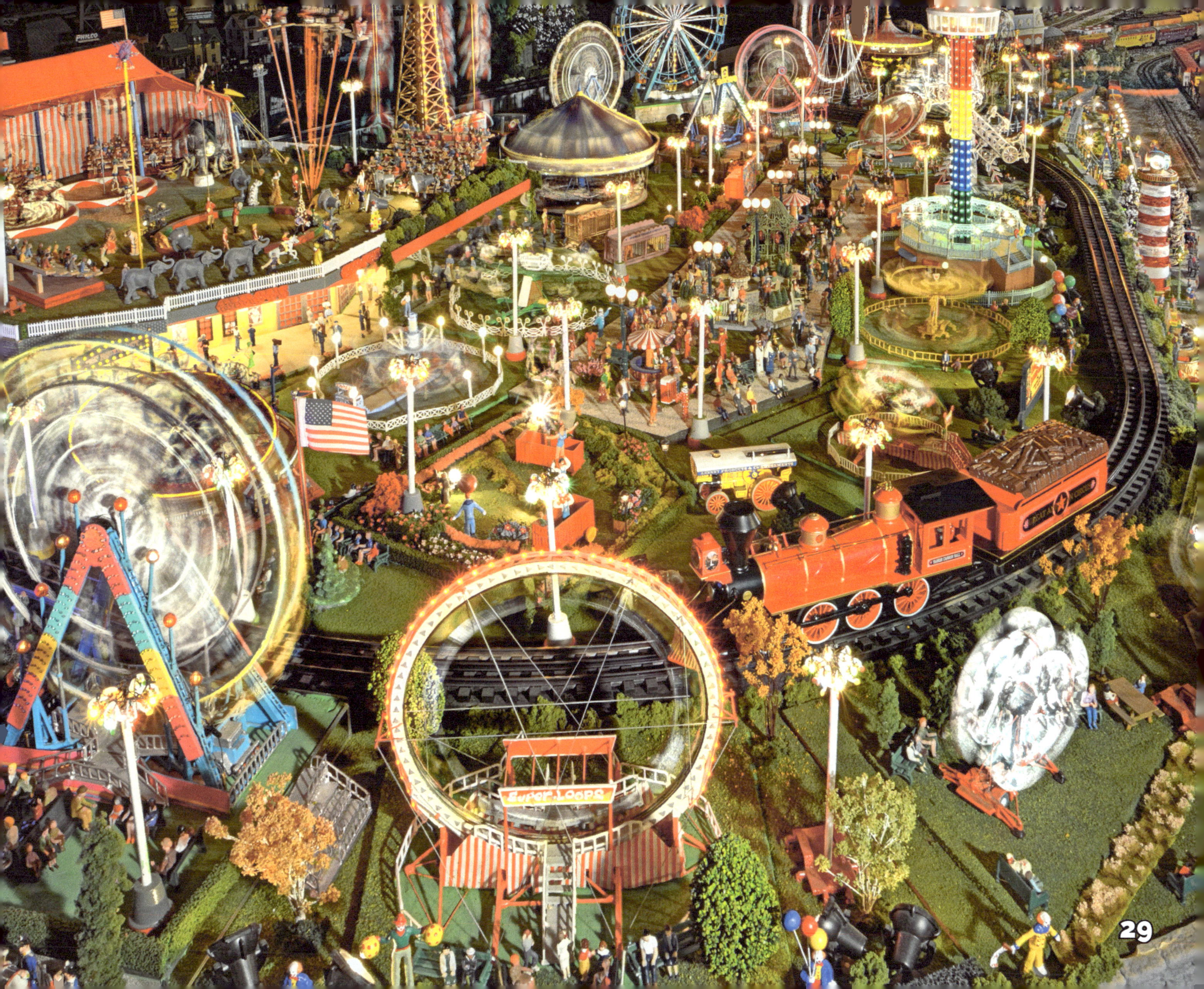

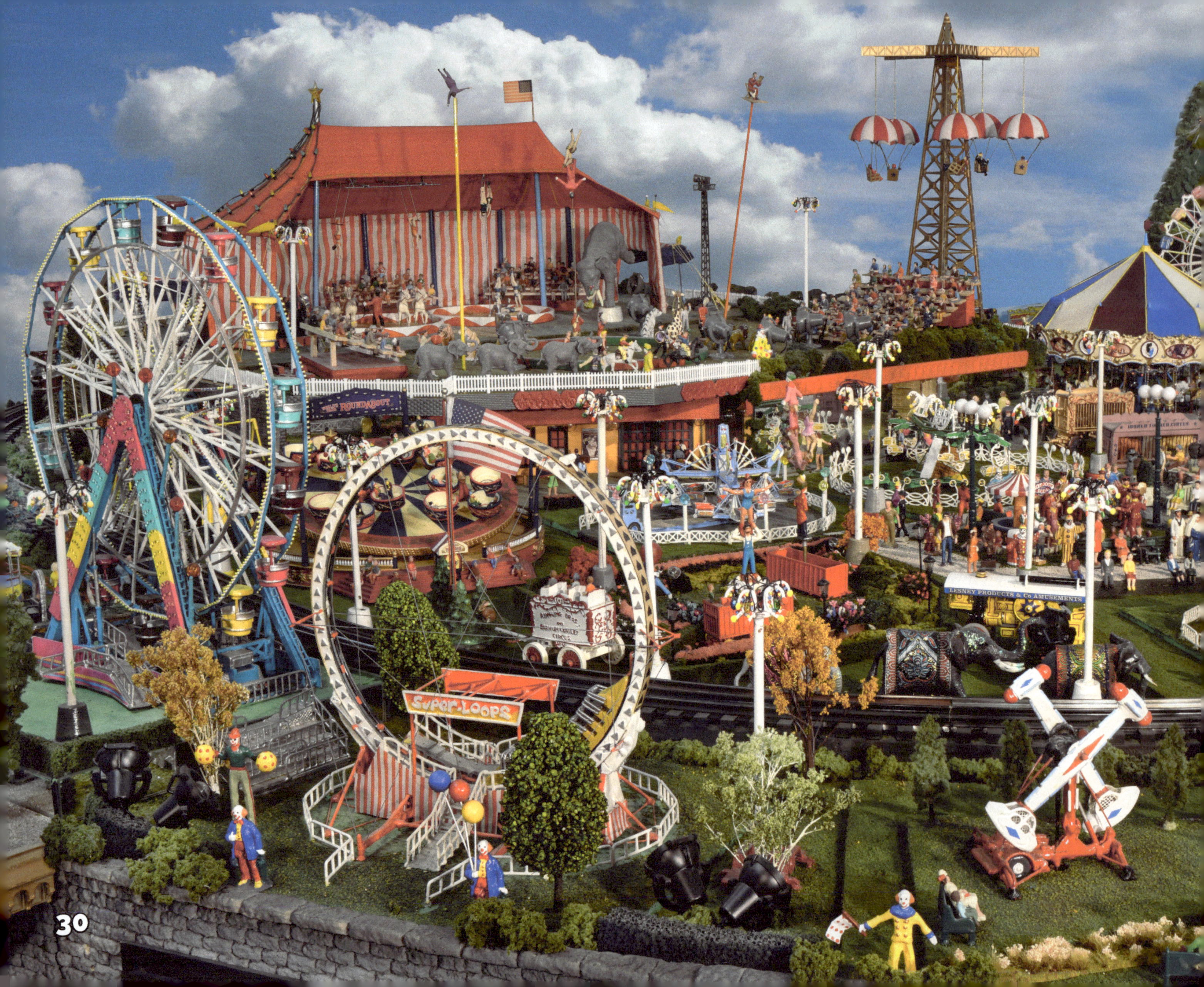

Super-LOOPS
LESNEY PRODUCTS & Co AMUSEMENTS

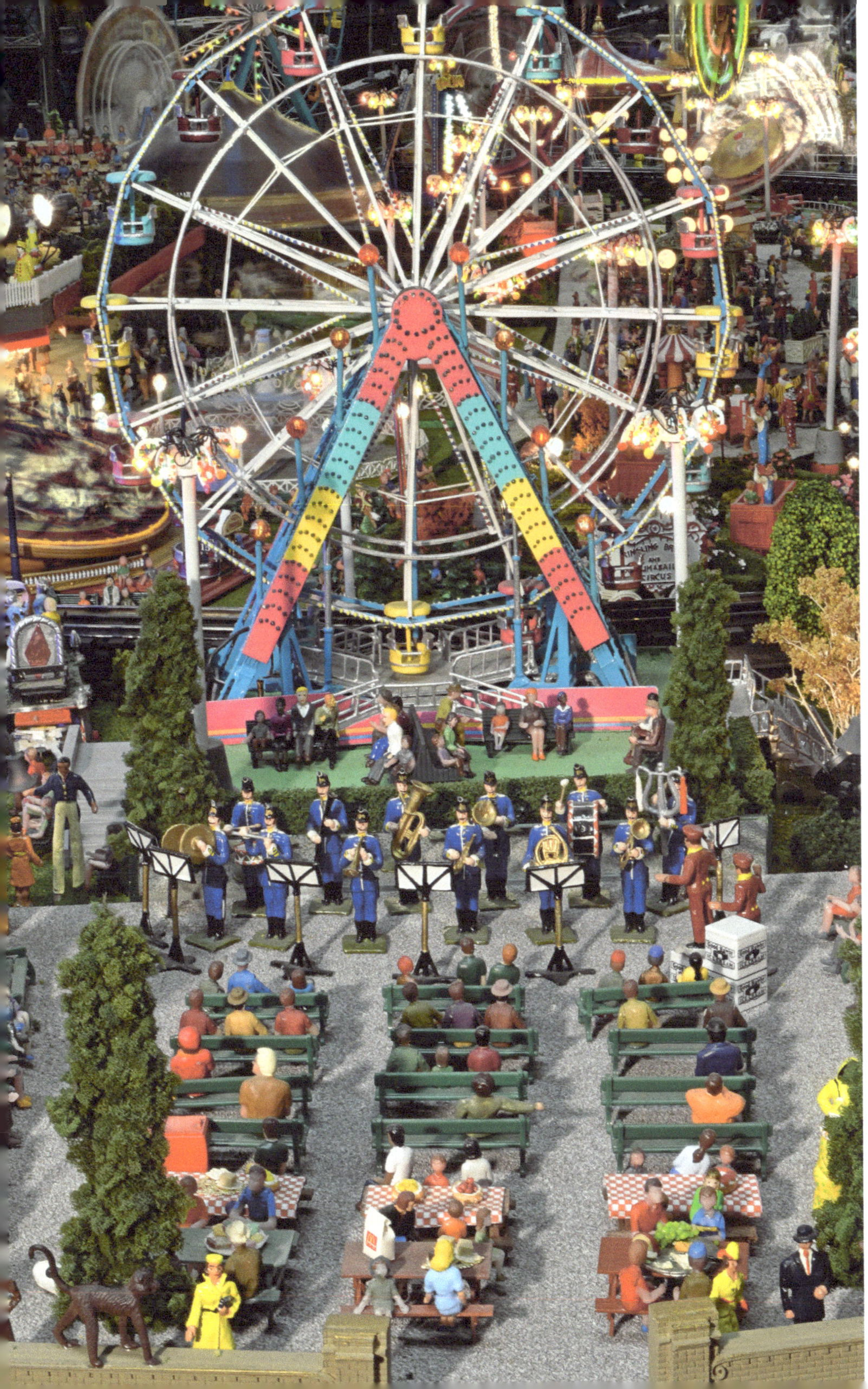

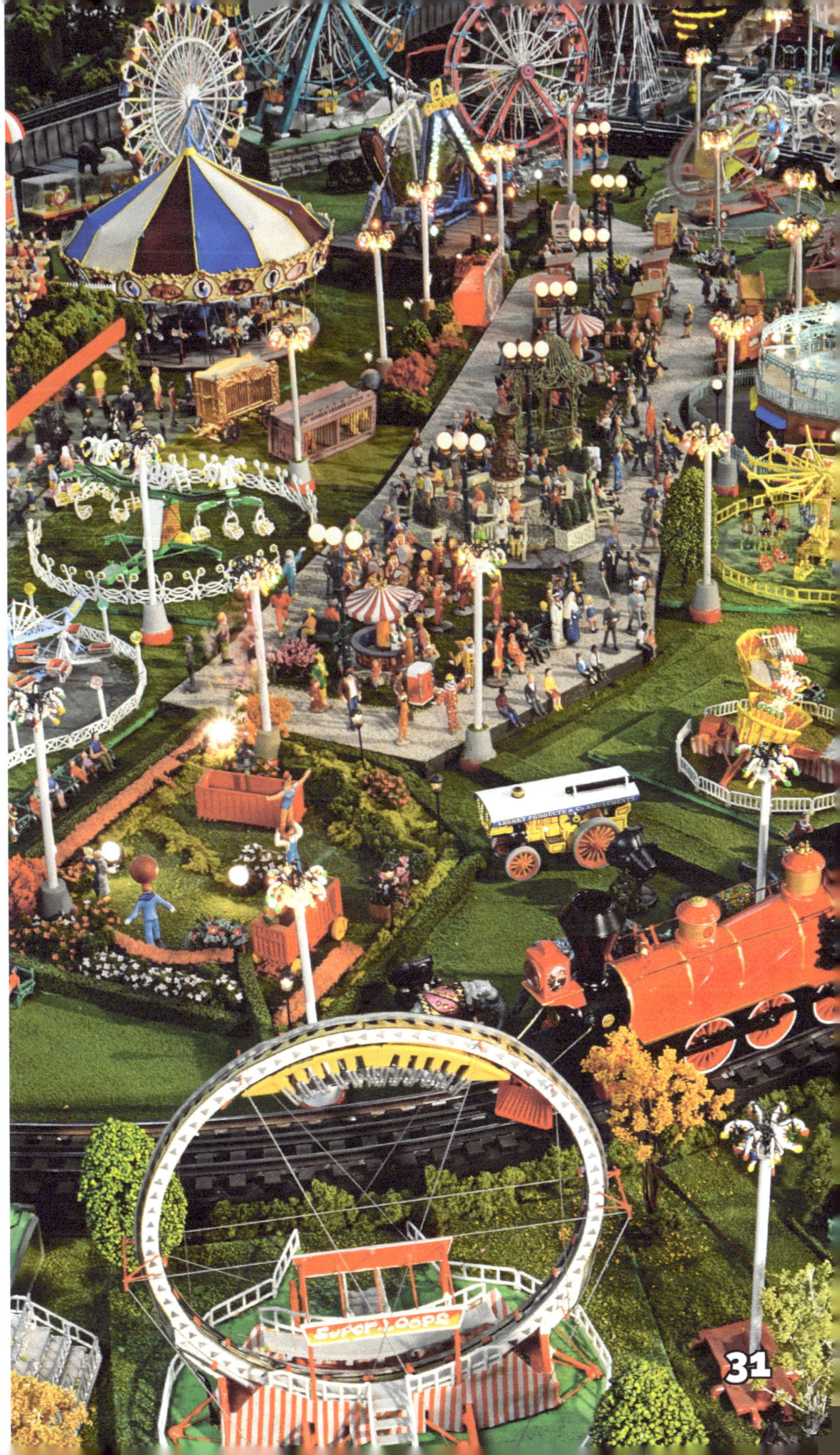

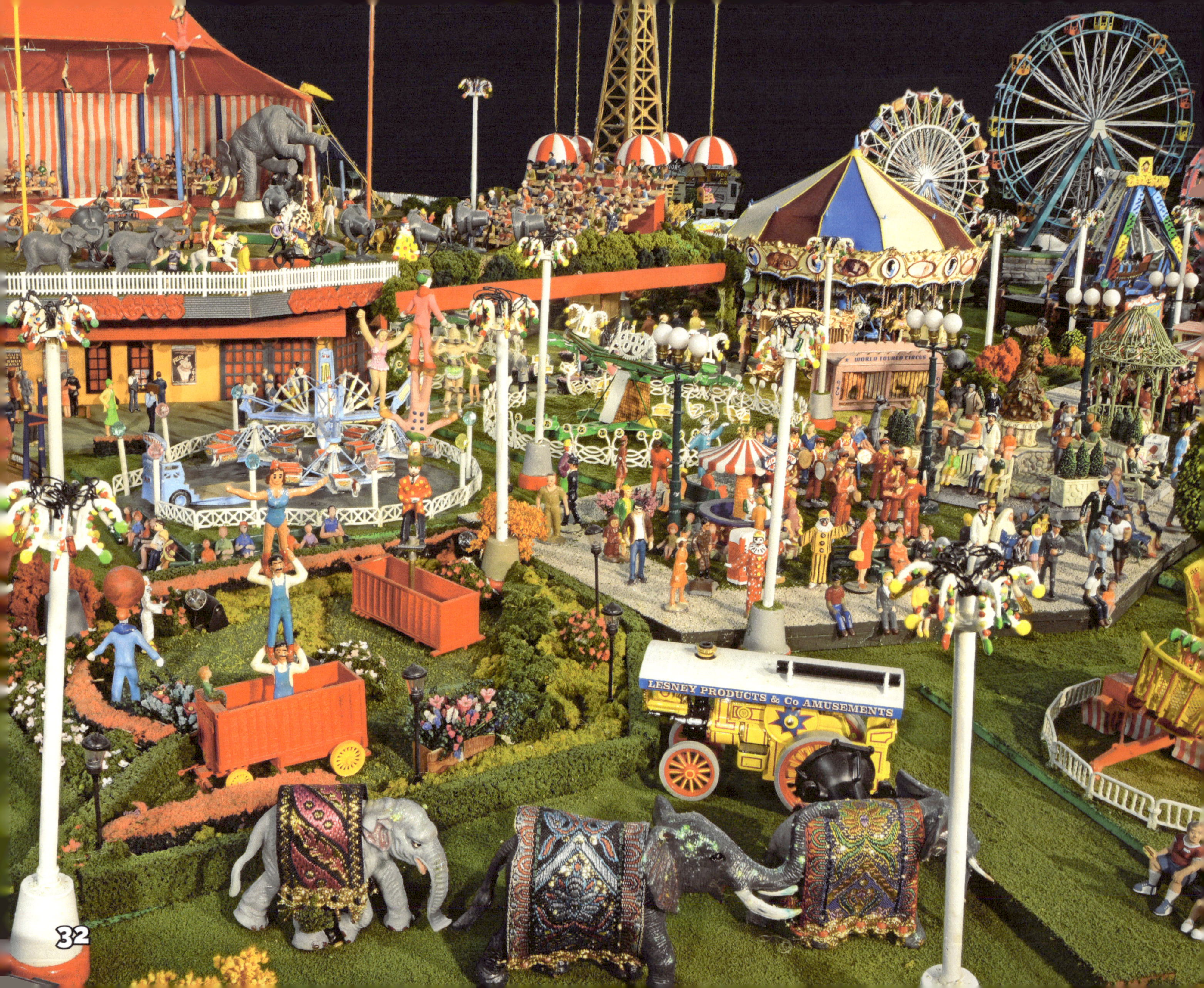
LESNEY PRODUCTS & Co AMUSEMENTS
WORLD TOURED CIRCUS

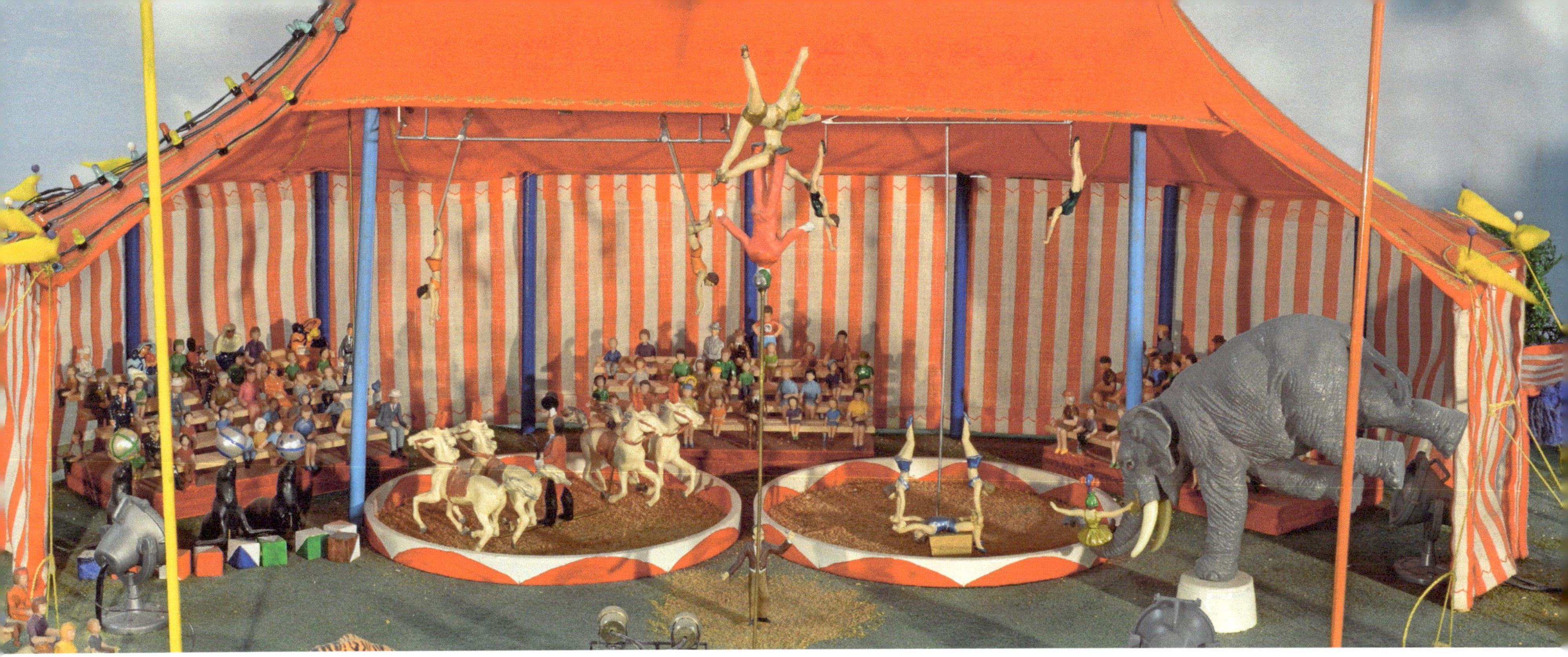

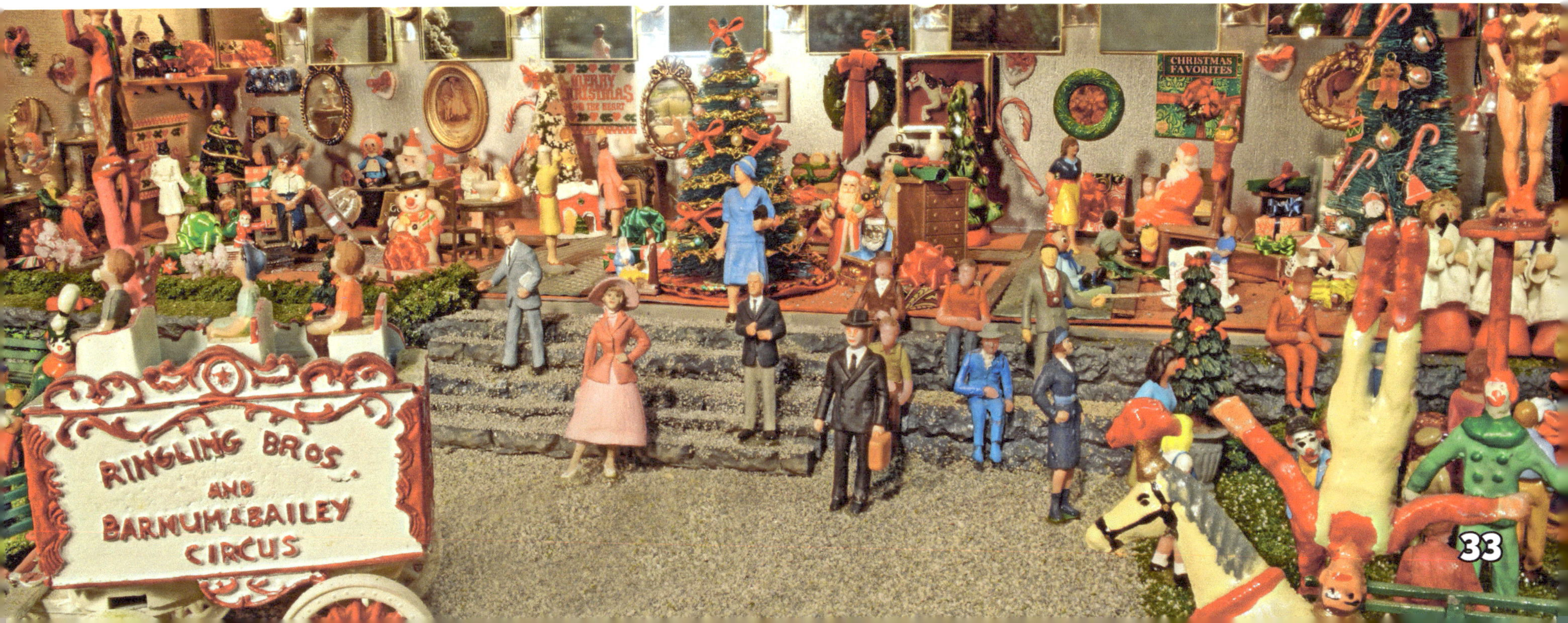

RINGLING BROS.
AND
BARNUM & BAILEY
CIRCUS

CHRISTMAS
FAVORITES

MERRY CHRISTMAS

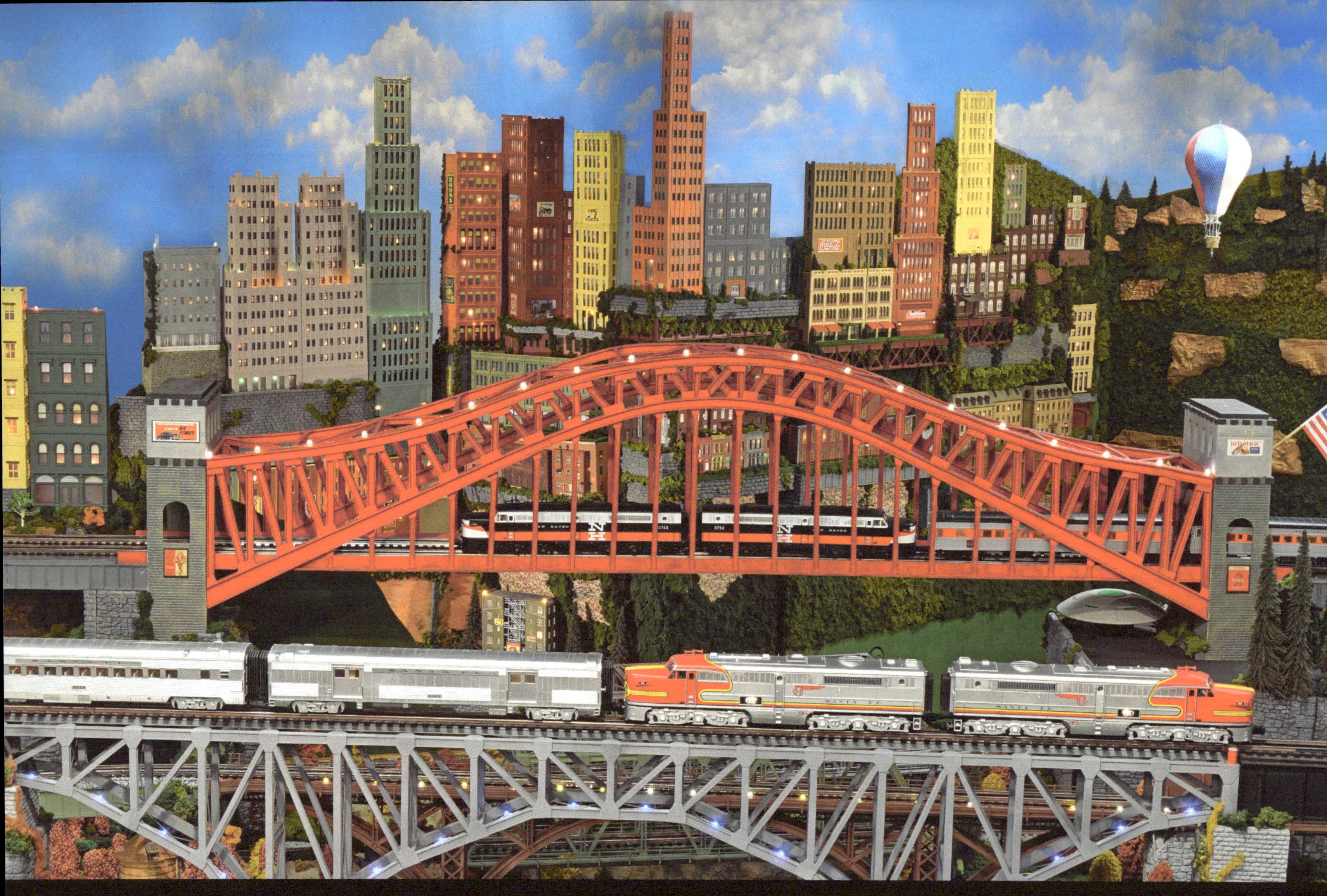

The Distant City Backdrop

In order to create the illusion of distance, I used HO scale kits to build this city backdrop. Using a smaller scale for distant buildings provides a more realistic view. It's called "forced perspective."

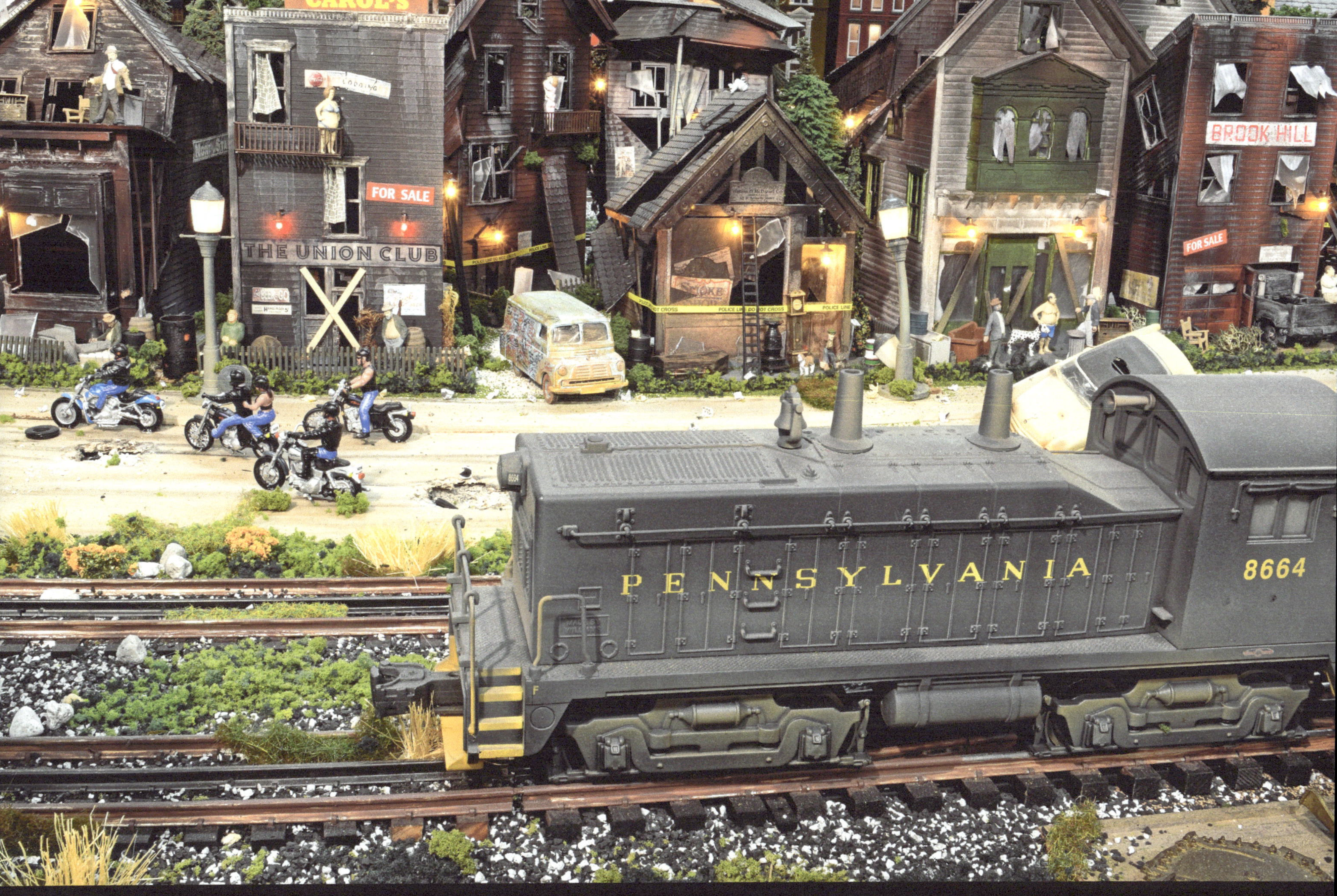

Life in The Bottoms

Life in The Bottoms is rugged. This neighborhood is not safe. The sole remaining
factory is closing. Potholes are big enough to swallow entire cars!

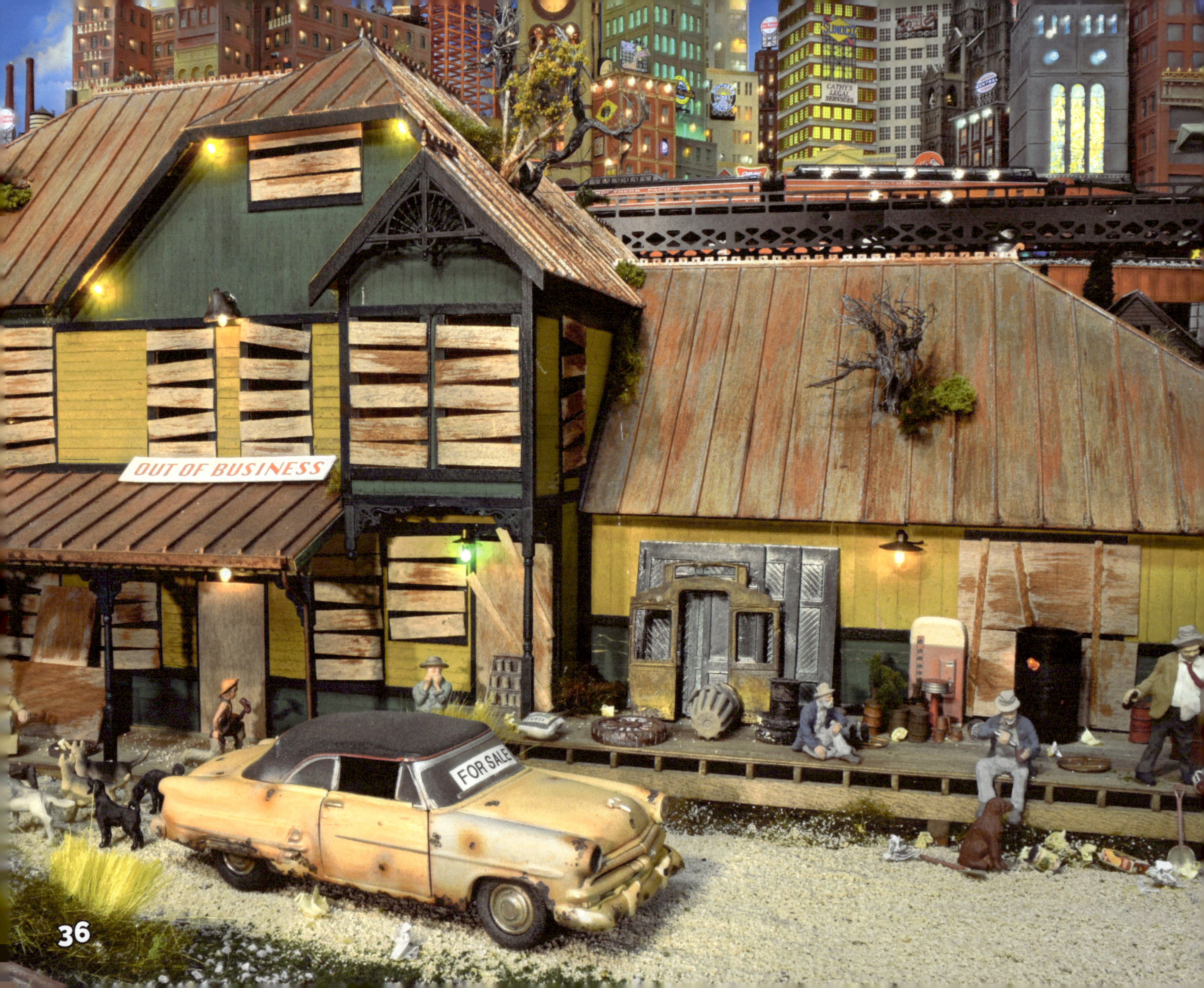

OUT OF BUSINESS
FOR SALE

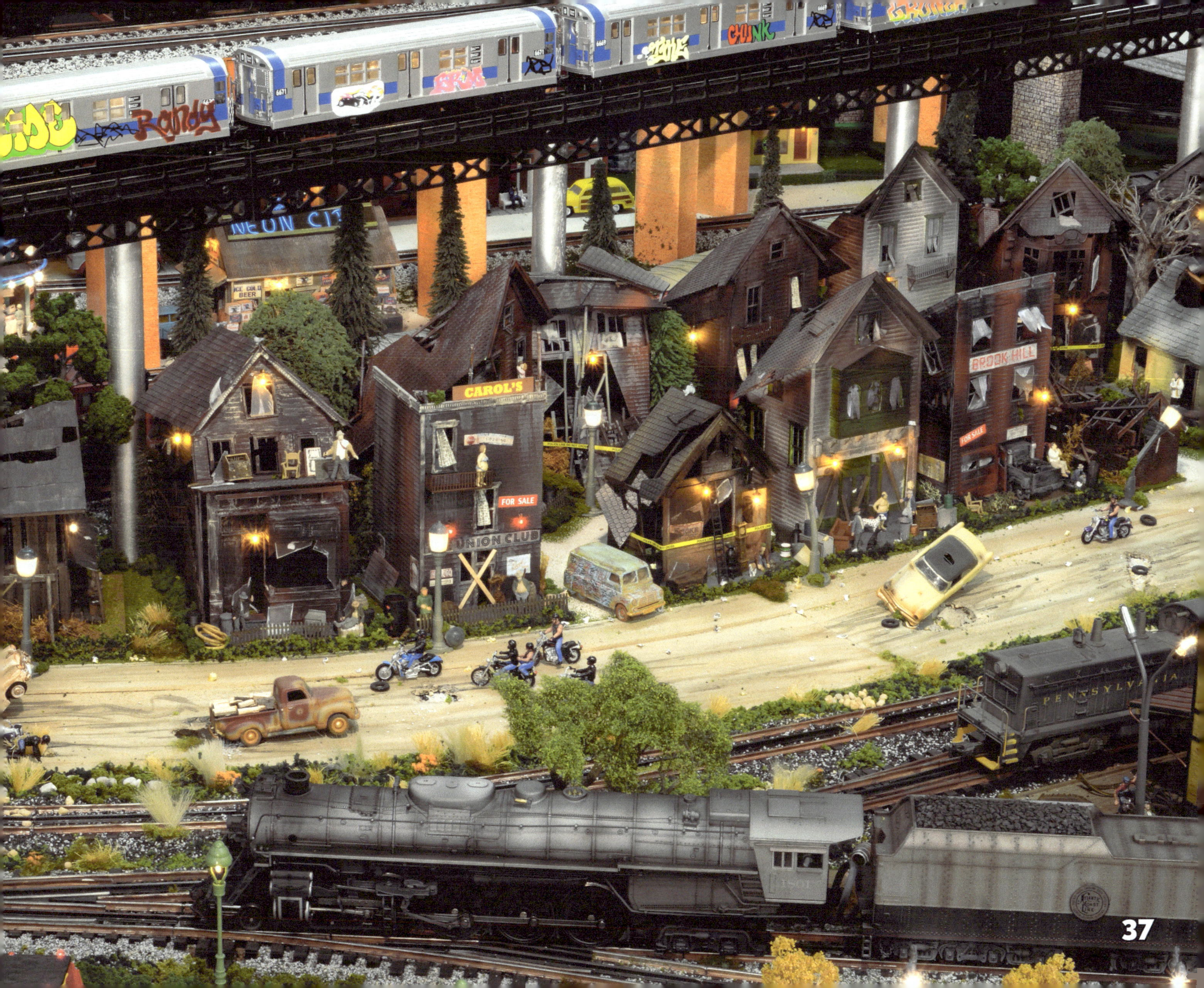

CHUNK
GRUNGE
Randy
NEON CITY
ICE COLD BEER
CAROL'S
FOR SALE
UNION CLUB
BROOK HILL
FOR SALE
PENNSYLVANIA

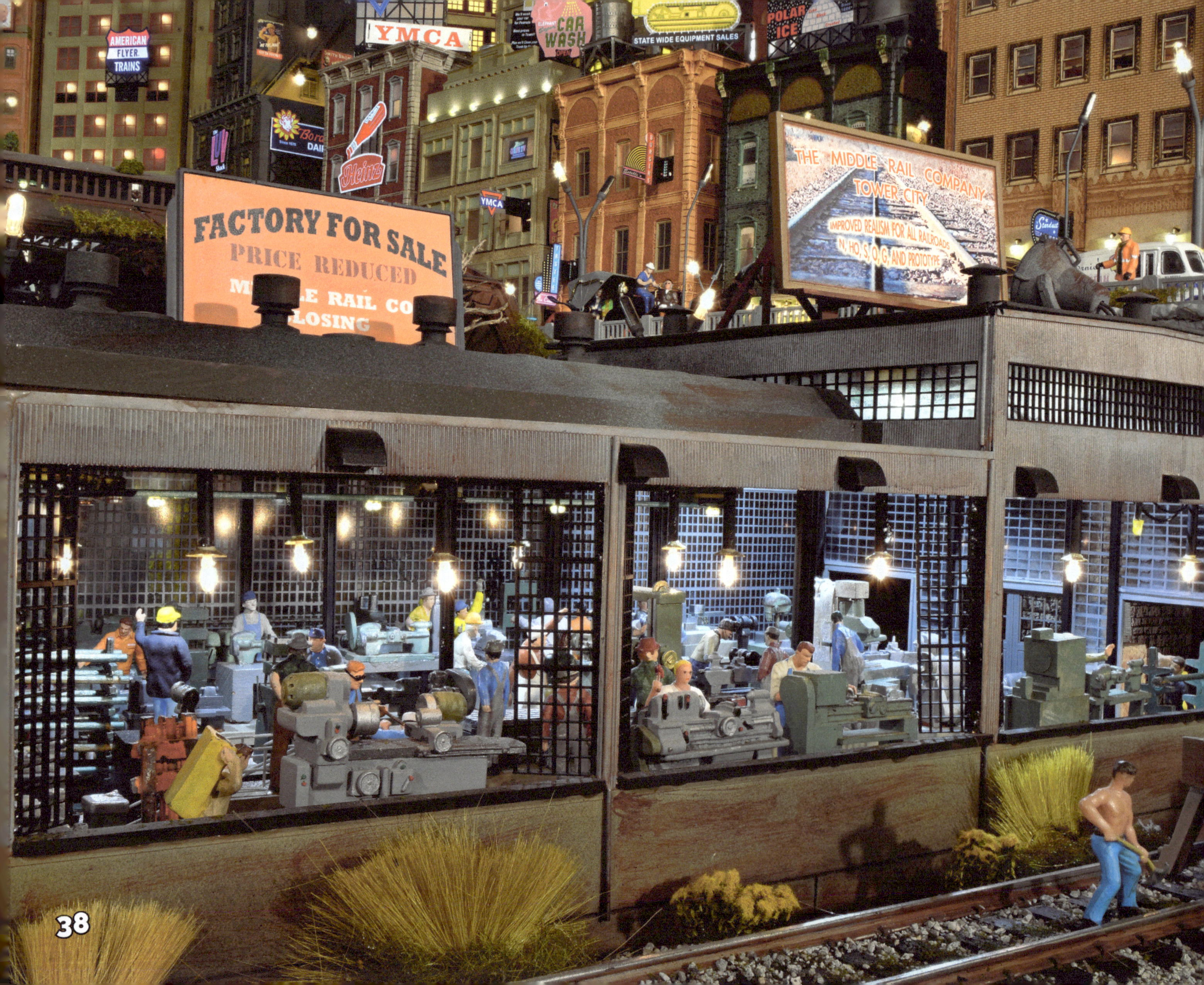
AMERICAN FLYER TRAINS
YMCA
CAR WASH
POLAR ICE
STATE WIDE EQUIPMENT SALES
Heinz
DAIRY
YMCA
THE MIDDLE RAIL COMPANY
TOWER CITY
IMPROVED REALISM FOR ALL RAILROADS
N, HO, S, O, G, AND PROTOTYPE
FACTORY FOR SALE
PRICE REDUCED
MIDDLE RAIL CO
CLOSING

Life Below The Tracks

This is life in the city near The Bottoms, below the tracks.

Down at the end of the street the fire department is dealing with a small office fire.

Those "shady-looking" characters standing by the phone booth are not drug dealers. Neither is the little boy in the blue shirt in the car.

They are photos of my grandsons, placed into this image via Photoshop.

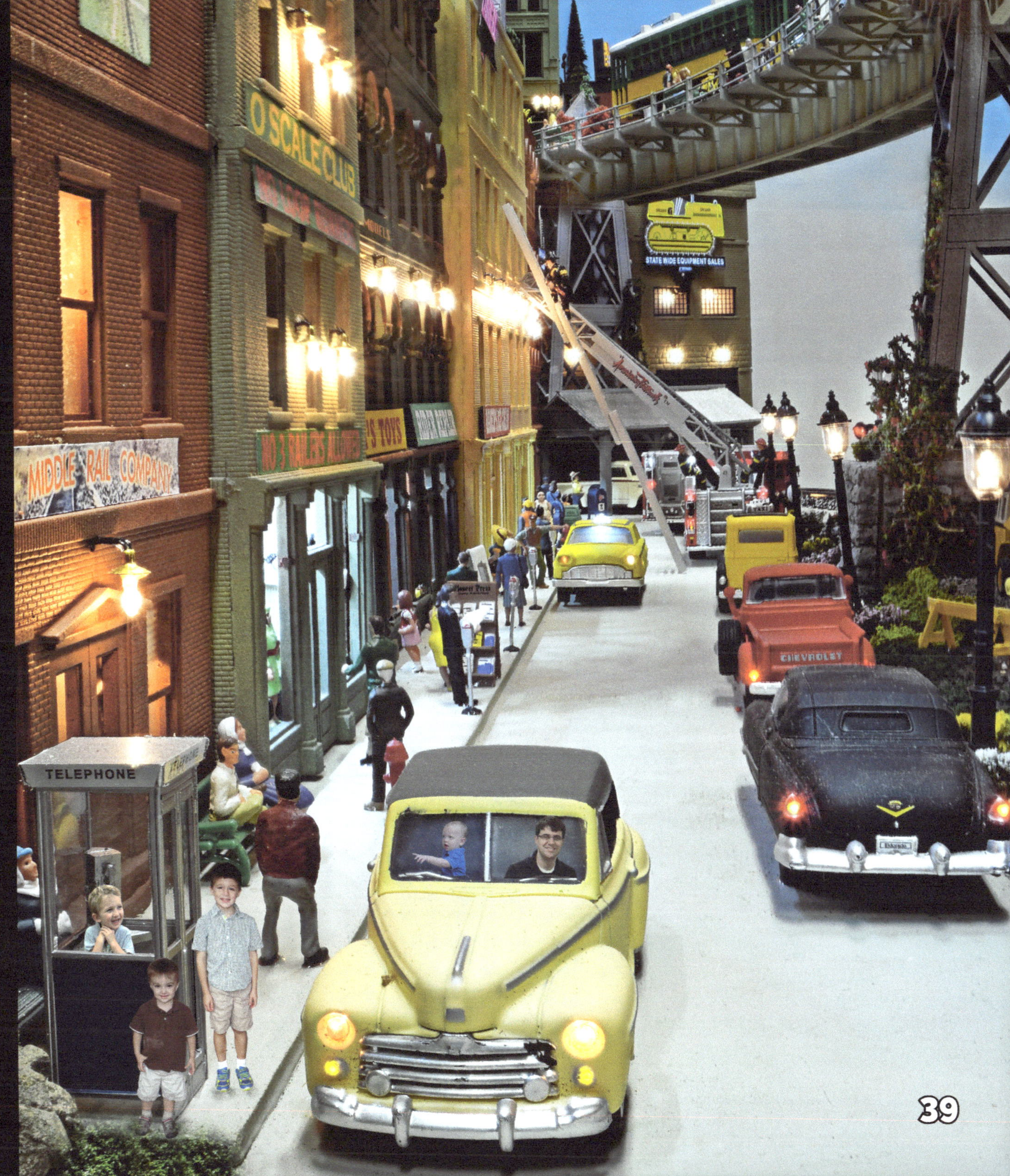

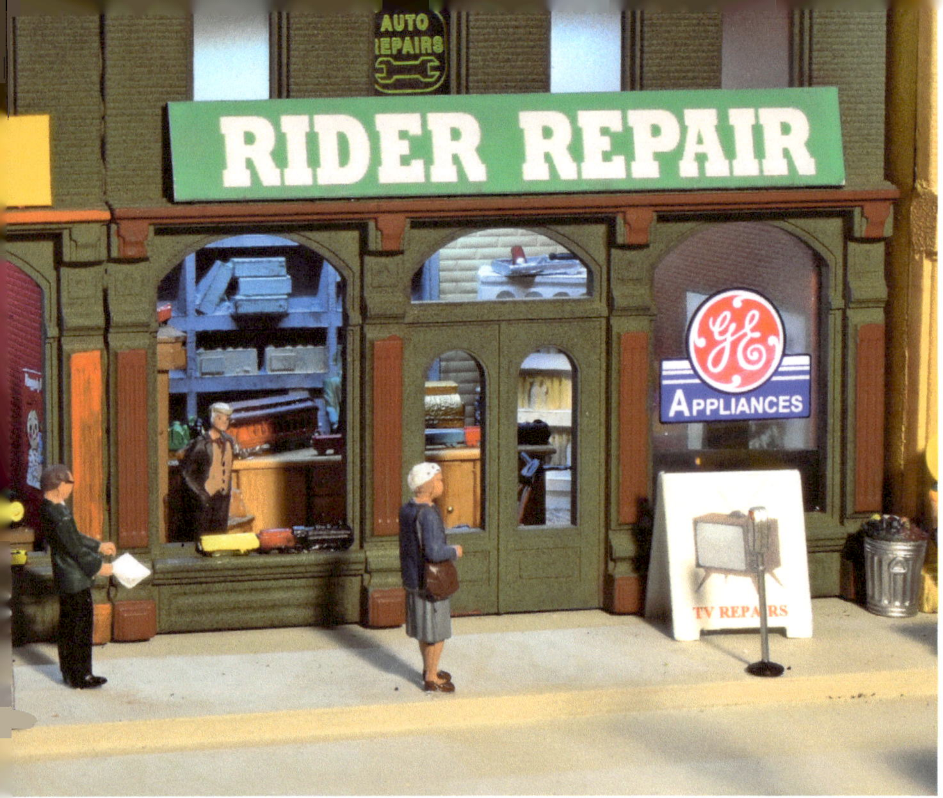

AUTO REPAIRS
RIDER REPAIR
GE
APPLIANCES
TV REPAIRS

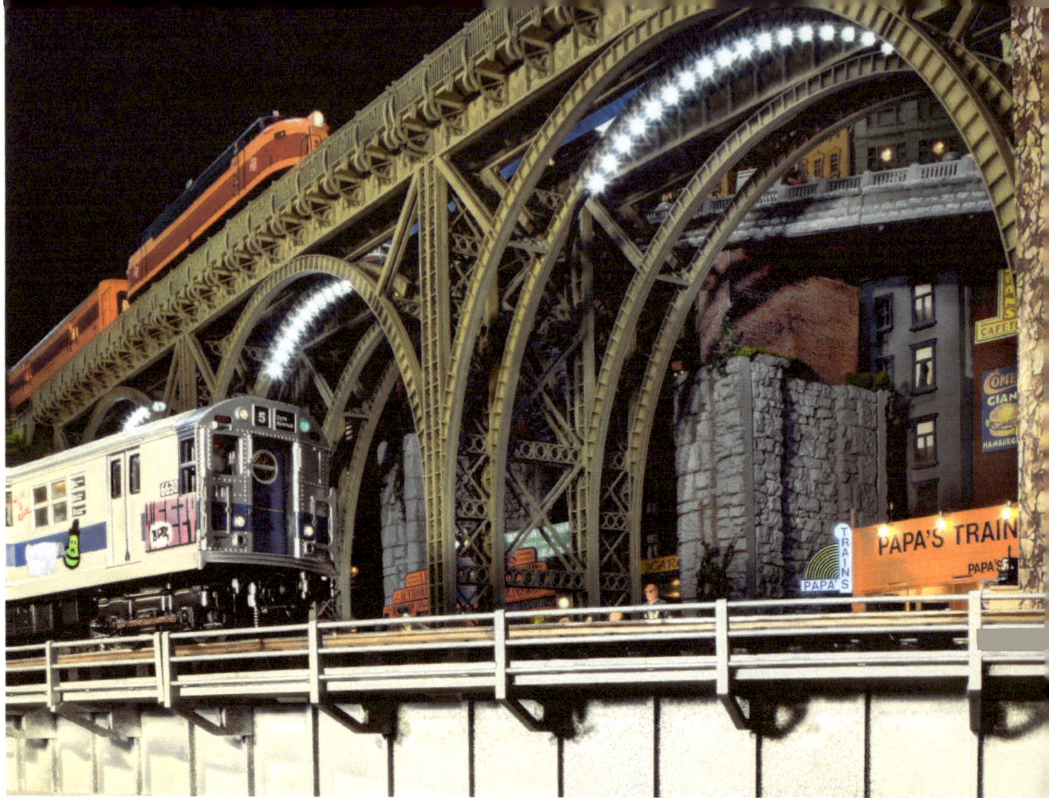

S
PAPA'S TRAIN
PAPA'S

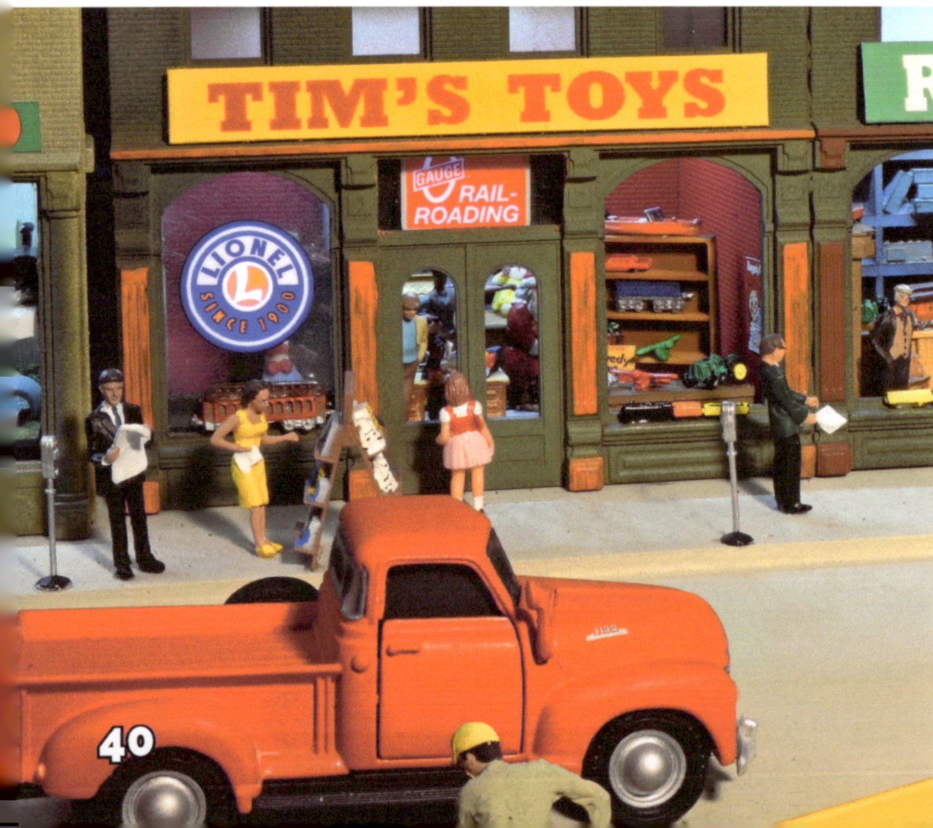

TIM'S TOYS
O GAUGE RAIL-ROADING
LIONEL SINCE 1900
R
40

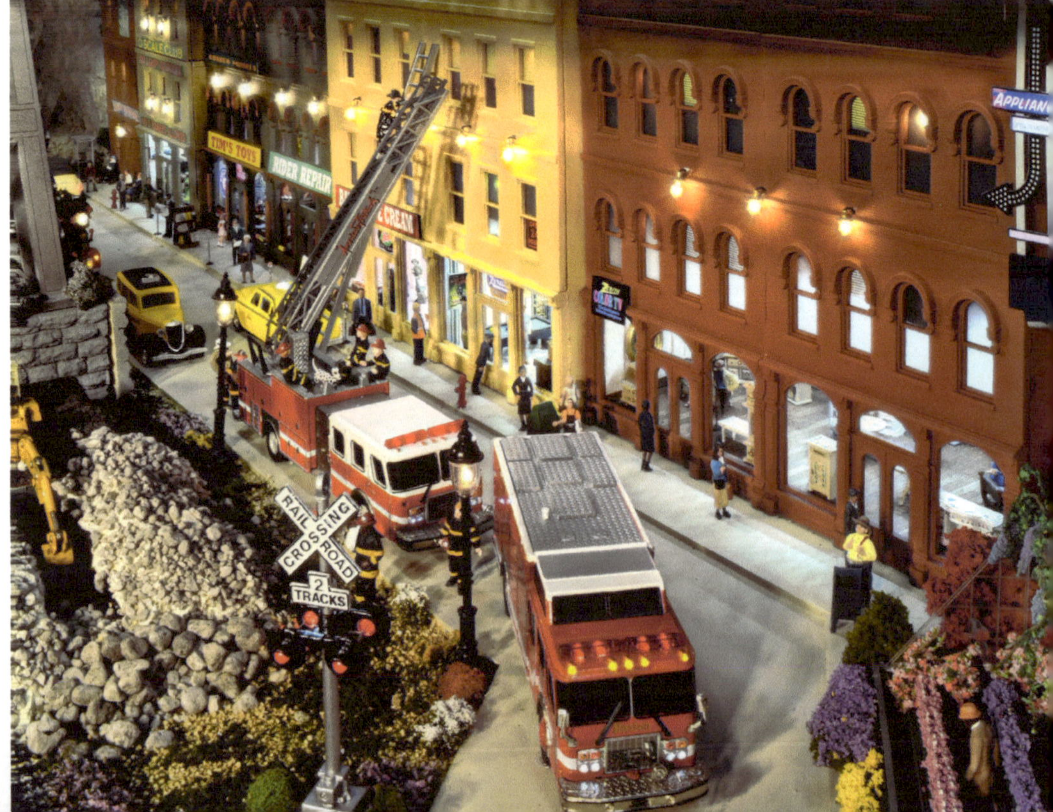

TIM'S TOYS
RIDER REPAIR
APPLIAN
RAILROAD CROSSING
2 TRACKS

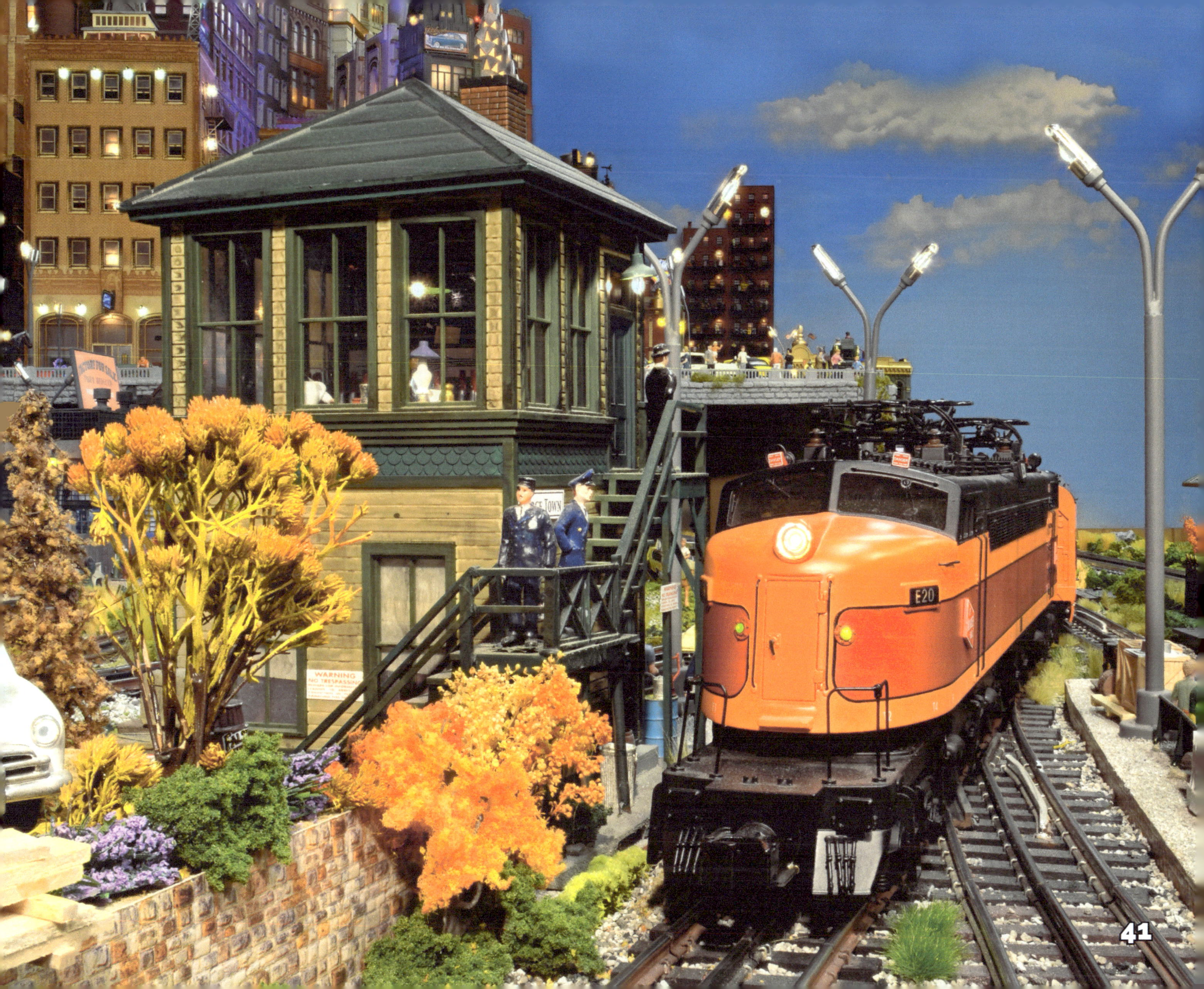

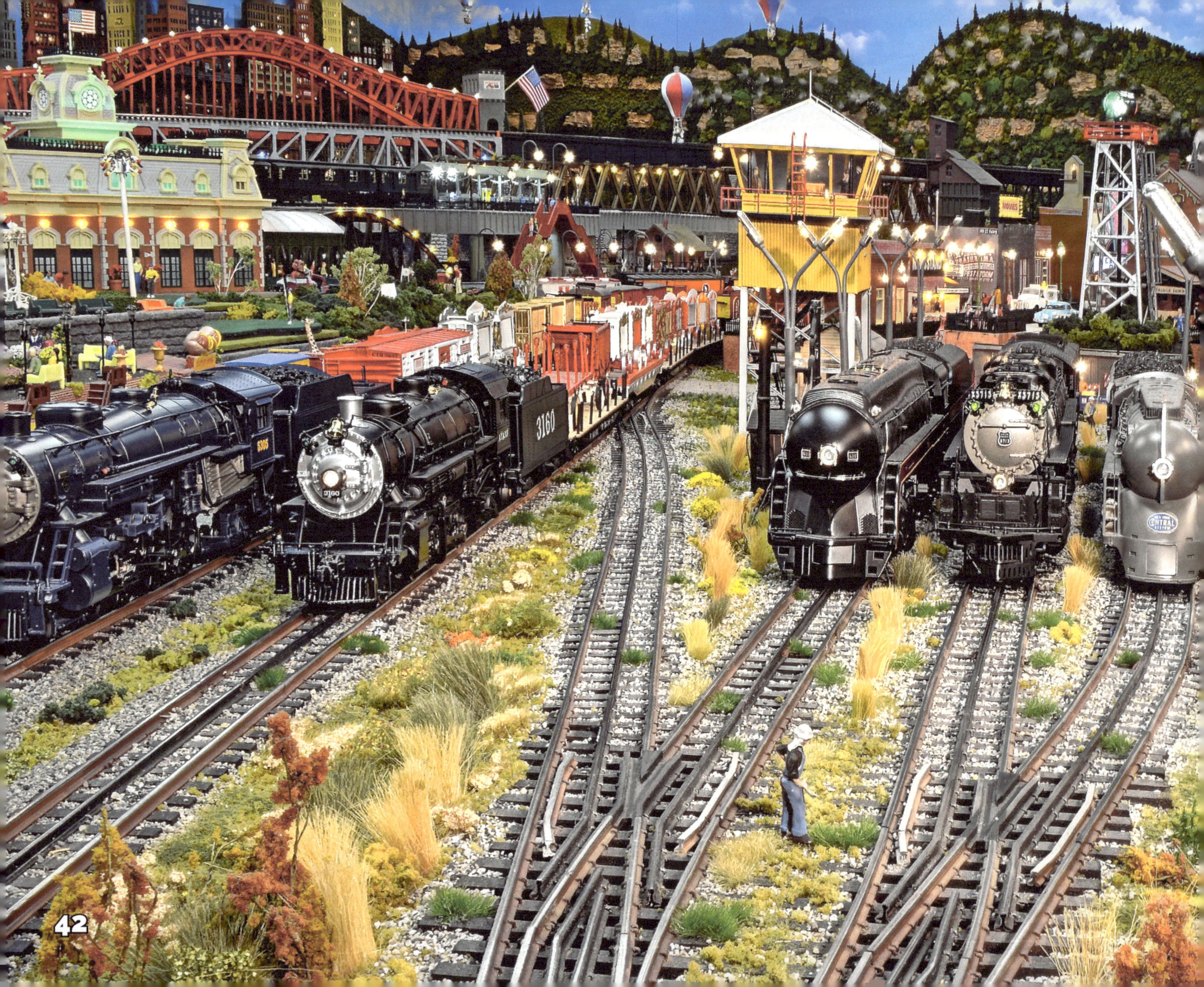

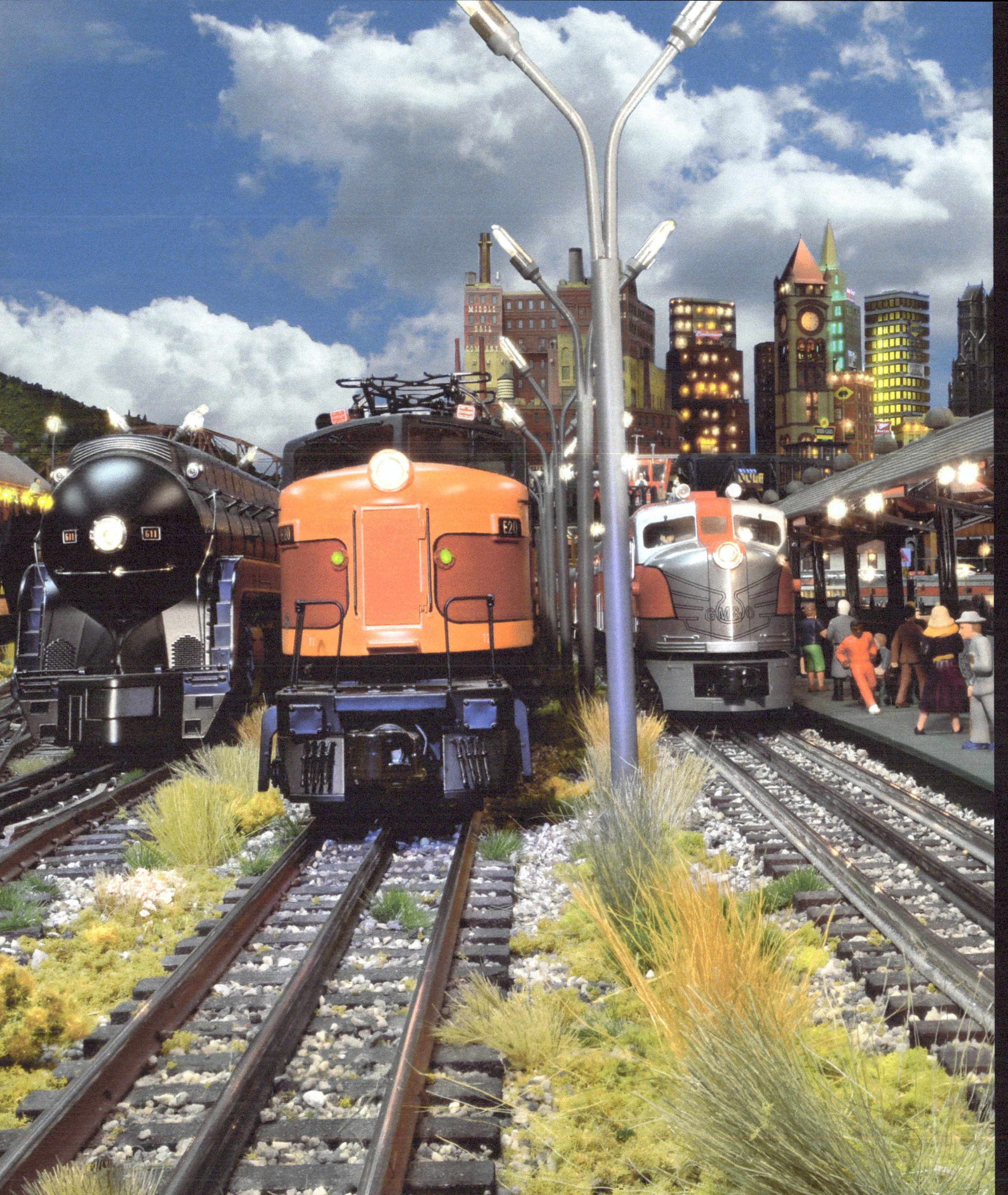

Trackwork

I wanted my train operations to be smooth, quiet and trouble-free.

I achieved that goal by building level and sturdy layout framework and using homasote sheeting, cork roadbed, GarGraves track and Ross switches.

I found most of my ideas and the materials for building the scenery and detailing the layout at Scenic Express.

GarGraves Track
www.gargraves.com

Ross Switches
www.rossswitches.com

Scenery Express
www.sceneryexpress.com

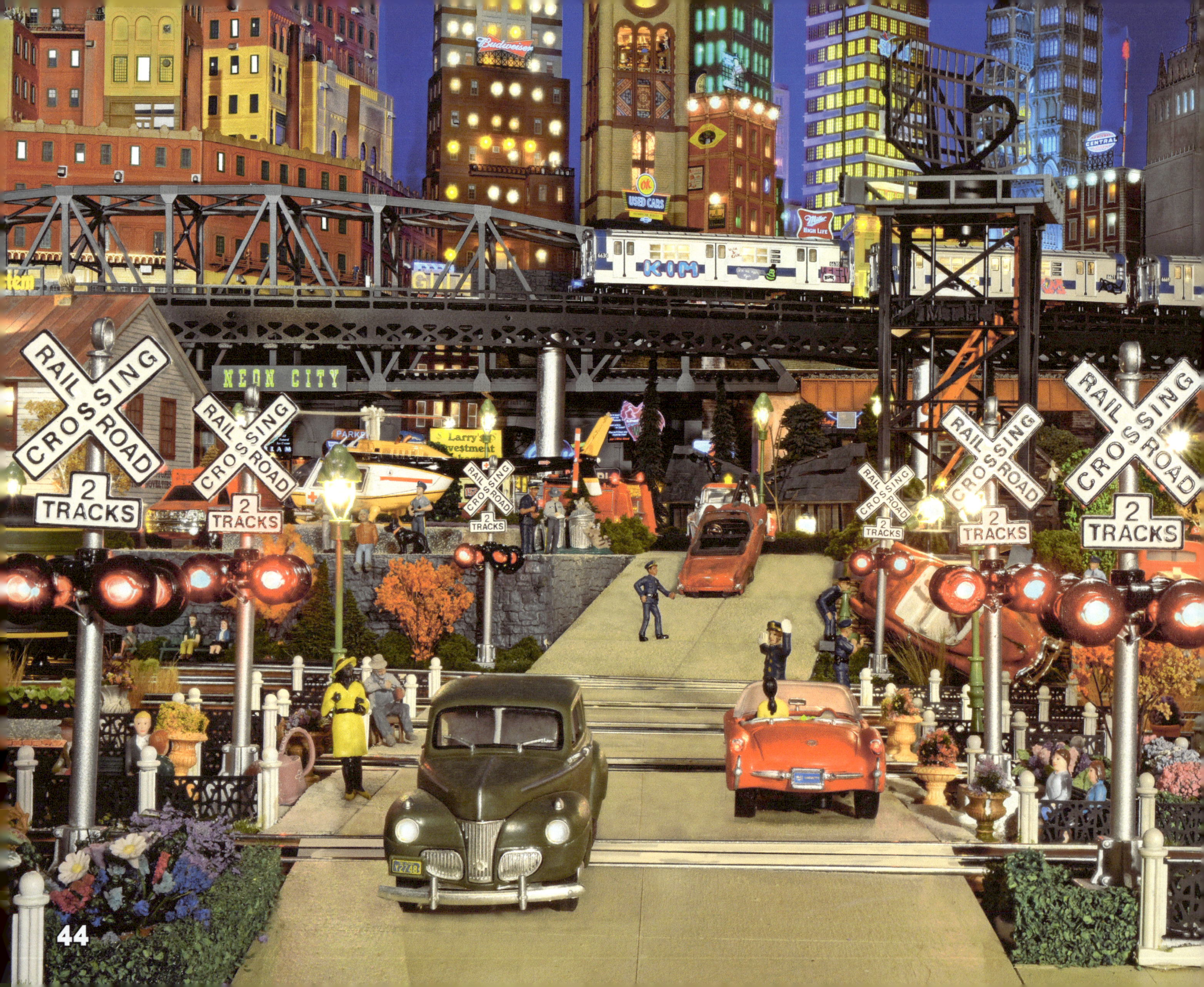

Budweiser
Miller High Life
OK USED CARS
CENTRAL
NEON CITY
Larry's Investment
PARK
RAIL ROAD CROSSING
2 TRACKS
RAIL ROAD CROSSING
2 TRACKS
RAIL ROAD CROSSING
2 TRACKS
RAIL ROAD CROSSING
2 TRACKS
RAIL ROAD CROSSING
2 TRACKS
KIM
Y2748

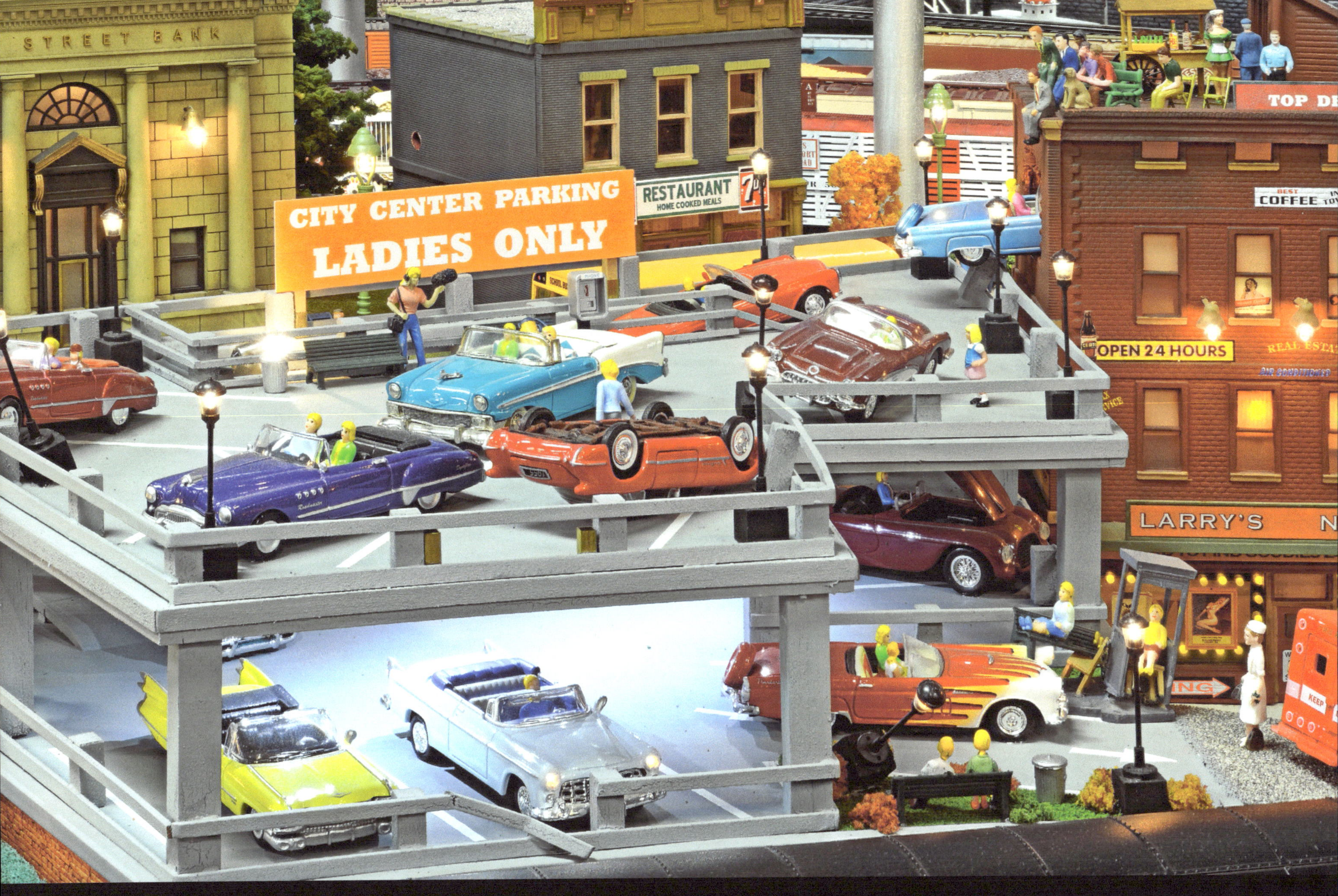

The "Ladies Only" Parking Lot

Would you want to park in this hazardous area? The men watching from
the roof top of Larry's Novelties are enjoying the afternoon's activities.

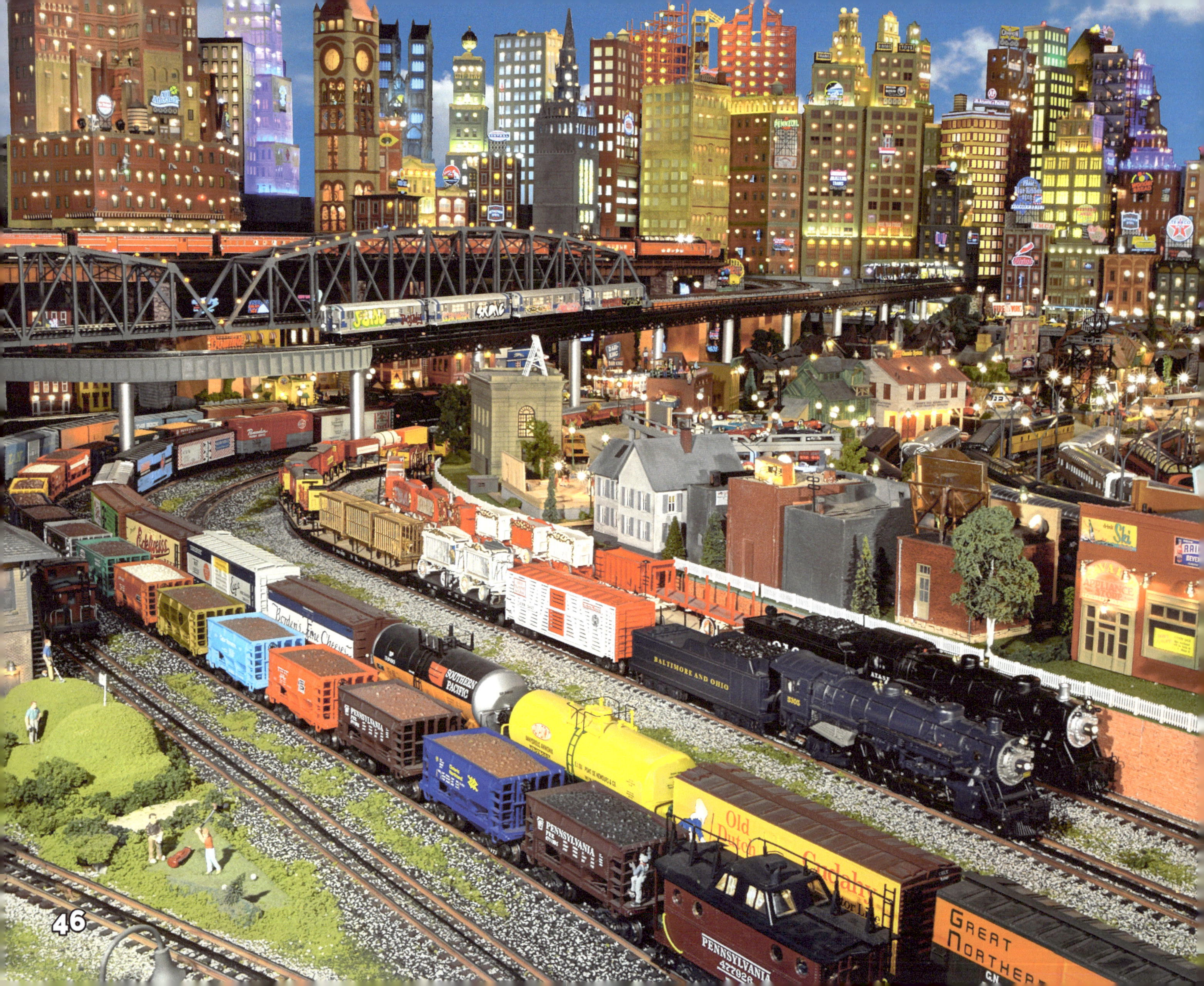

Pennzoil
Texaco
Borden's Fine Cheese
SOUTHERN PACIFIC
BALTIMORE AND OHIO
PENNSYLVANIA
Old Dutch
GREAT NORTHERN
PENNSYLVANIA
Ski

The Stations of Tower City

There are several passenger and transit stations located throughout the bustling metropolis of Tower City.

These days, trains operate daily due to frequent visits from my grandchildren!

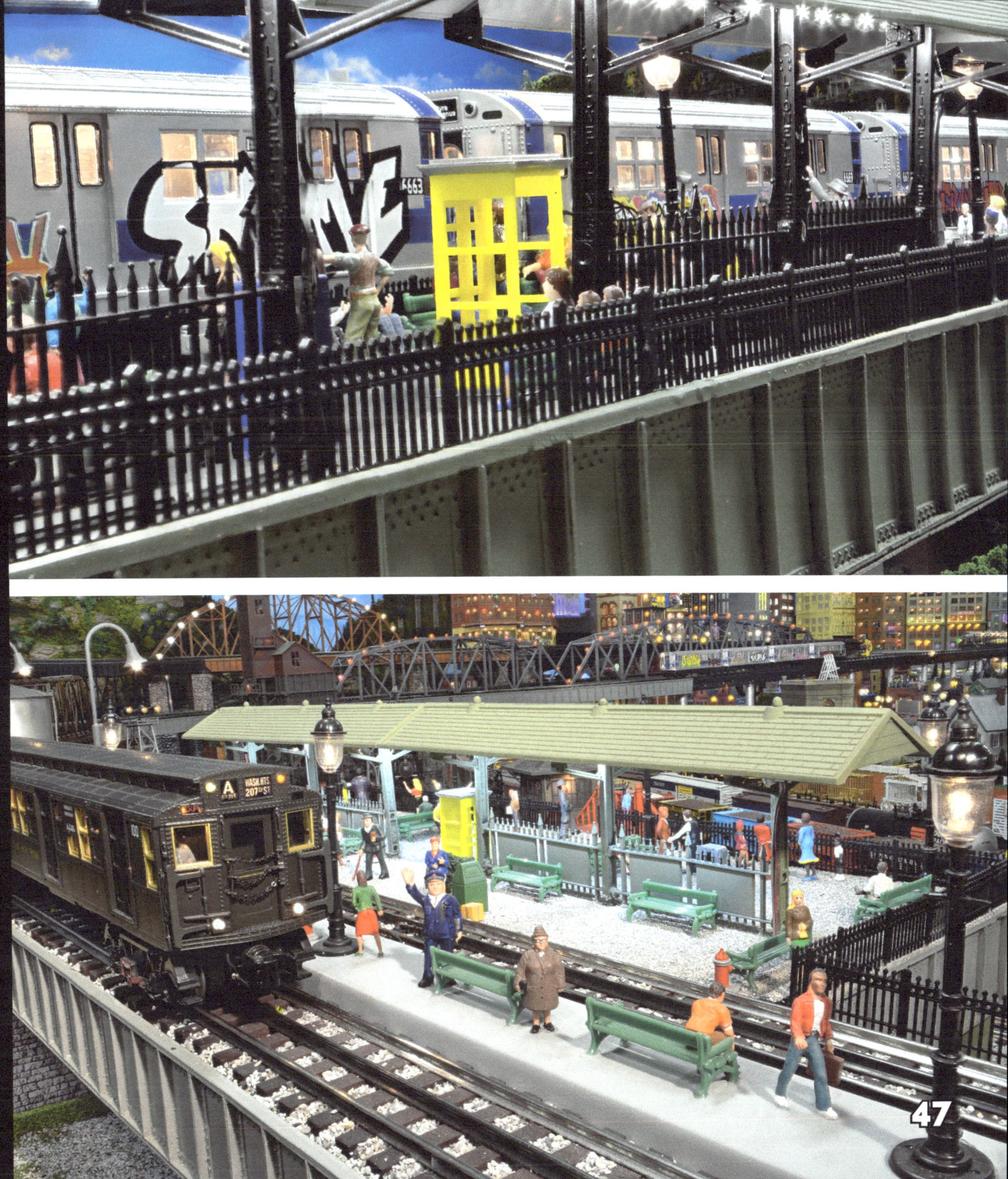

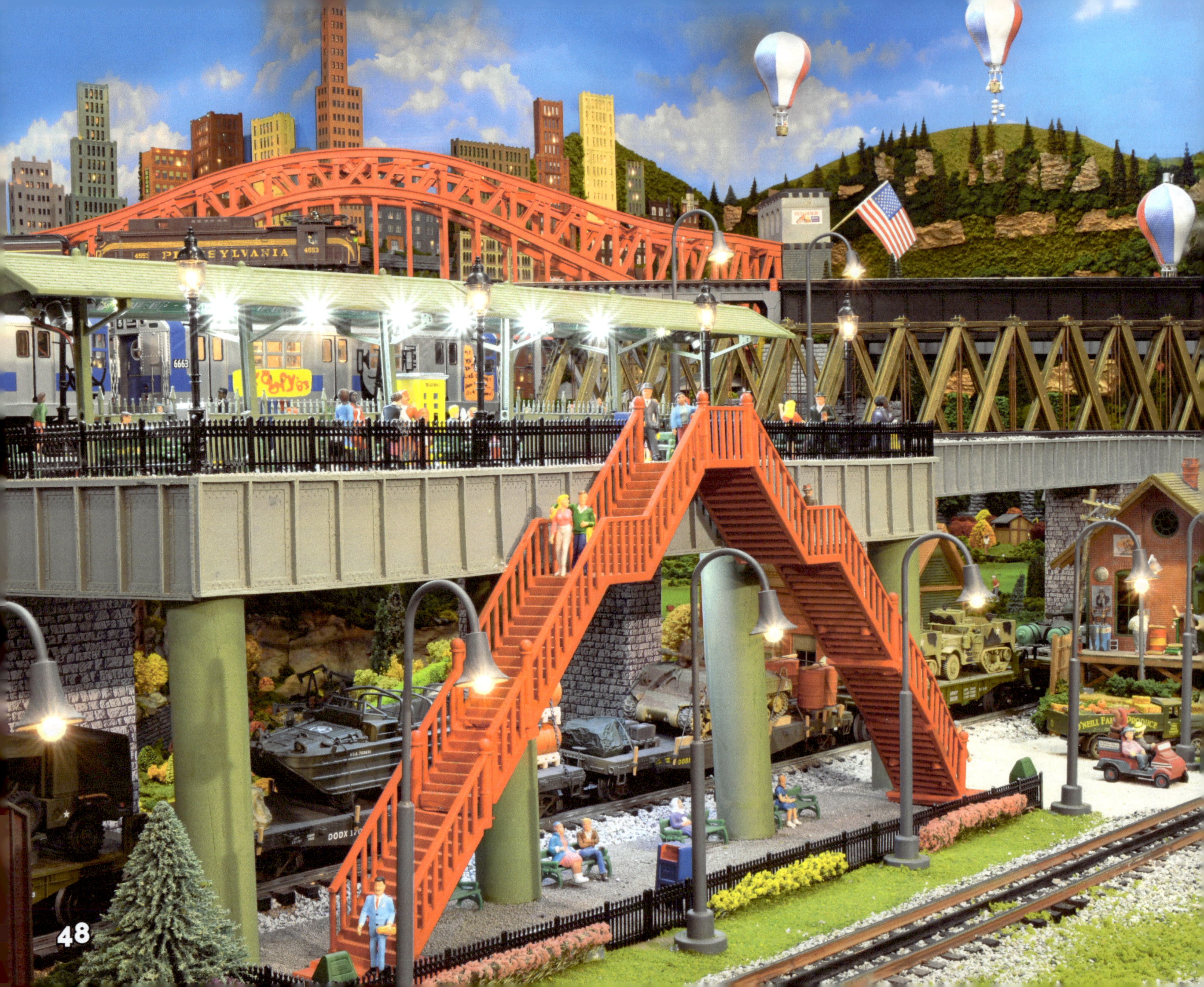
PENNSYLVANIA 4553
6663
O'NEILL FARM PRODUCE
DODX 170

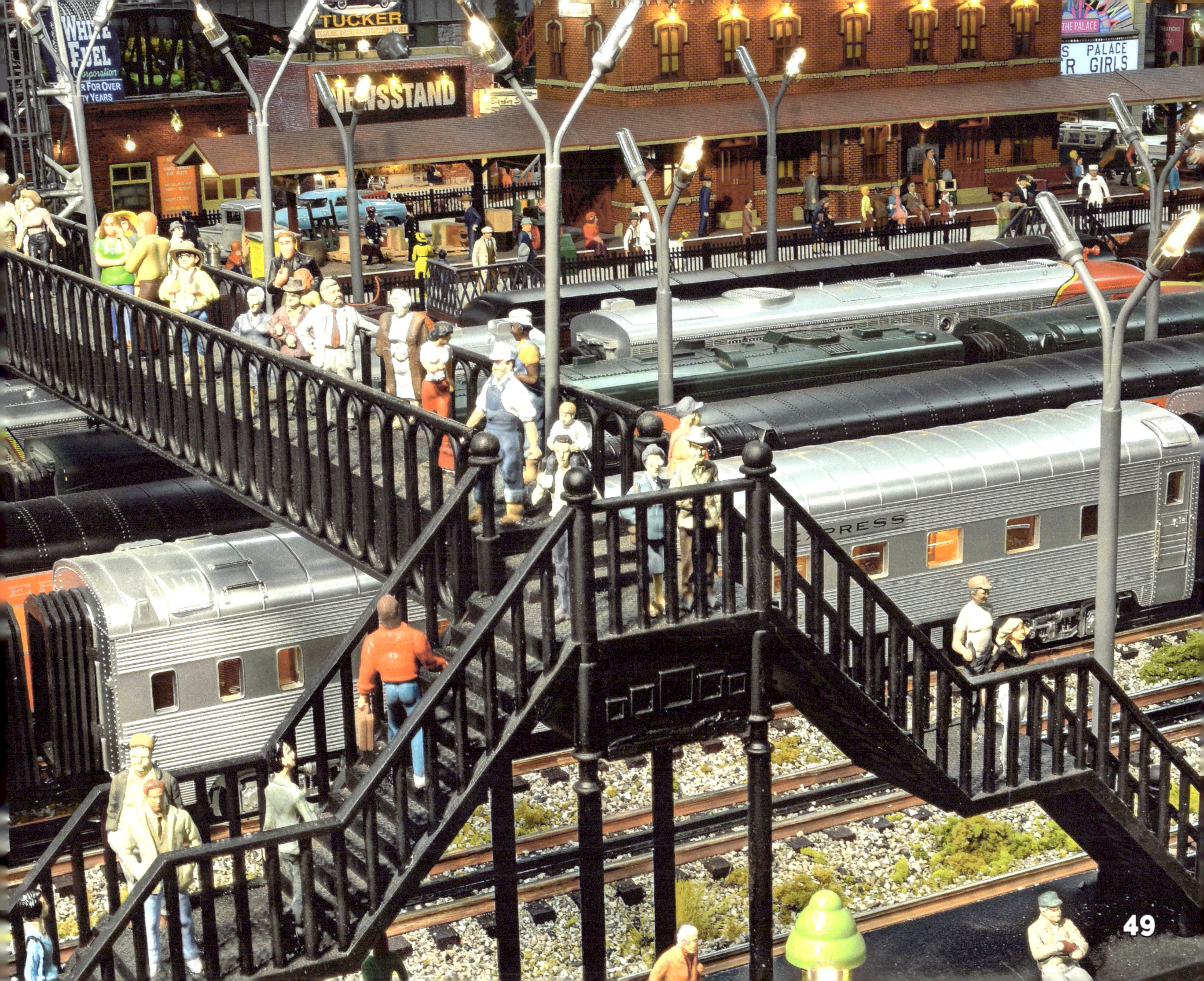

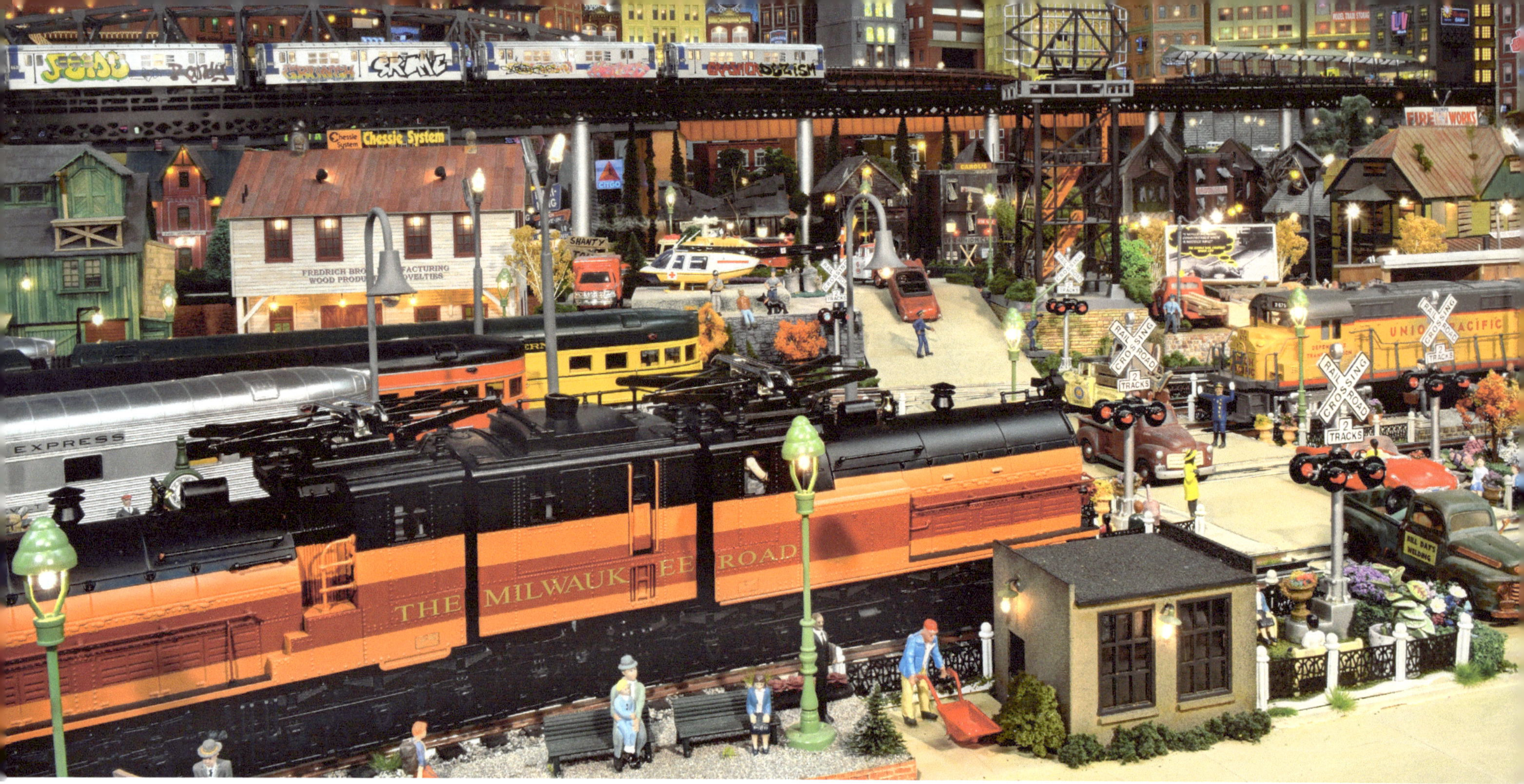

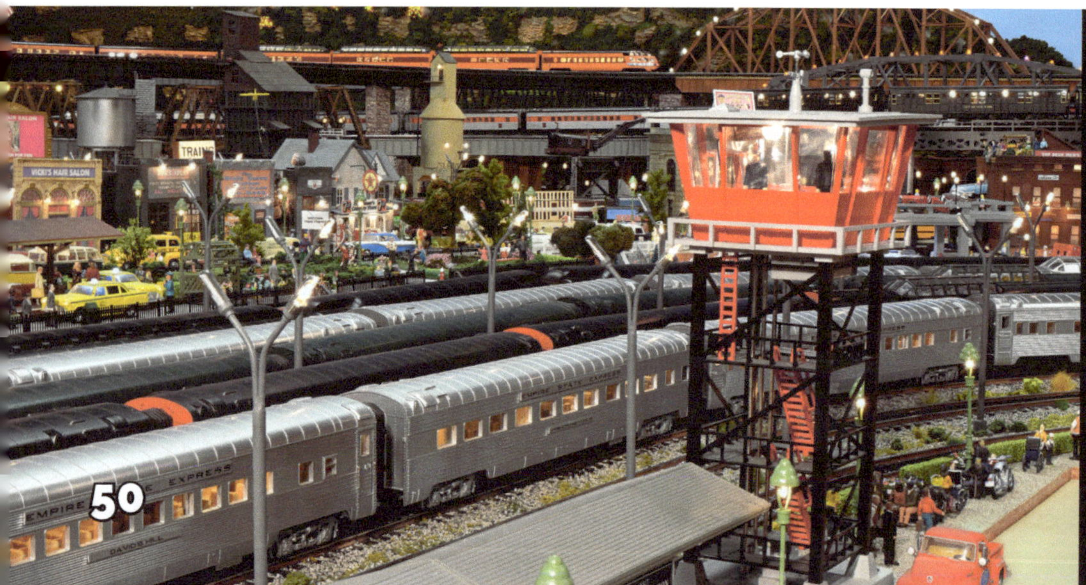

Traveling to Tower City

Passenger and commuter trains are heading to Tower City. The trains will pass through The Bottoms, so be sure to stay on board until you reach the City Center Station!

I hope you have a great visit in Tower City.

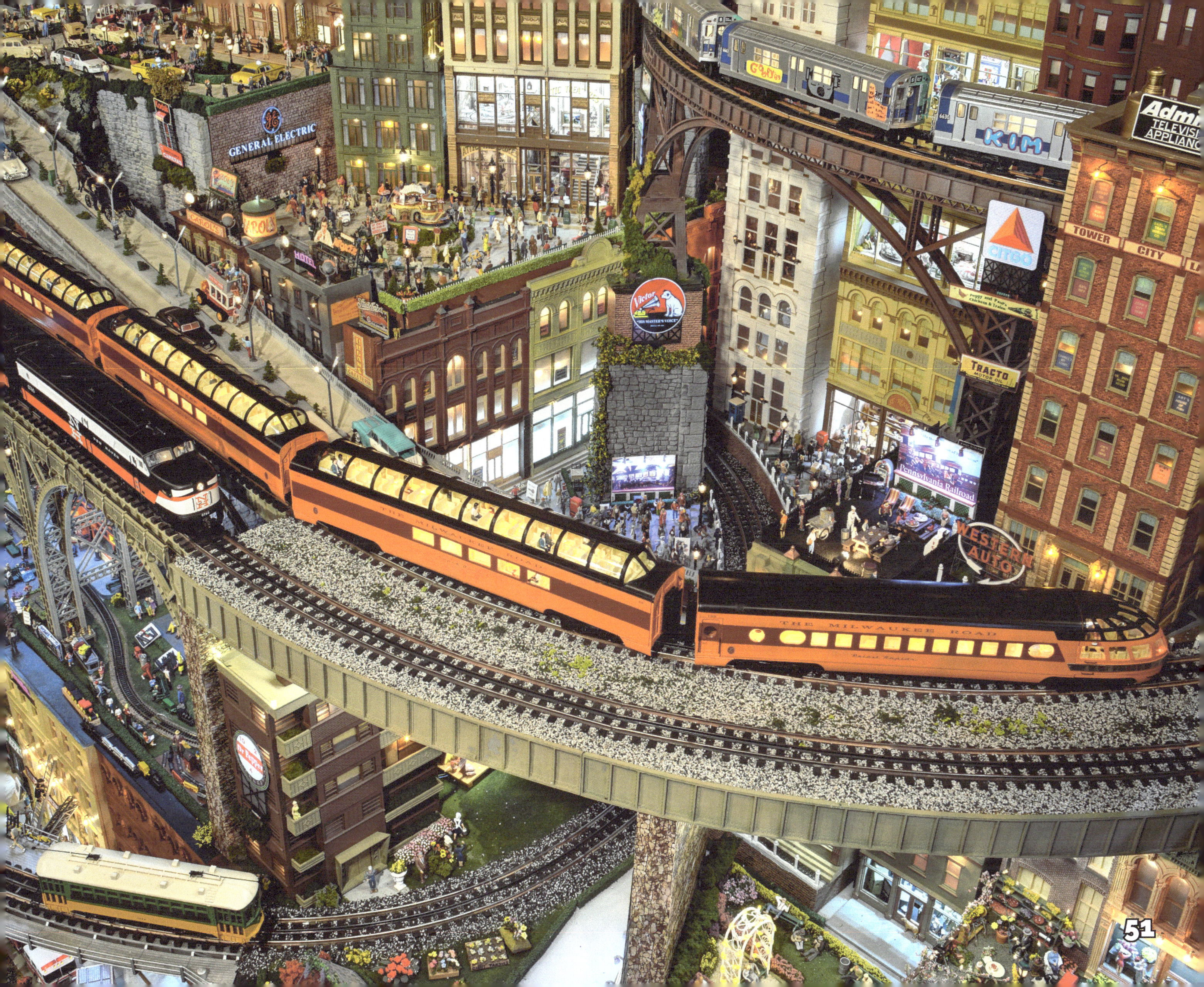

GENERAL ELECTRIC
GE
citgo
TOWER CITY
Admiral
TELEVISION
APPLIANC
Victor
"HIS MASTER'S VOICE"
TRACTO
Pennsylvania Railroad
WESTERN AUTO
THE MILWAUKEE ROAD
KIM

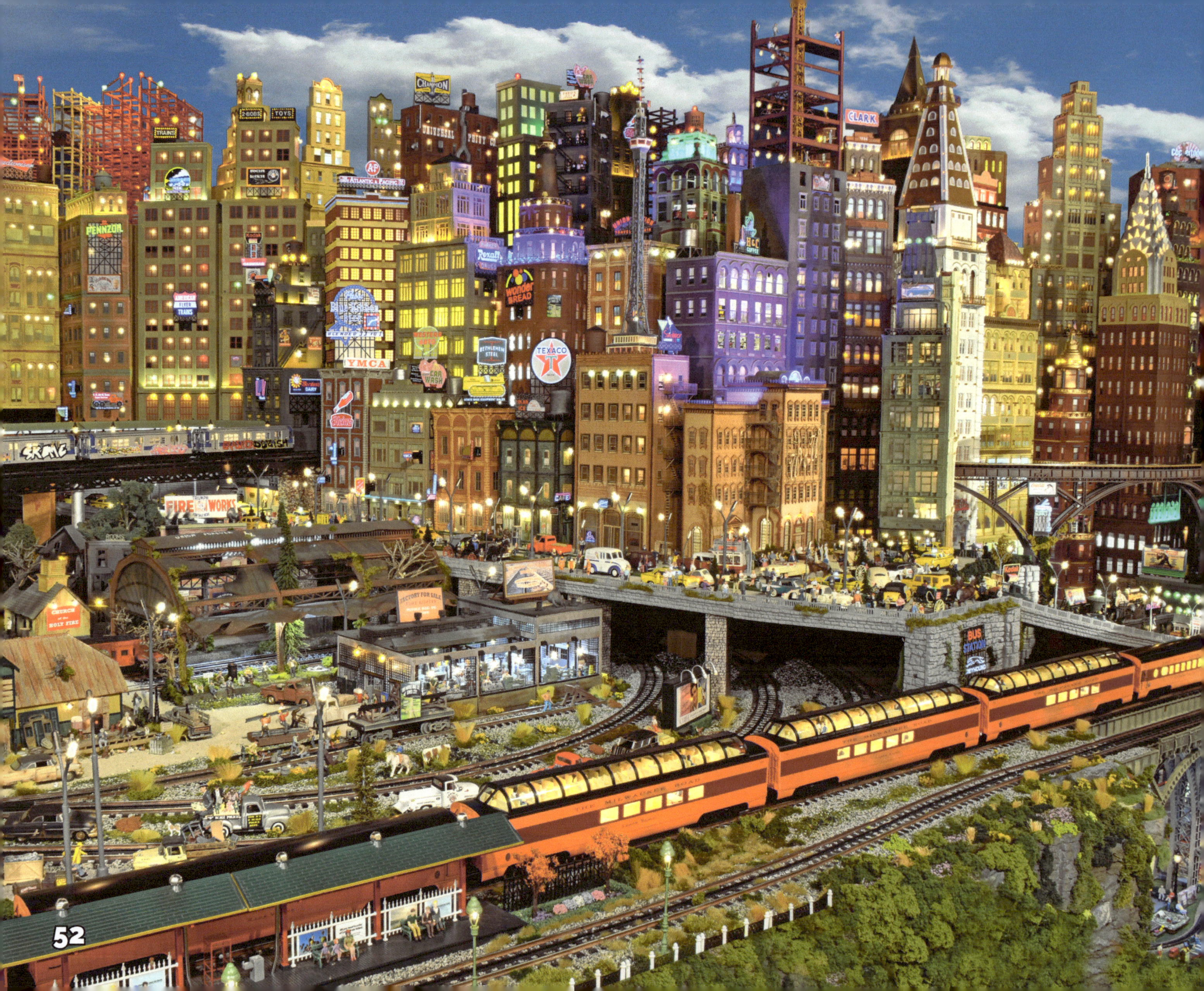

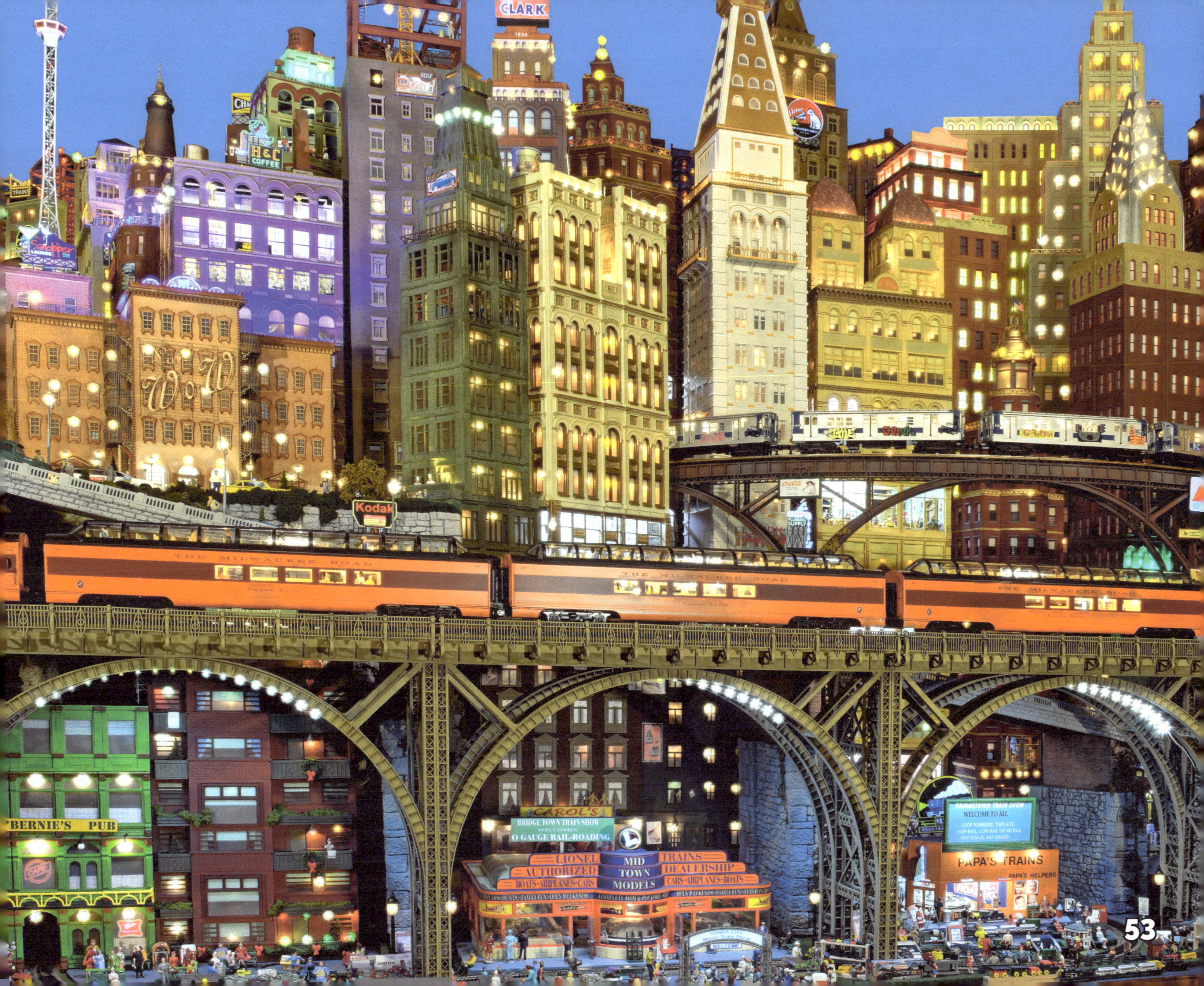

CLARK
1854
GULF
H&C COFFEE
Kodak
THE MILWAUKEE ROAD
THE MILWAUKEE ROAD
THE MILWAUKEE ROAD
BERNIE'S PUB
CAROL'S
WELCOMES
O GAUGE RAIL-ROADING
LIONEL
AUTHORIZED
BOATS-AIRPLANES-CARS
MID TOWN MODELS
TRAINS
DEALERSHIP
CARS-AIRPLANES-BOATS
BRIDGE TOWN TRAINSHOW
WELCOME TO ALL
PAPA'S TRAINS
PAPA'S HELPERS

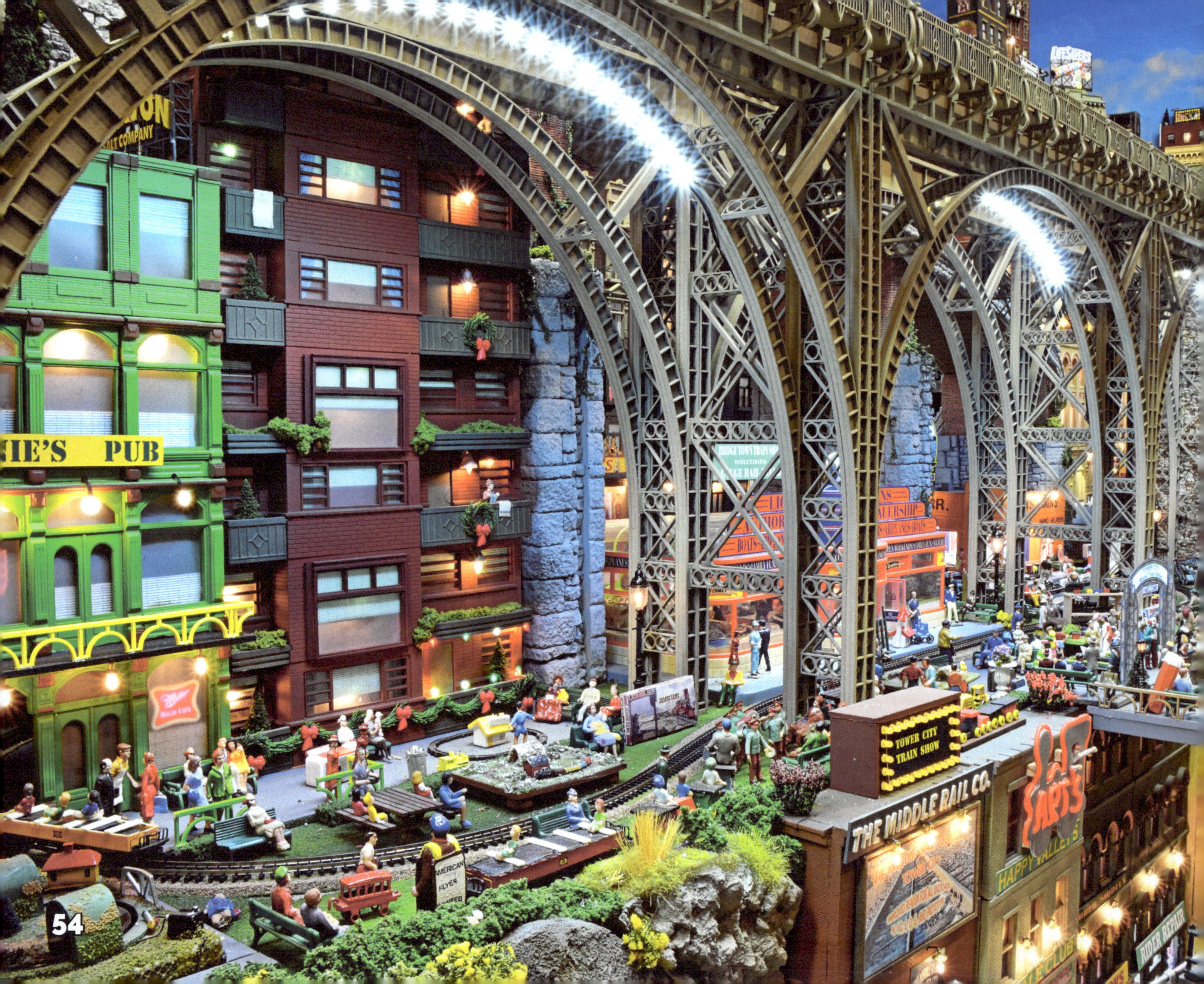

HIE'S PUB
Miller HIGH LIFE
TOWER CITY TRAIN SHOW
THE MIDDLE RAIL CO.
HAPPY VALLEY
AMERICAN FLYER
LIFESAVERS

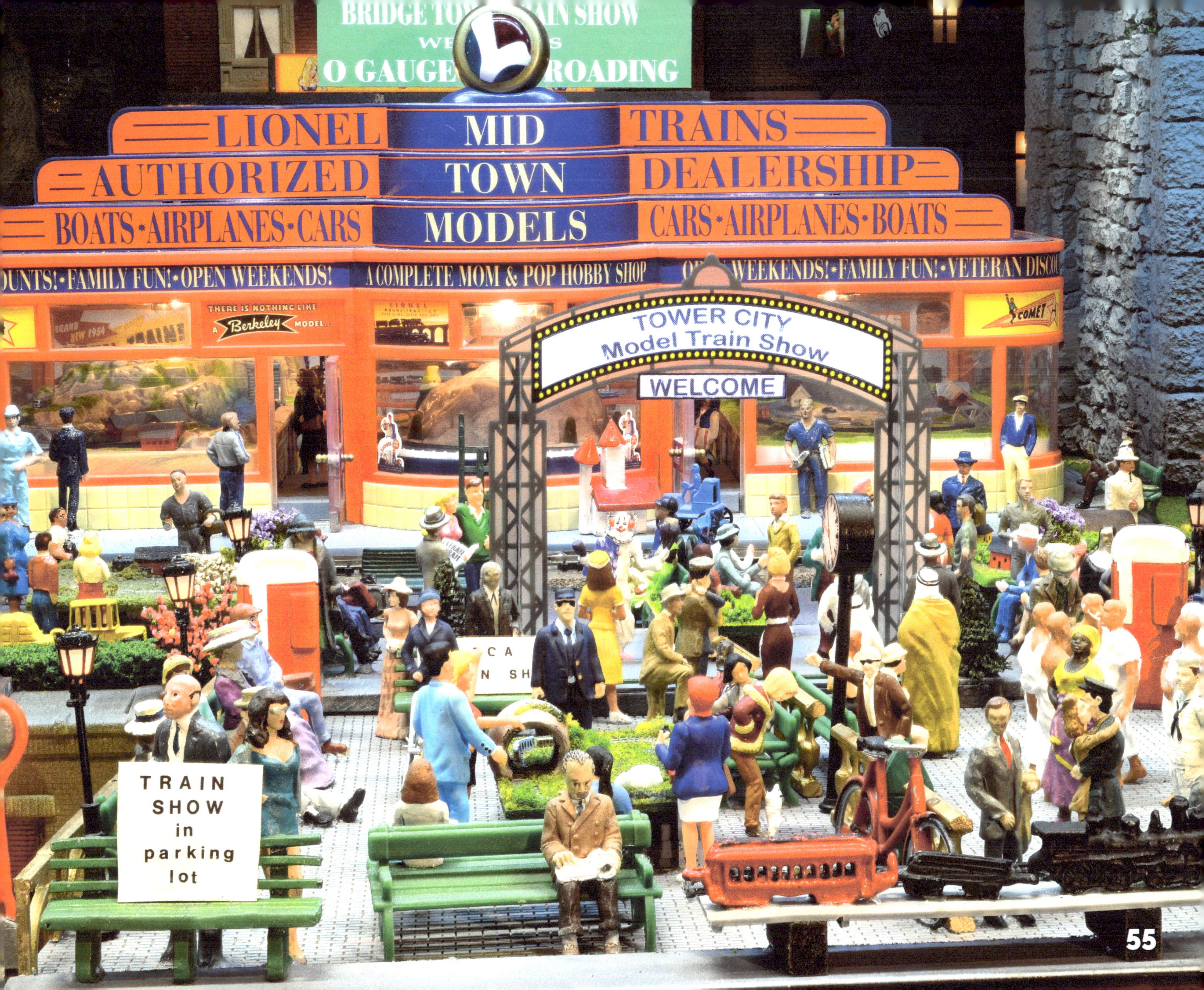

BRIDGE TOWN TRAIN SHOW
WELCOMES
O GAUGE RAILROADING
LIONEL MID TRAINS
AUTHORIZED TOWN DEALERSHIP
BOATS · AIRPLANES · CARS MODELS CARS · AIRPLANES · BOATS
DISCOUNTS! · FAMILY FUN! · OPEN WEEKENDS! A COMPLETE MOM & POP HOBBY SHOP OPEN WEEKENDS! · FAMILY FUN! · VETERAN DISCO
THERE IS NOTHING LIKE A Berkeley Model...
BRAND NEW 1954
LIONEL
COMET
TOWER CITY
Model Train Show
WELCOME
TRAIN SHOW in parking lot

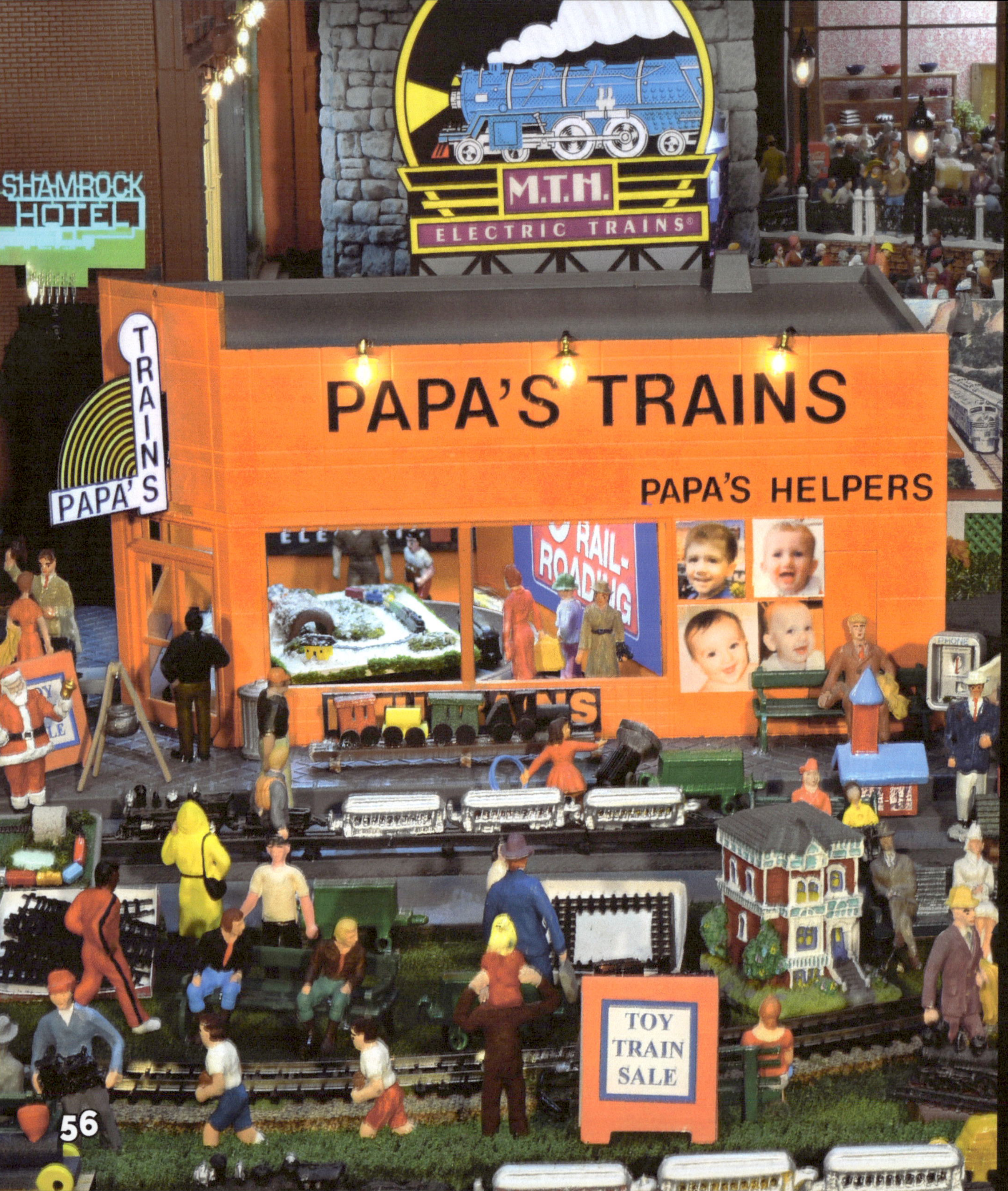

Model Trains in Tower City

The local train stores and weekend train shows are where you go to buy model trains in Tower City.

Big crowds always gather at the train shows held under the city's arched trestle.

Papa's Trains store has just opened! Papa's Trains competes with the Lionel store by offering a new line of toy trains manufactured by MTH Electric Trains.

Lionel Trains
www.lionel.com

MTH Electric Trains
www.mthtrains.com

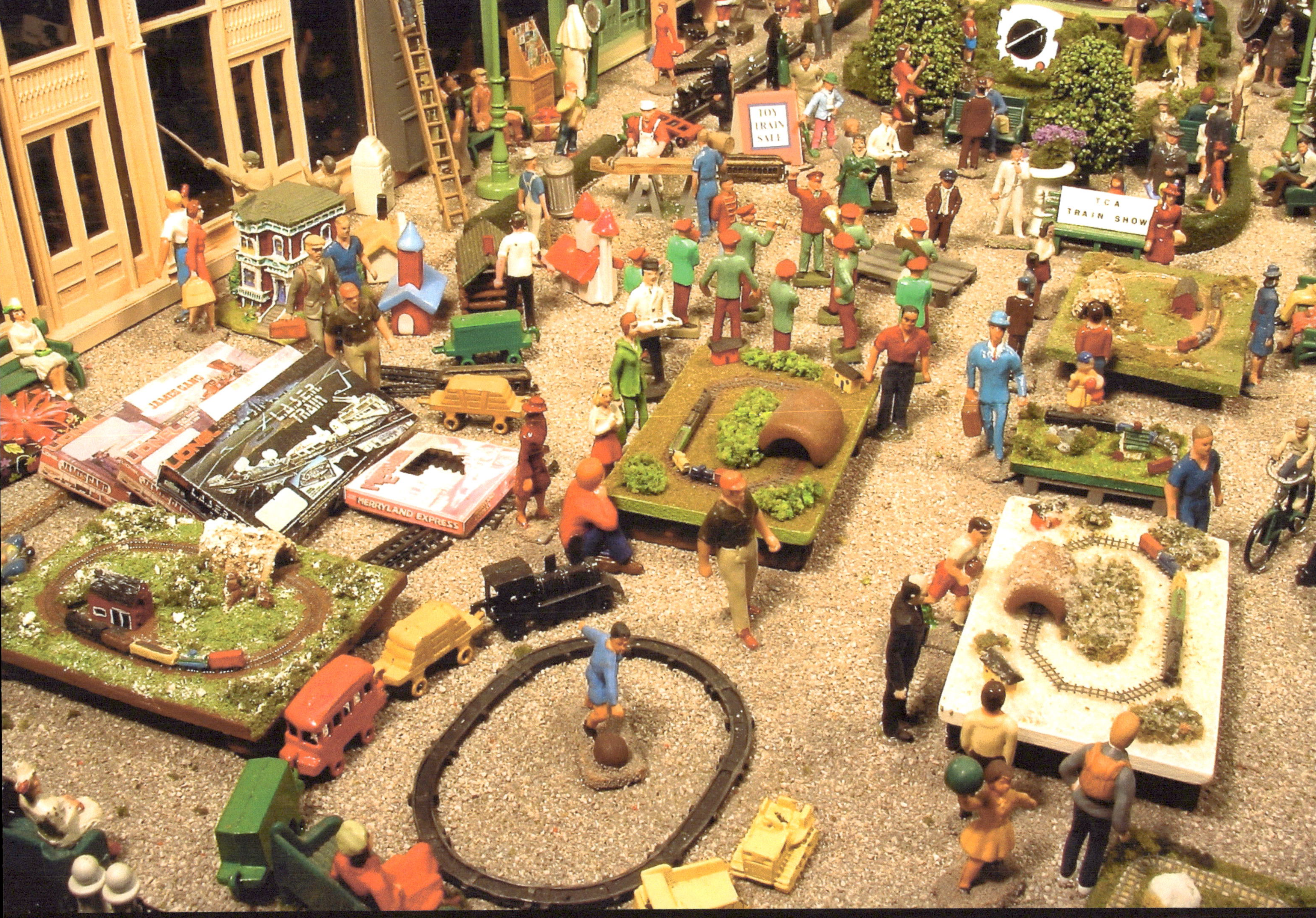

Train Show at the Mall

Everything I used to make this train show was purchased from various doll house stores and shows.

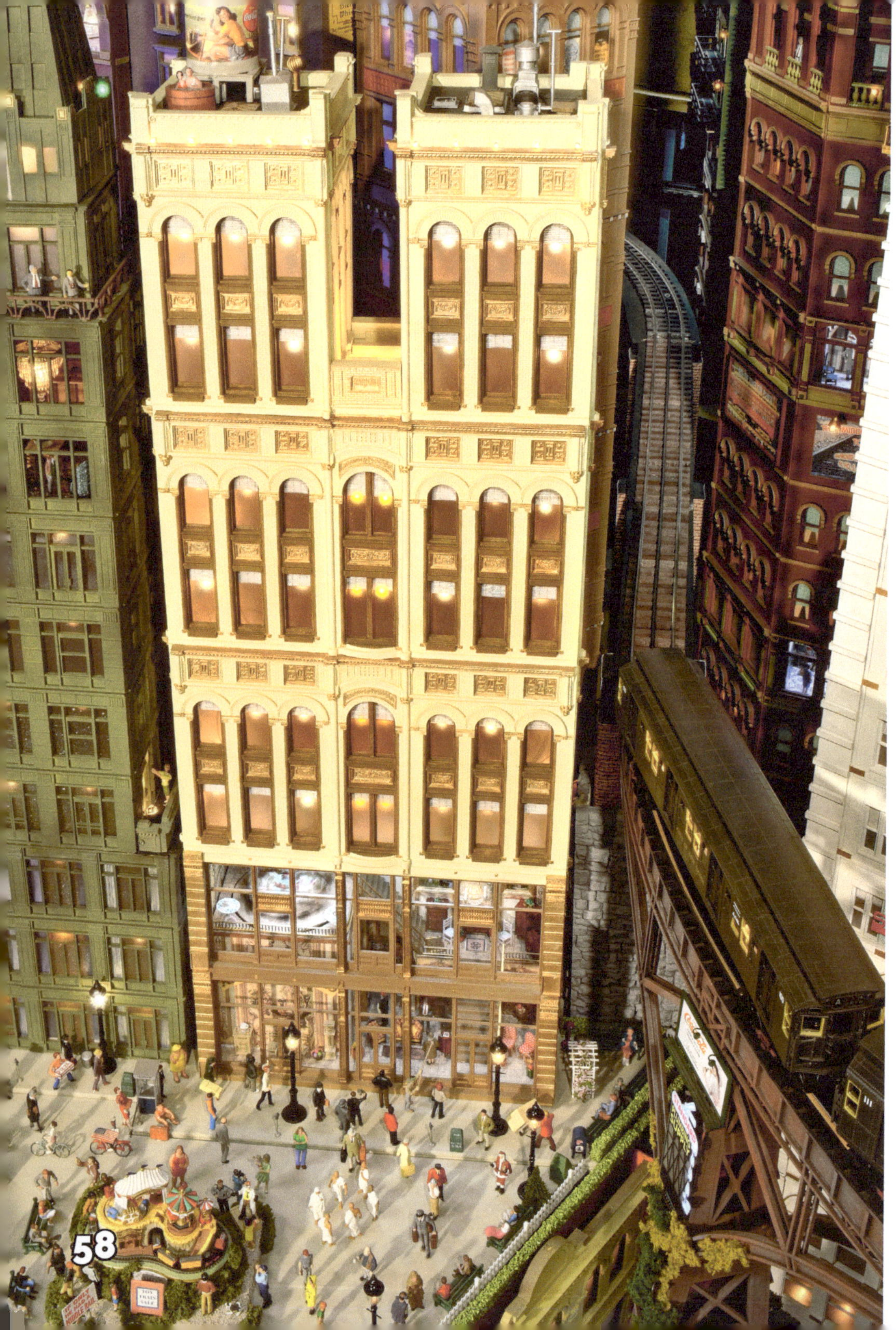

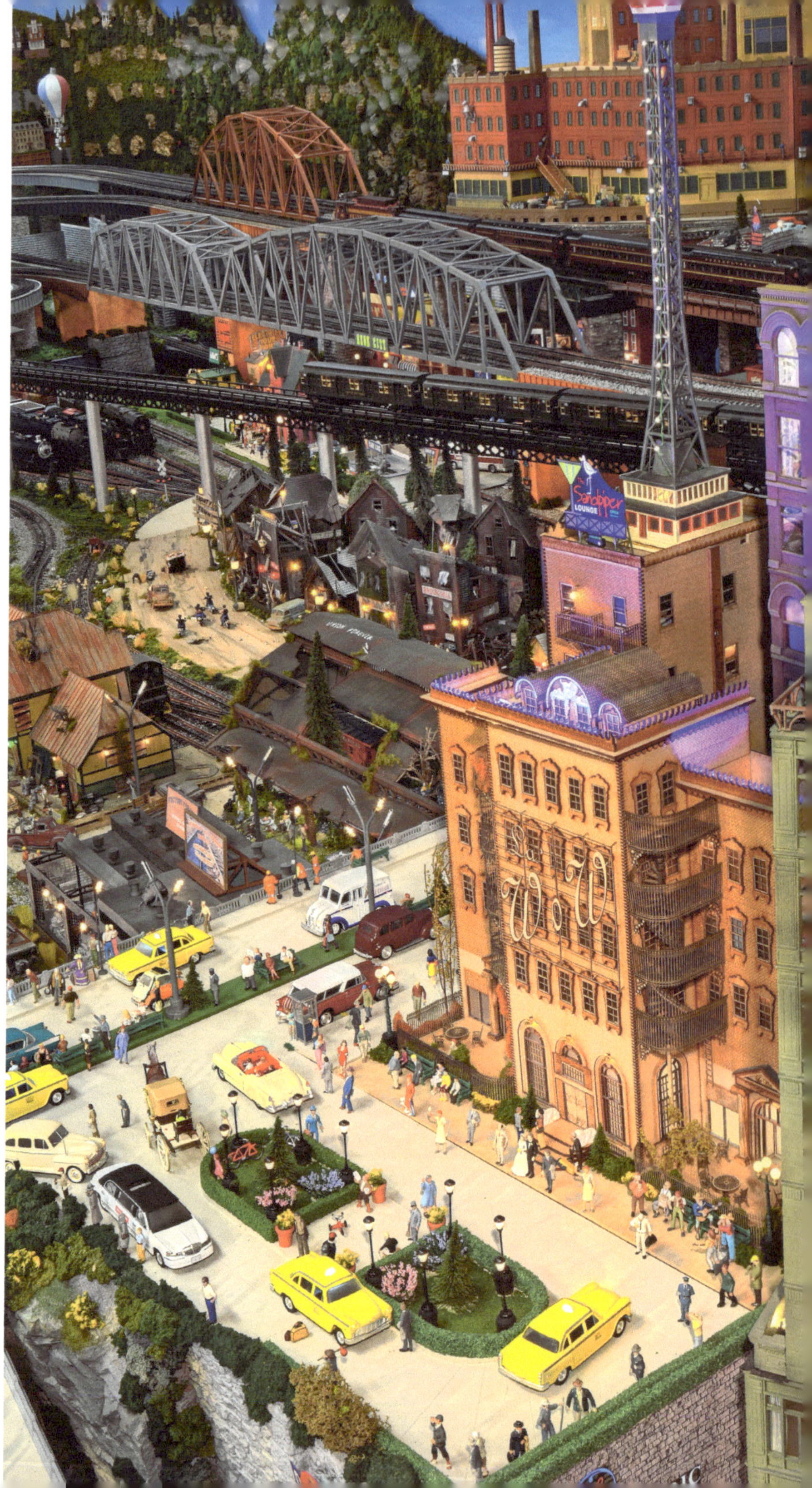

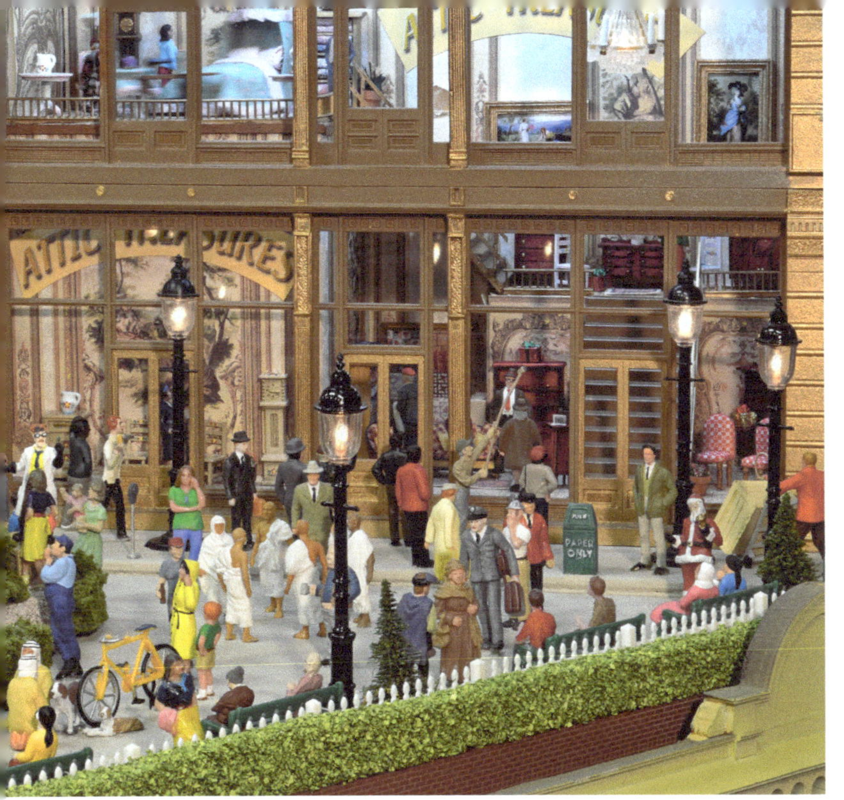

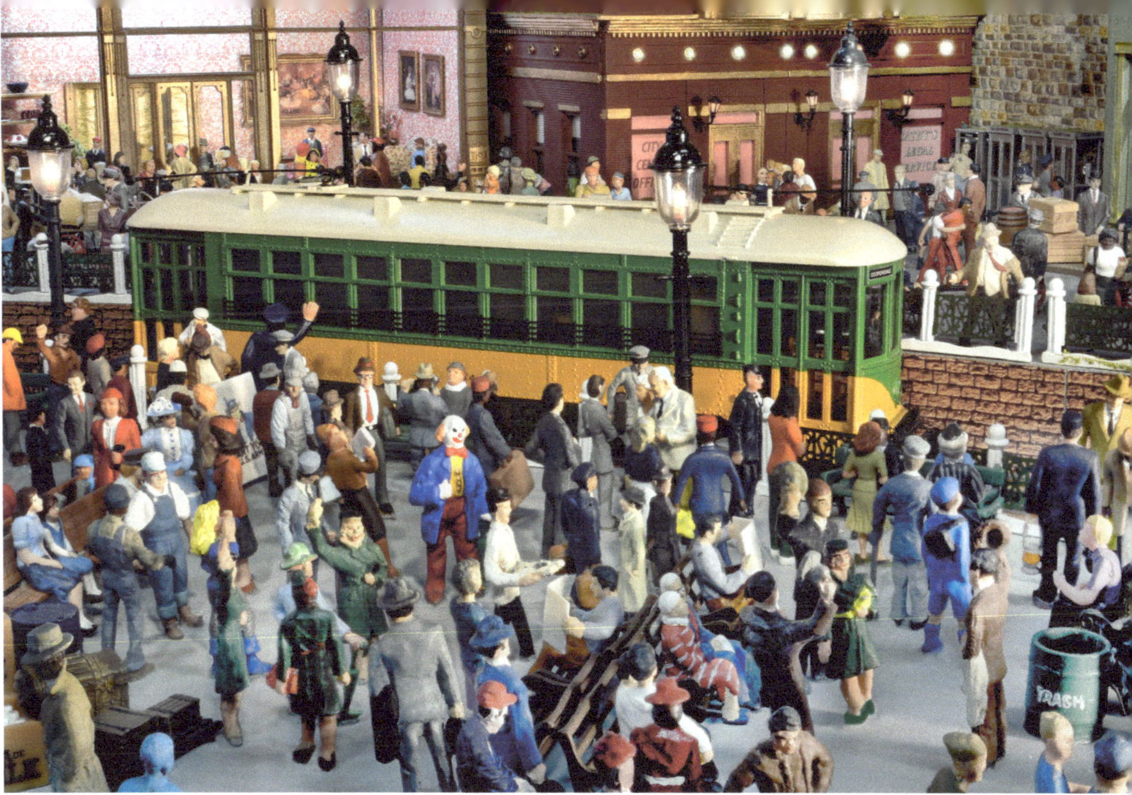

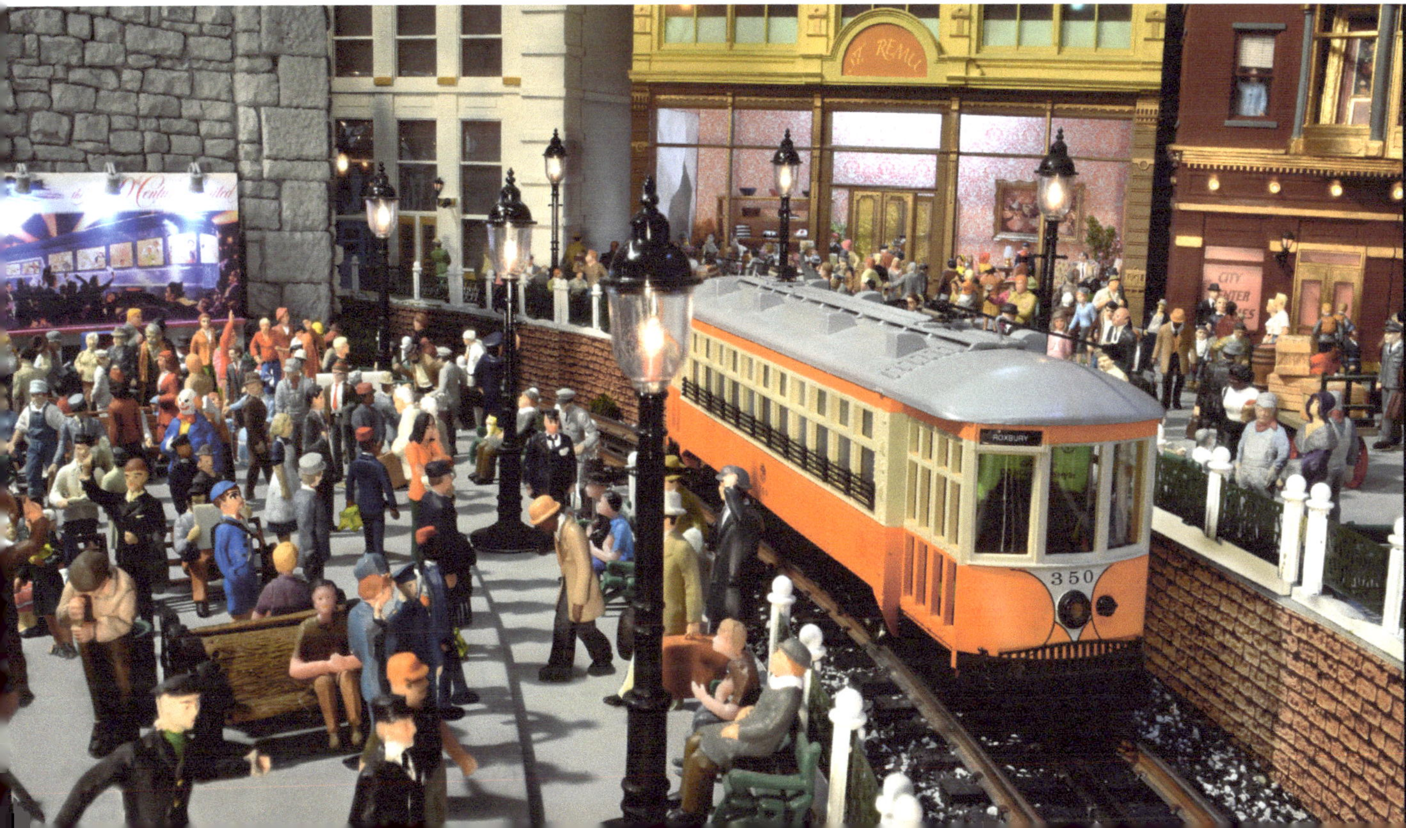

The Crowded City

The plazas, streets, trolleys stops, sidewalks and stores are packed with holiday afternoon shoppers in Tower City.

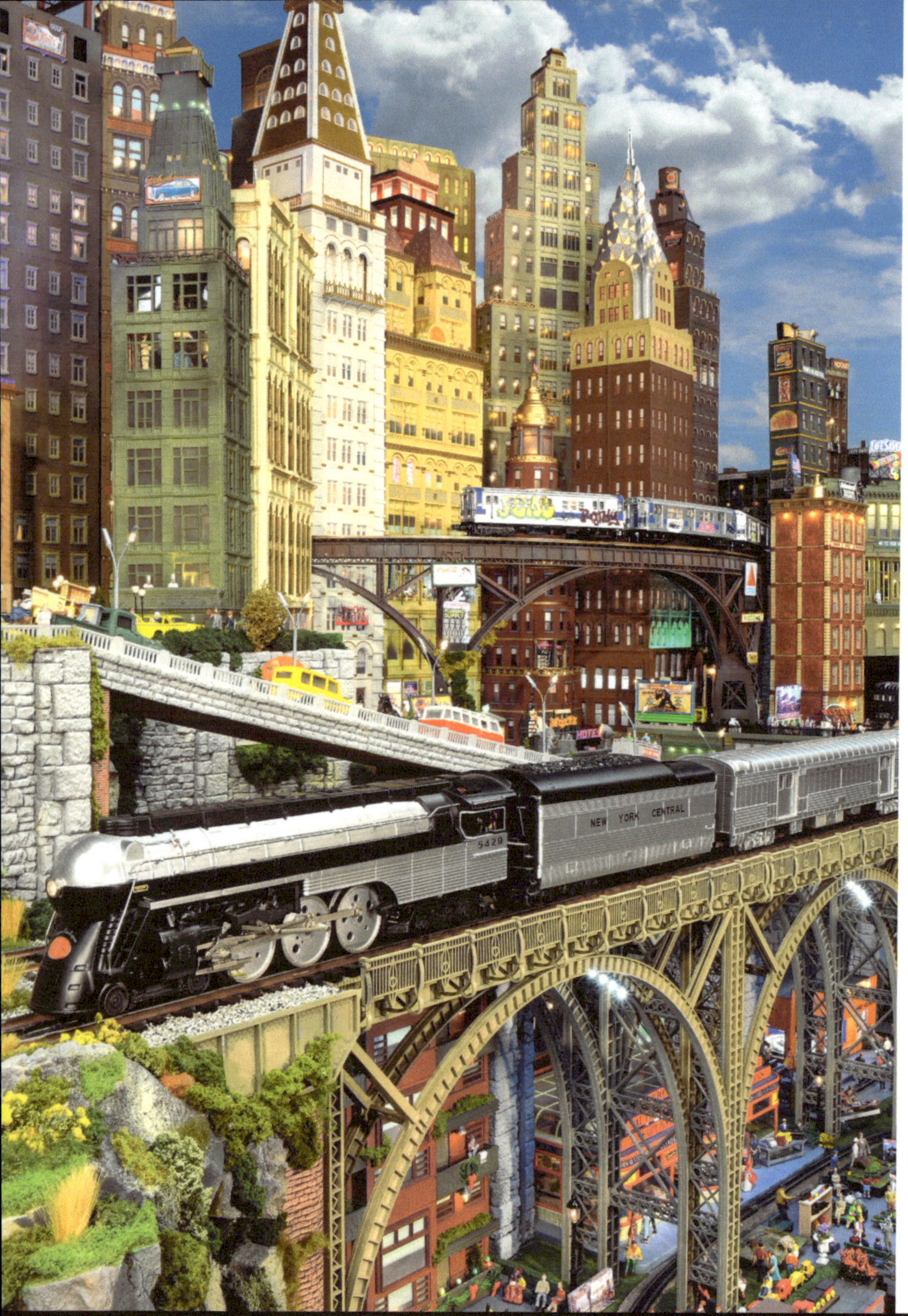

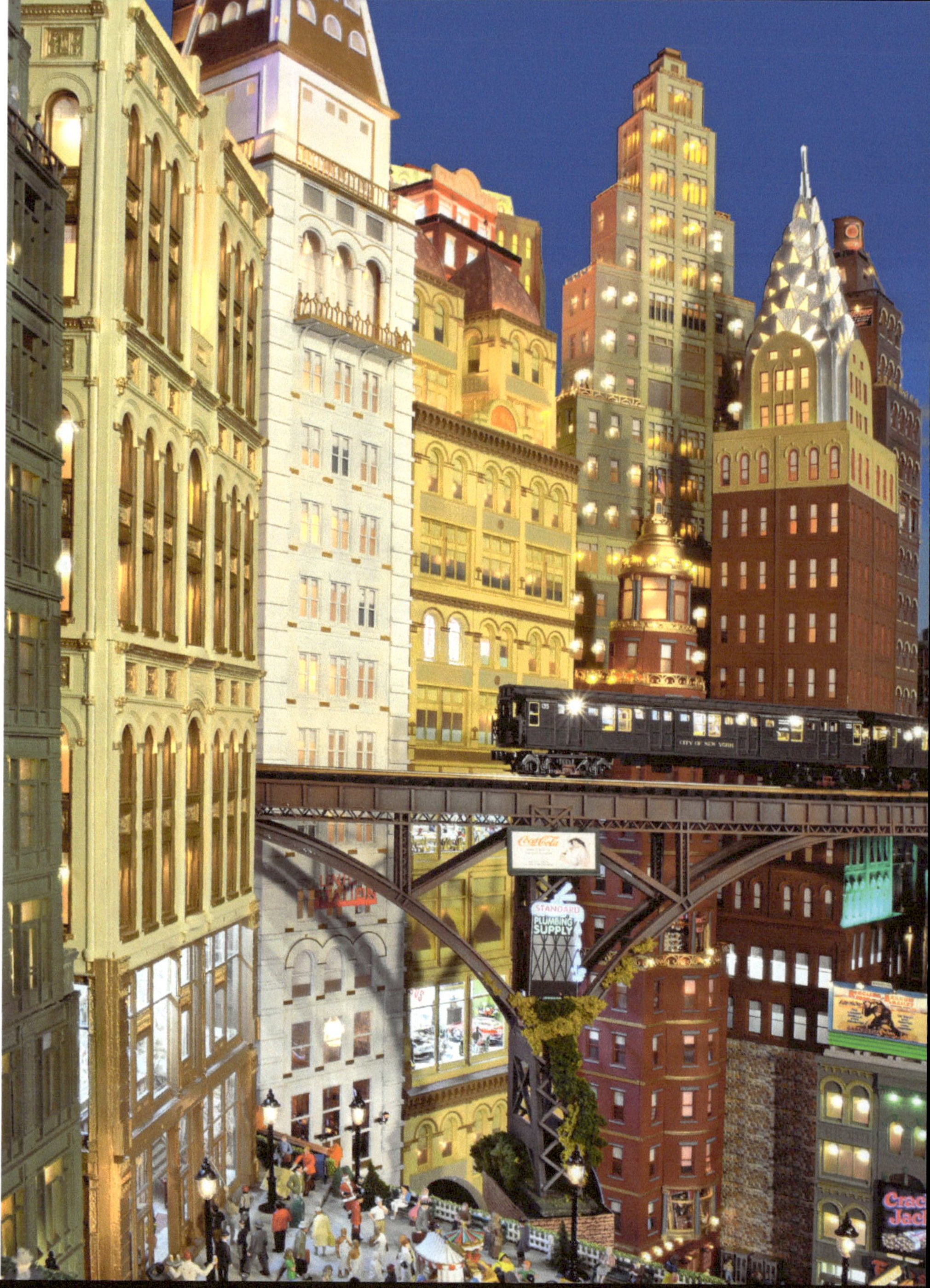

Arriving in Tower City

Passenger trains and elevated mass transit trains arrive in Tower City.
Get ready for crowds, noise and busy traffic.

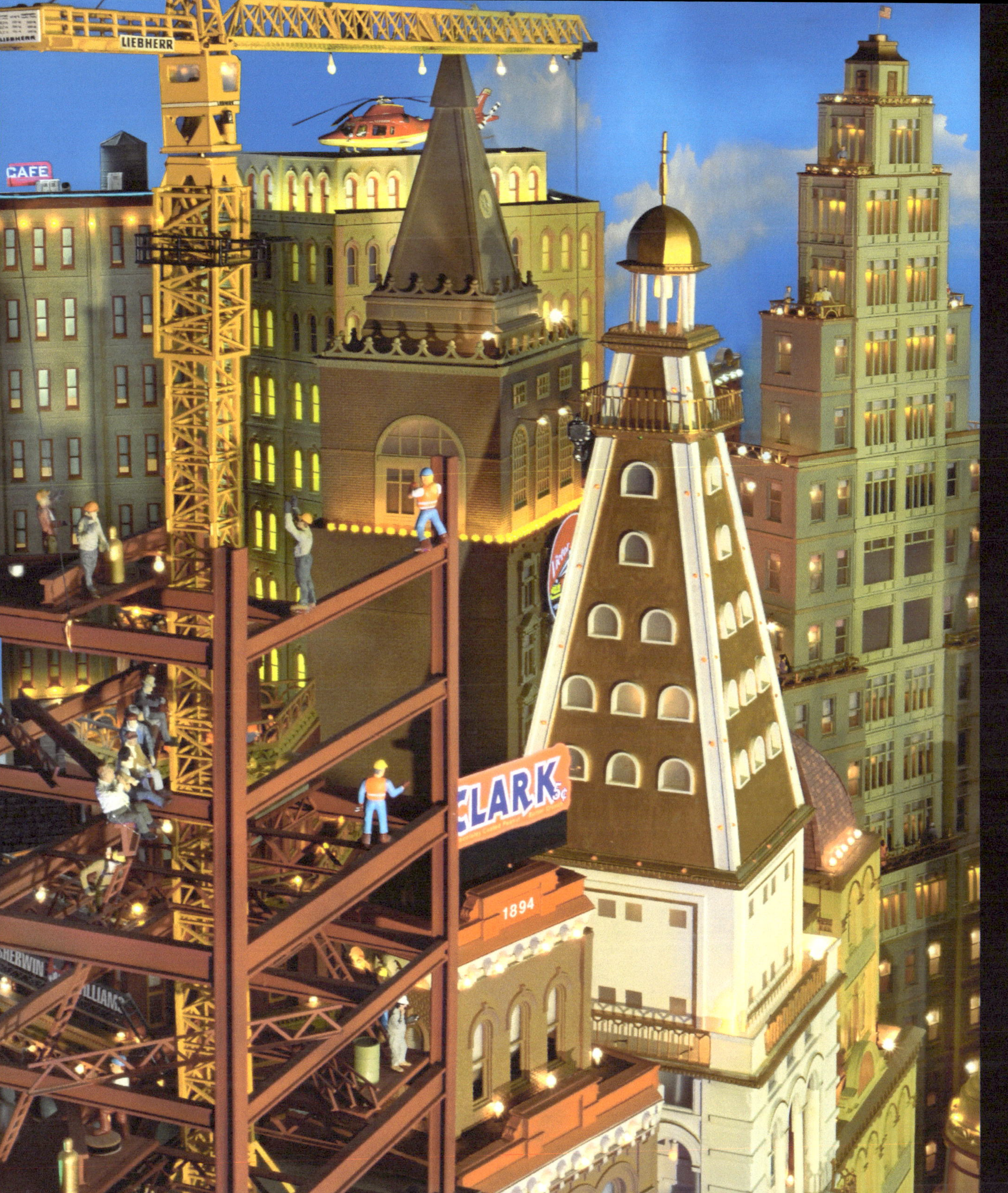

Skyscrapers!

The steel skeleton of a new sky-scraper soars into the sky above Tower City.

The buildings in Tower City are de-signed in the style of United States tall city buildings of the 1930's and 1940's.

The majority of the Tower City sky-scrapers are kitbashed from 2 and 3-story building kits made by Ameri-Towne, Korber Models and Design Preservation Models.

Ameri-Towne
www.ogaugerr.com

Korber Models
www.korbermodels.com

Design Preservation Models
Sold through various hobby dealers.

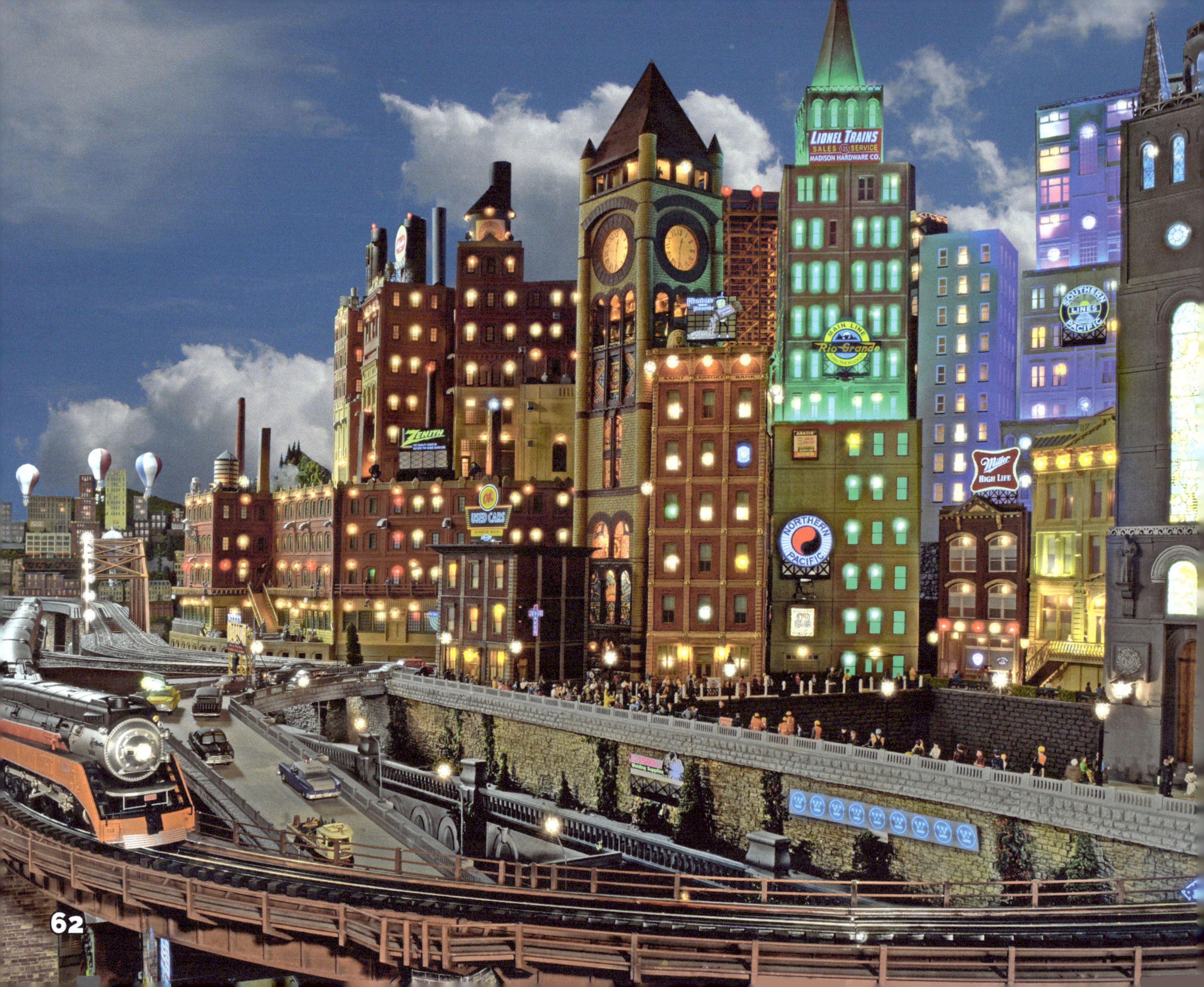

LIONEL TRAINS
SALES SERVICE
MADISON HARDWARE CO.
MAIN LINE
Rio Grande
USED CARS
ZENITH
SAINT LAWRENCE BANK
NORTHERN PACIFIC
SOUTHERN PACIFIC LINES
Miller
HIGH LIFE

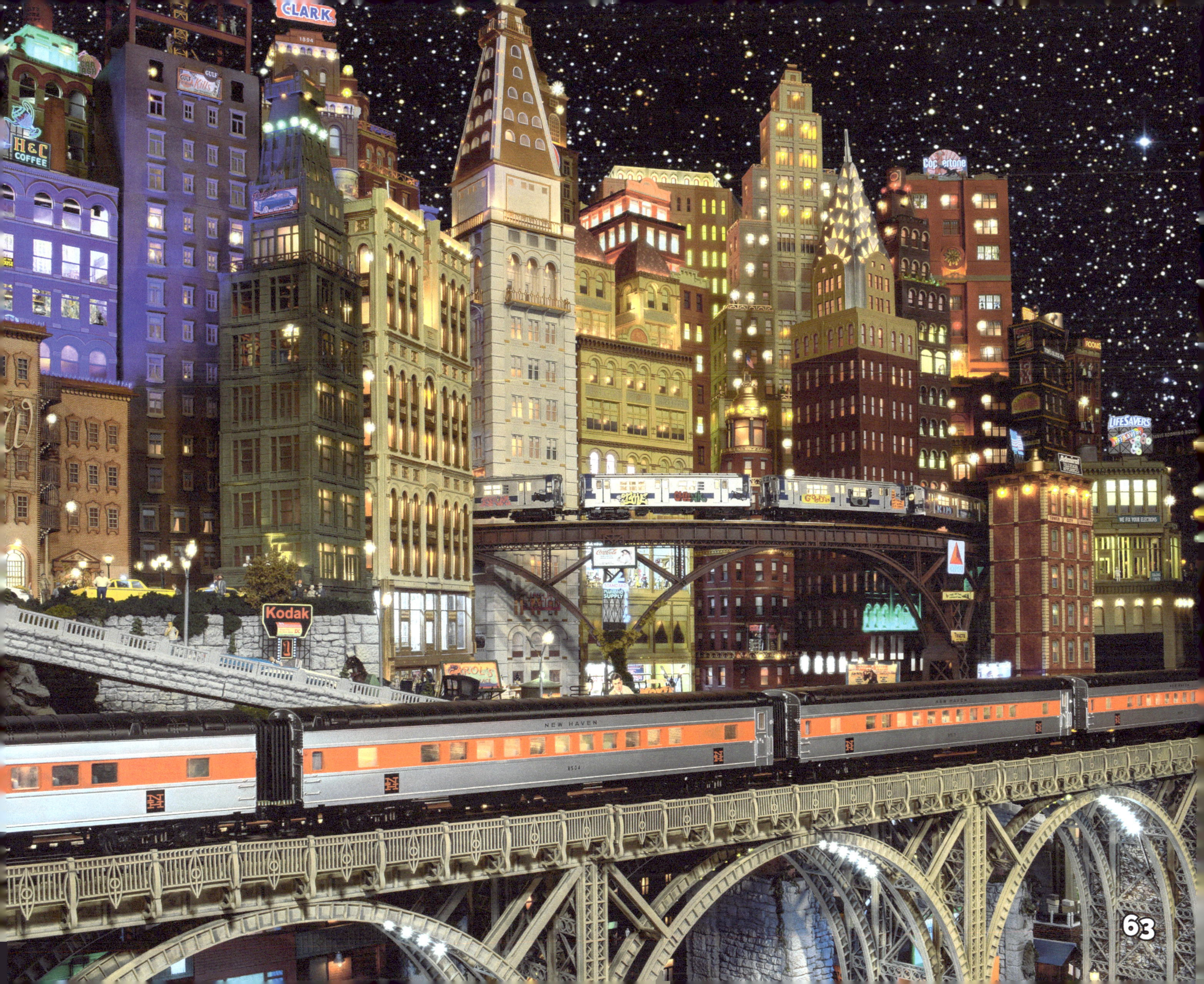

CLARK
H&C COFFEE
GULF
Coppertone
LifeSavers
Kodak
NEW HAVEN
NEW HAVEN

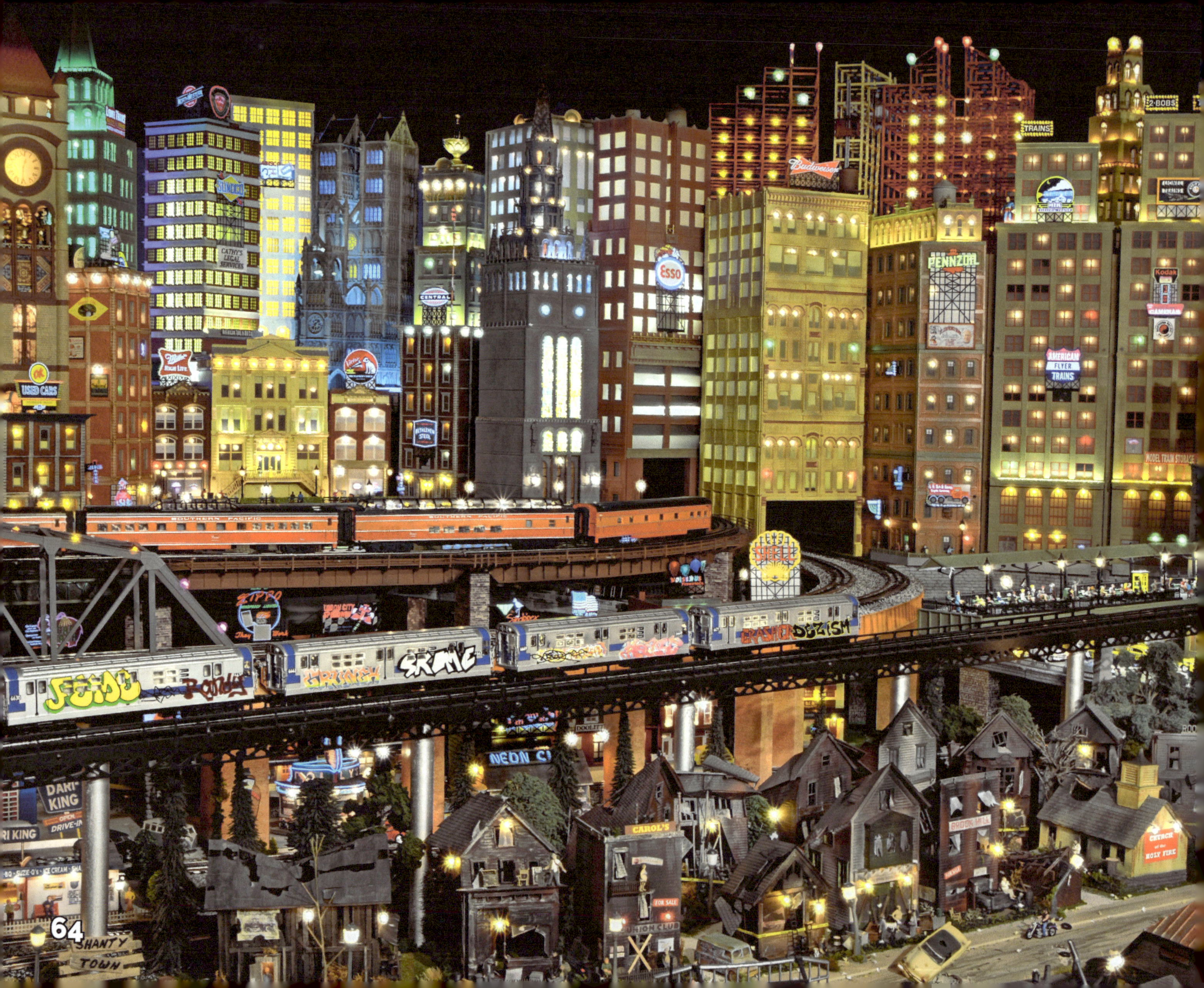
SHANTY
TOWN
64

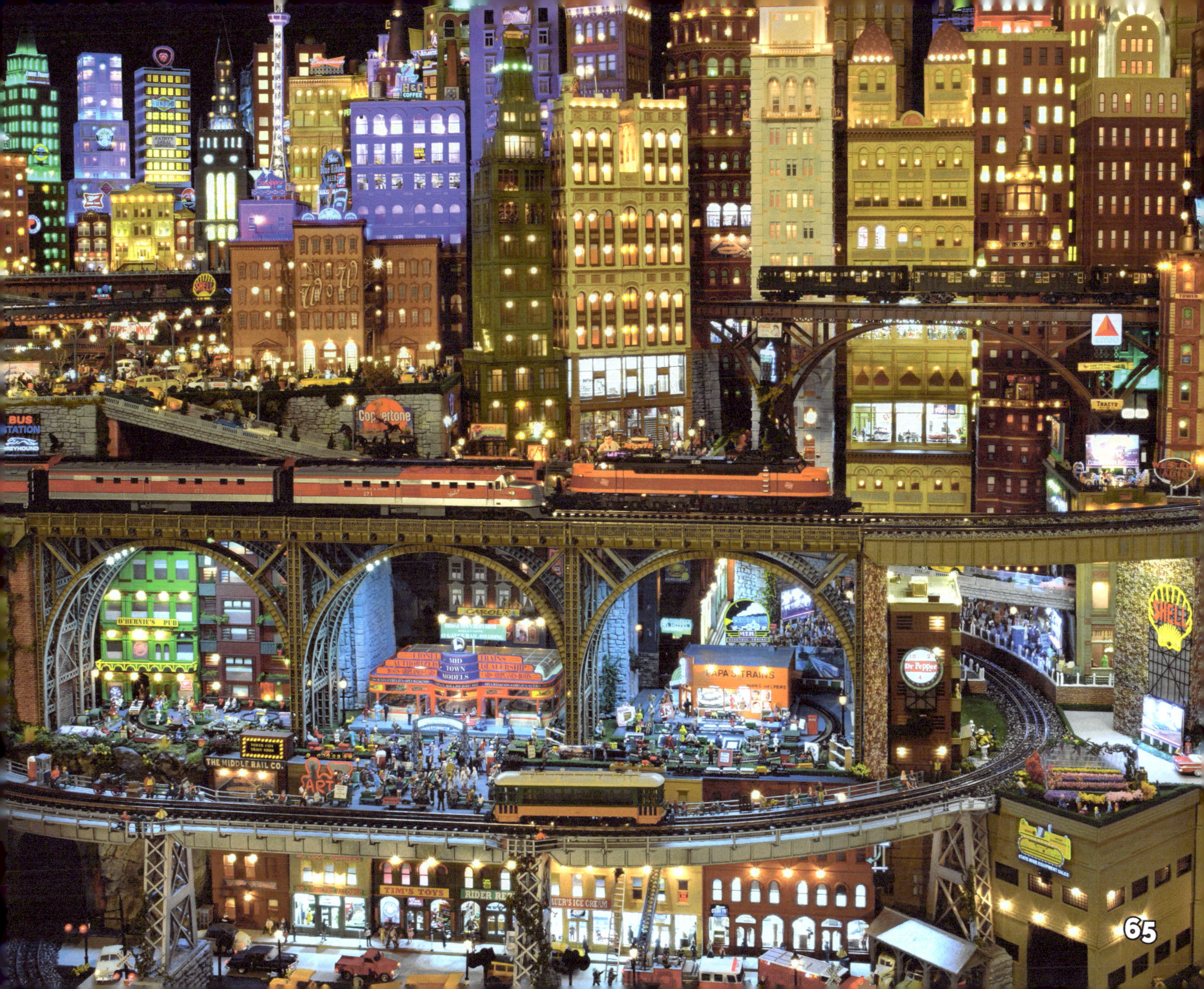

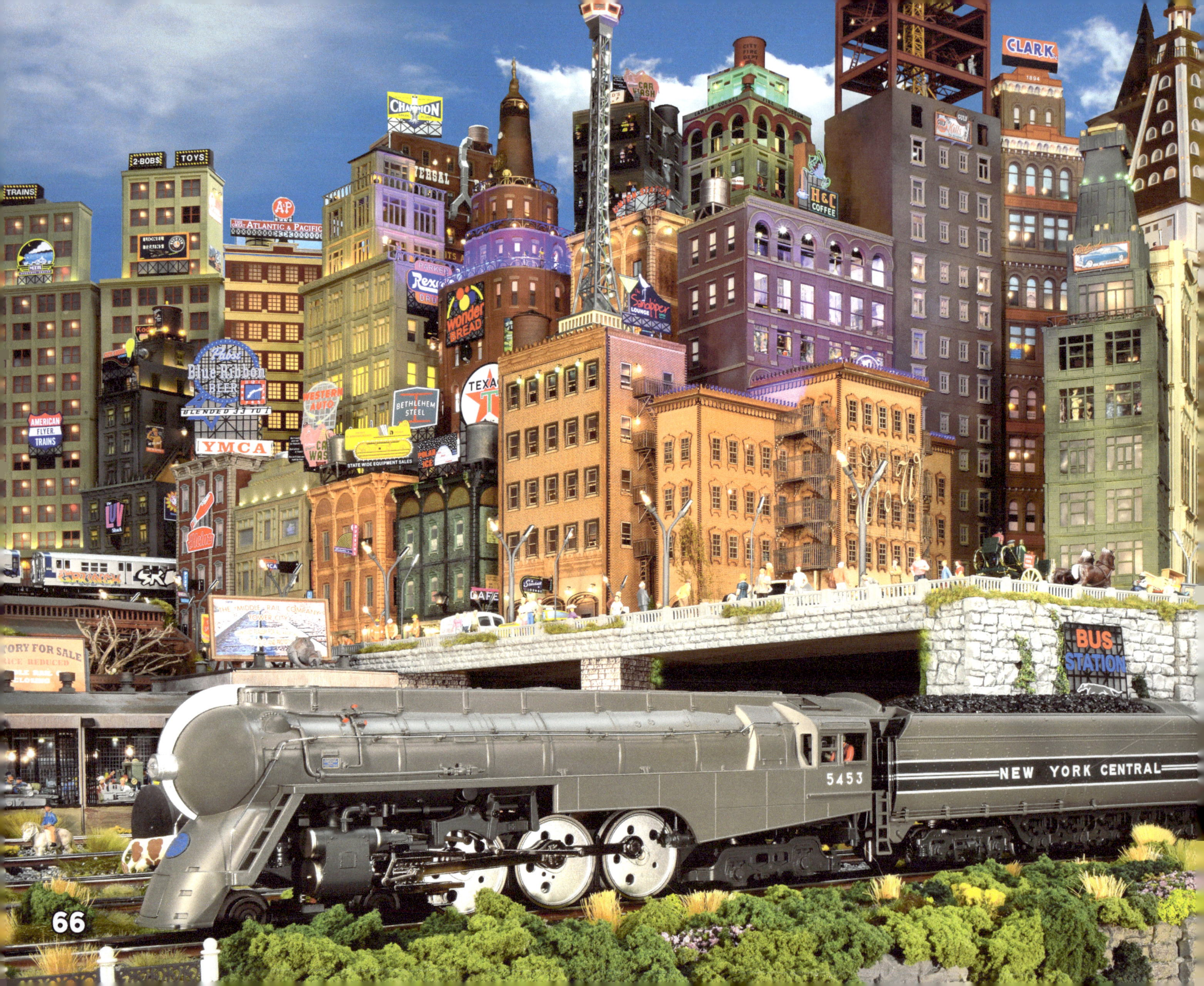

NEW YORK CENTRAL
5453
BUS STATION
CLARK
2-BOBS TOYS
TRAINS
A&P
ATLANTIC & PACIFIC
CHAMPION
H&C COFFEE
Pabst Blue Ribbon BEER
BLENDED 33 TO 1
WESTERN AUTO
AMERICAN FLYER TRAINS
YMCA
CAR WASH
BETHLEHEM STEEL
TEXACO
Rexall DRUG
Wonder BREAD
Schlopey LOUNGE
CITY FIRE DEPT
FOR SALE
PRICE REDUCED
STATE WIDE EQUIPMENT SALES
CAFE

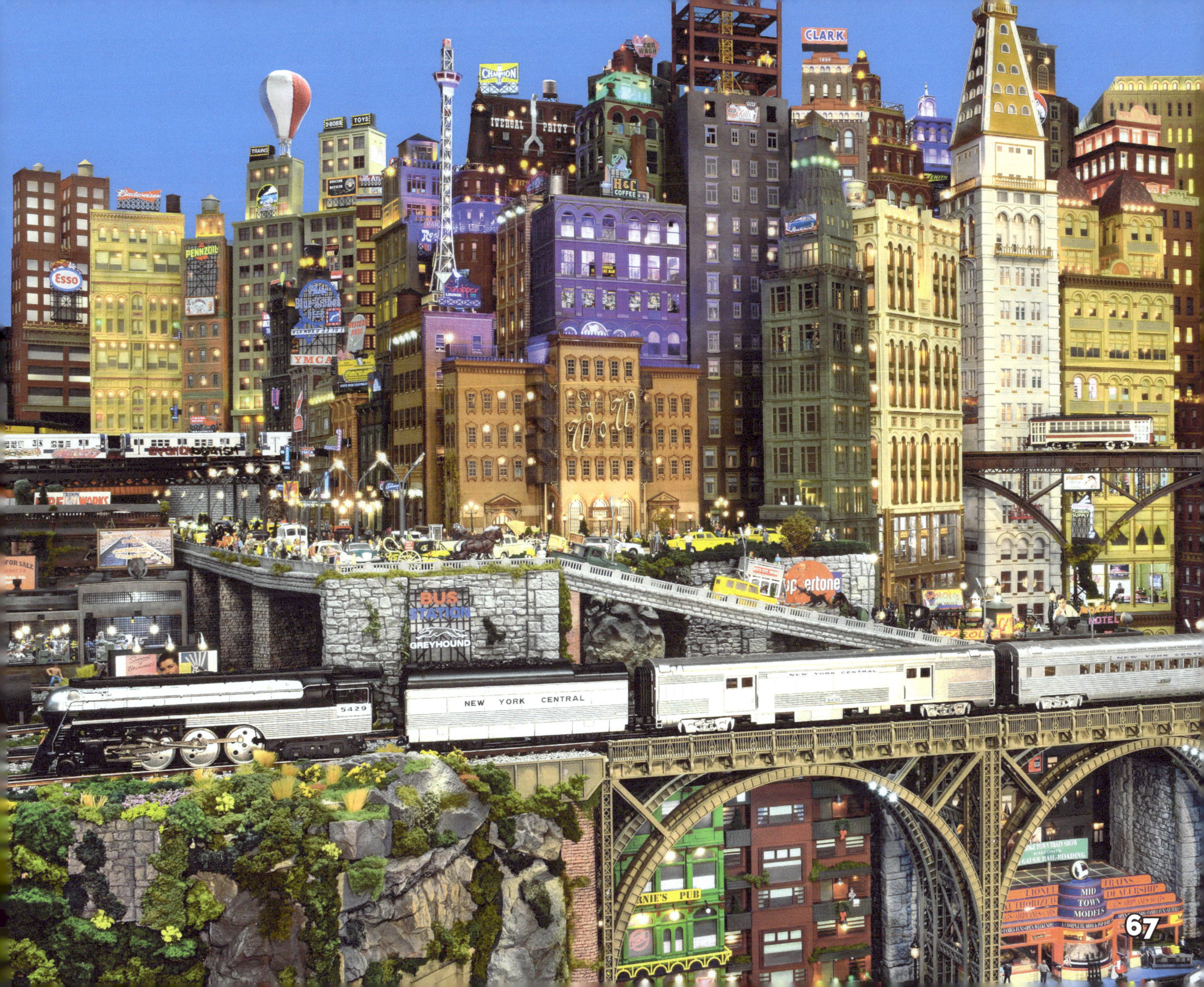

CLARK
Budweiser
ESSO
PENNZOIL
TOYS
TRAINS
YMCA
H&C COFFEE
CHAMPION
BUS STATION
GREYHOUND
NEW YORK CENTRAL
5429
NEW YORK CENTRAL
NEW YORK CENTRAL
NIE'S PUB

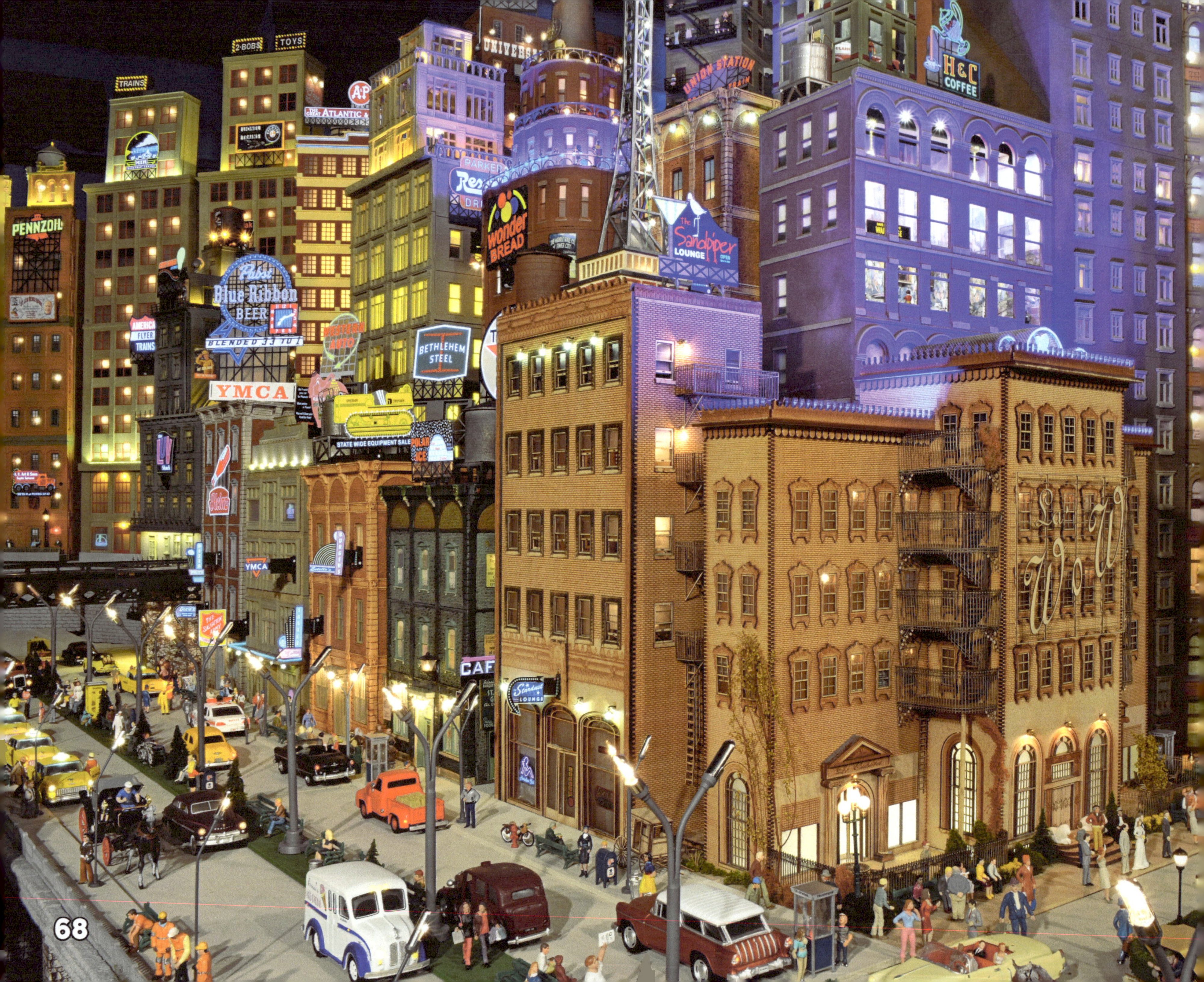

2-BOBS TOYS
TRAINS
UNIVERSE
UNION STATION
H & C COFFEE
PENNZOIL
A&P
ATLANTIC
AMERICA FLYER TRAINS
Pabst Blue Ribbon BEER
BLENDED 33 TO 1
YMCA
Wonder BREAD
The Sandpiper LOUNGE OPEN
BETHLEHEM STEEL
STATE WIDE EQUIPMENT SALE
POLAR ICE
CAFE
Stardust LOUNGE
68

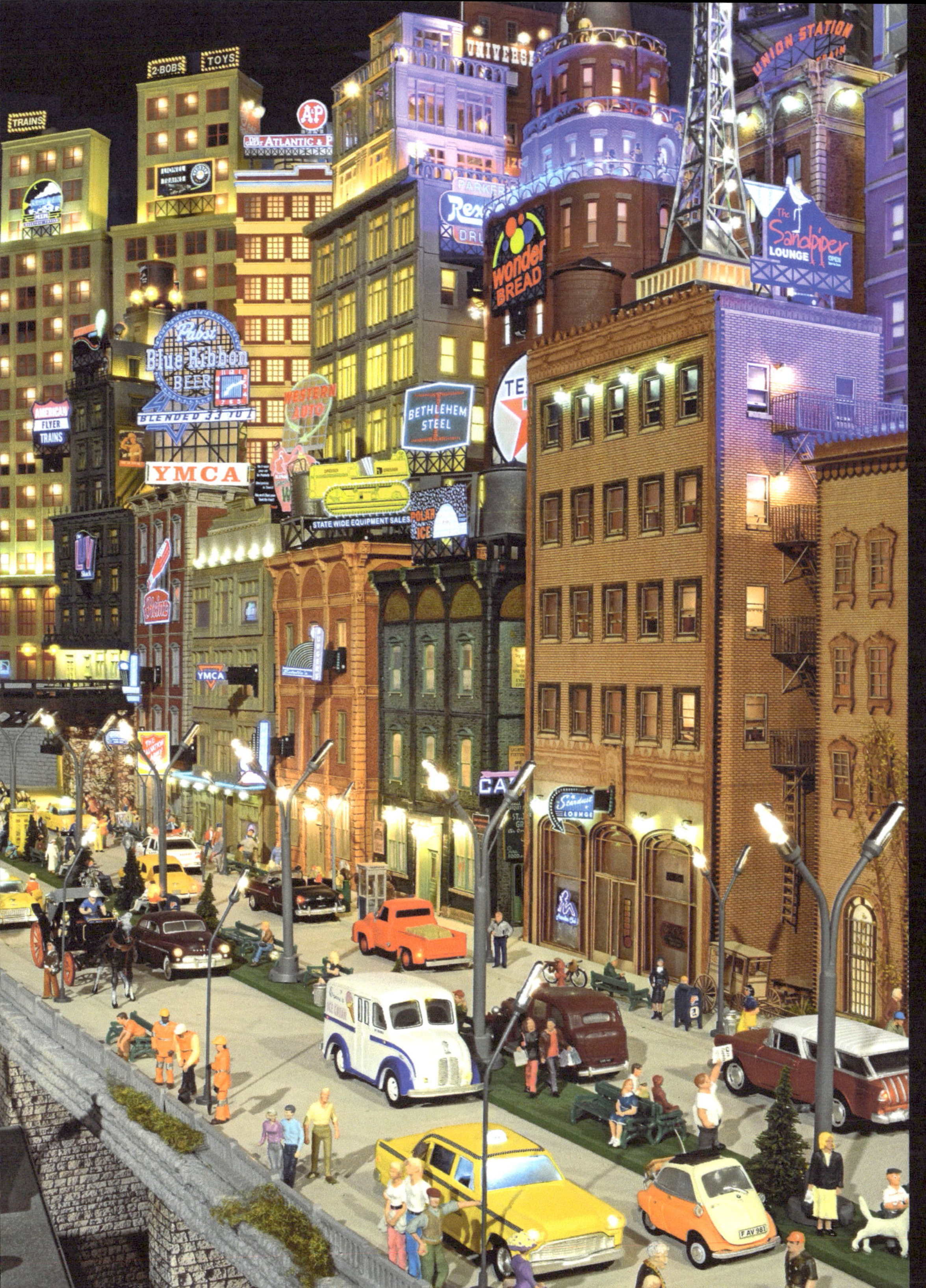

The Grand Boulevard

The Grand Boulevard of Tower City is a magical kingdom of lights!

The lighting supplies produced by Miniatronics, the colorful animated signs manufactured by Miller Engineering and the lighted vehicles made by Jack Pearce, all combine to make this city scene come to life.

Miniatronics
www.miniatronics.com

Miller Engineering
www.microstru.com

Jack Pearce
jack_pearce4@sympatico.ca

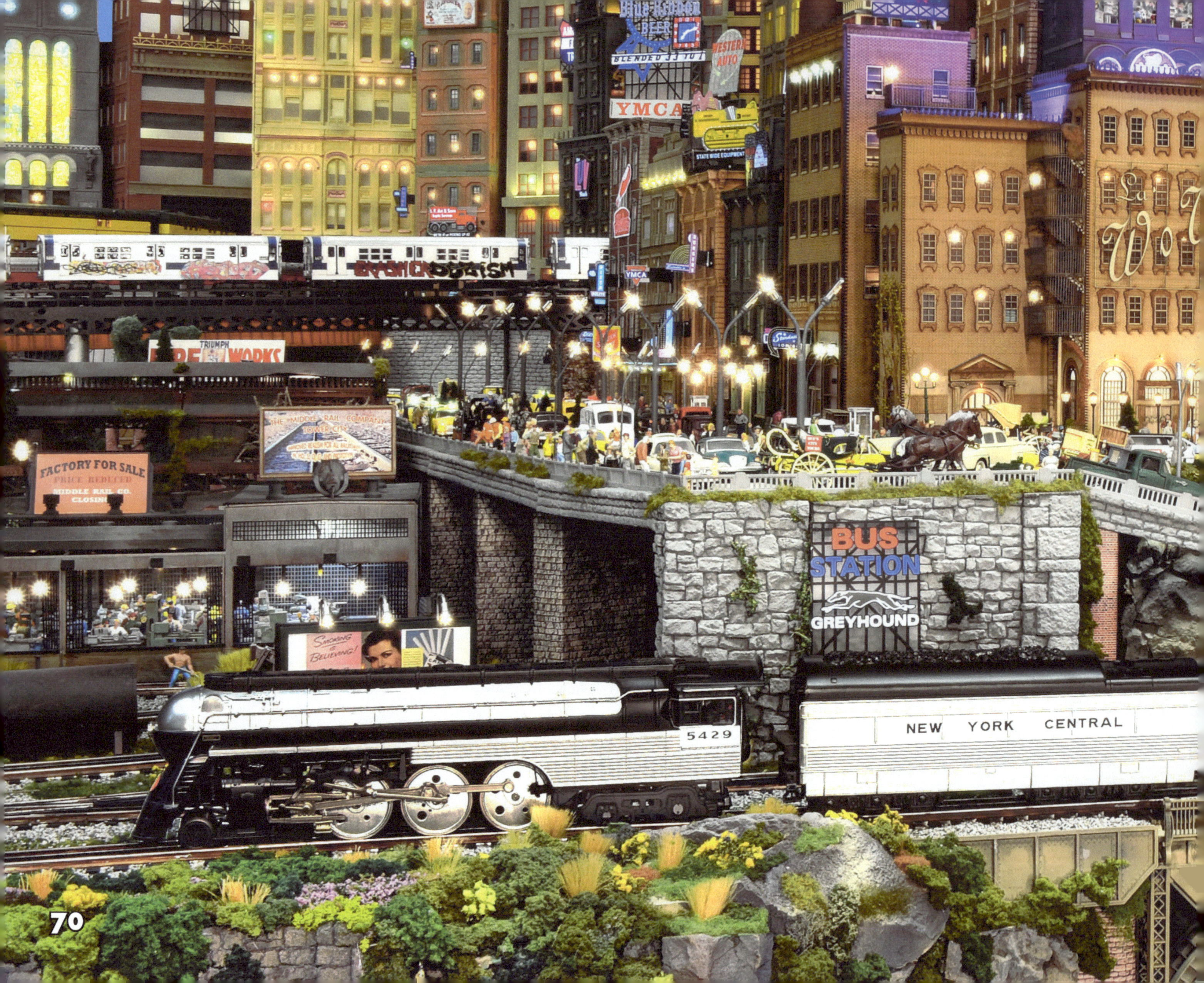

BEER
WESTERN AUTO
YMCA
FACTORY FOR SALE
PRICE REDUCED
MIDDLE RAIL CO. CLOSING
THE "MIDDLE RAIL COMPANY"
SMOKING IS BELIEVING!
BUS STATION
GREYHOUND
5429
NEW YORK CENTRAL
TRIUMPH
WORKS

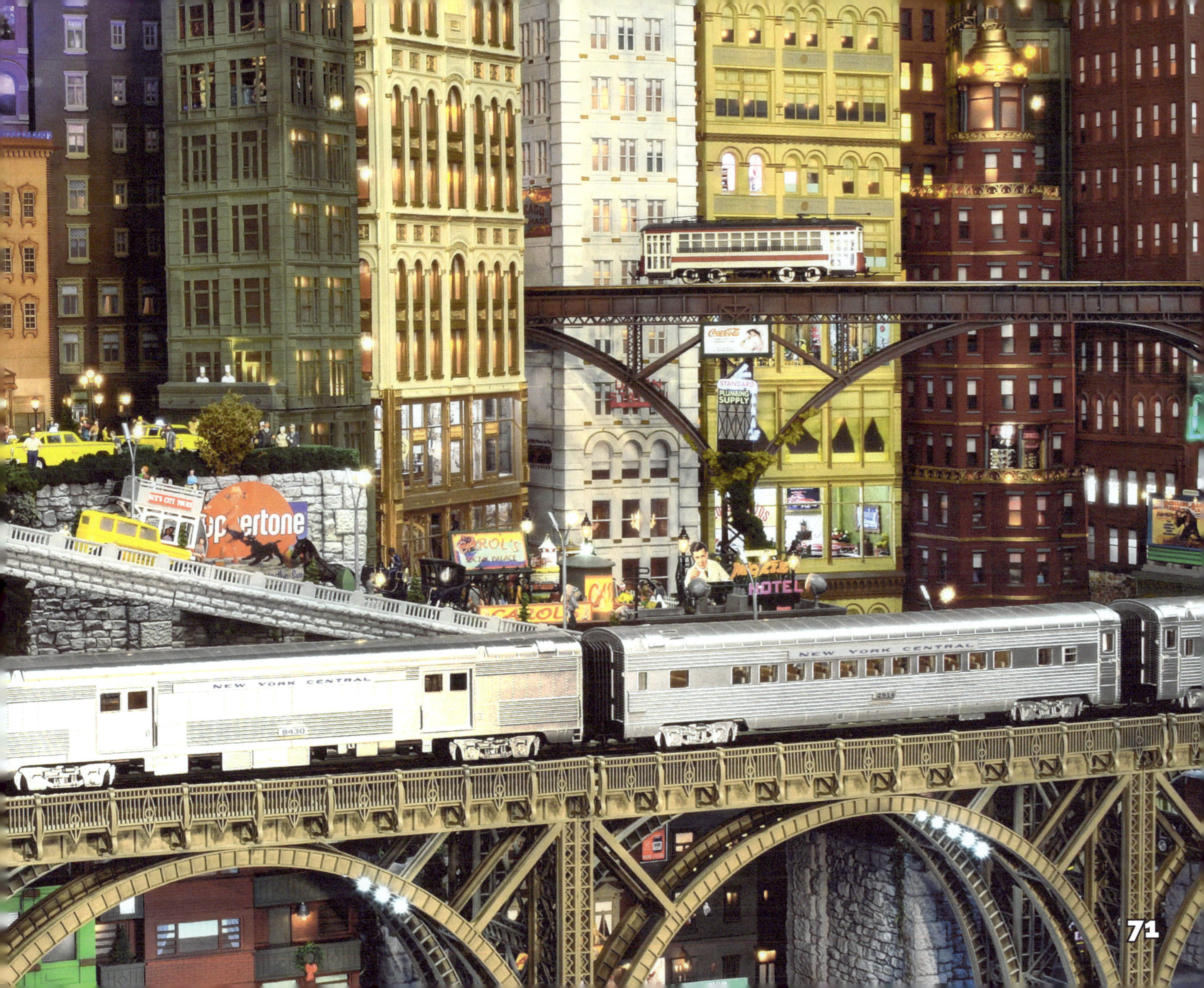

NEW YORK CENTRAL
NEW YORK CENTRAL
8430
HOTEL
Coppertone
Coca-Cola
STANDARD
PLUMBING
SUPPLY
CAROL'S

Building Room Interiors

You can pump up the entertainment level of your train layout by adding a few furnished interior rooms to your buildings! Your guests will have a great time looking in the windows and checking out all the tiny details. If you include a guest's name, hobby or special interest in a store window or hidden room, that will really spark their interest!

Many model railroaders have small, nearly completed or inactive layouts. Building a few humorous, entertaining or realistic interior rooms can provide that little something "extra" on the layout. Your family and friends will love exploring your miniature world in order to find their name or interest included in your train layout.

Room interiors should be in an easy to see location. The buildings should have large windows, great interior lighting and entertaining content. Inexpensive quarter inch scale furniture is available from Scenic Express. Another source of quarter inch scale detail pieces and furniture is Shapeways 3-D printing.

www.sceneryexpress.com
www.shapeways.com

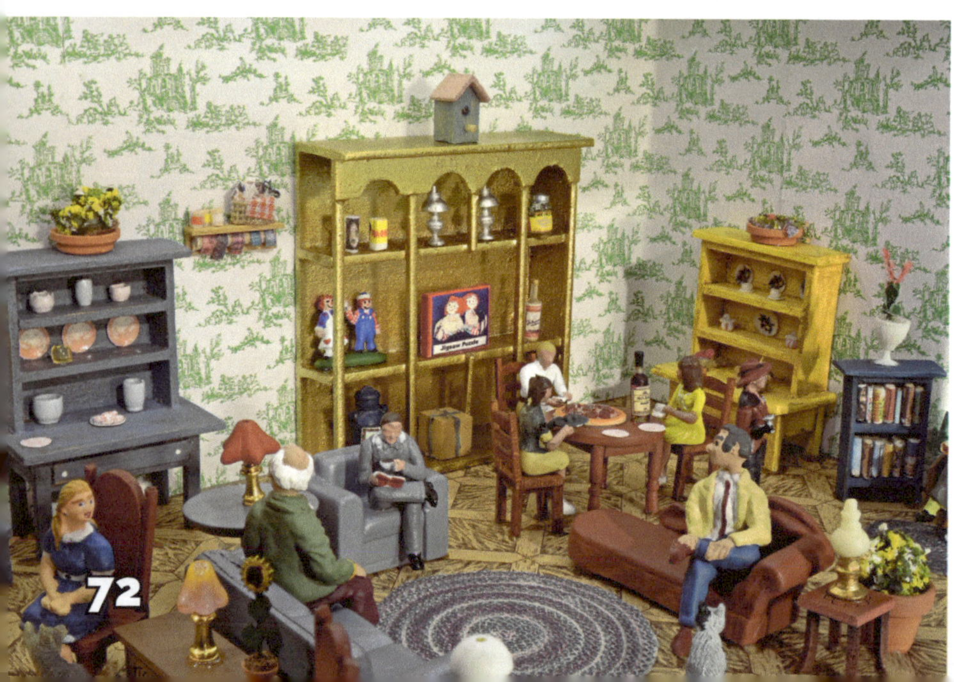

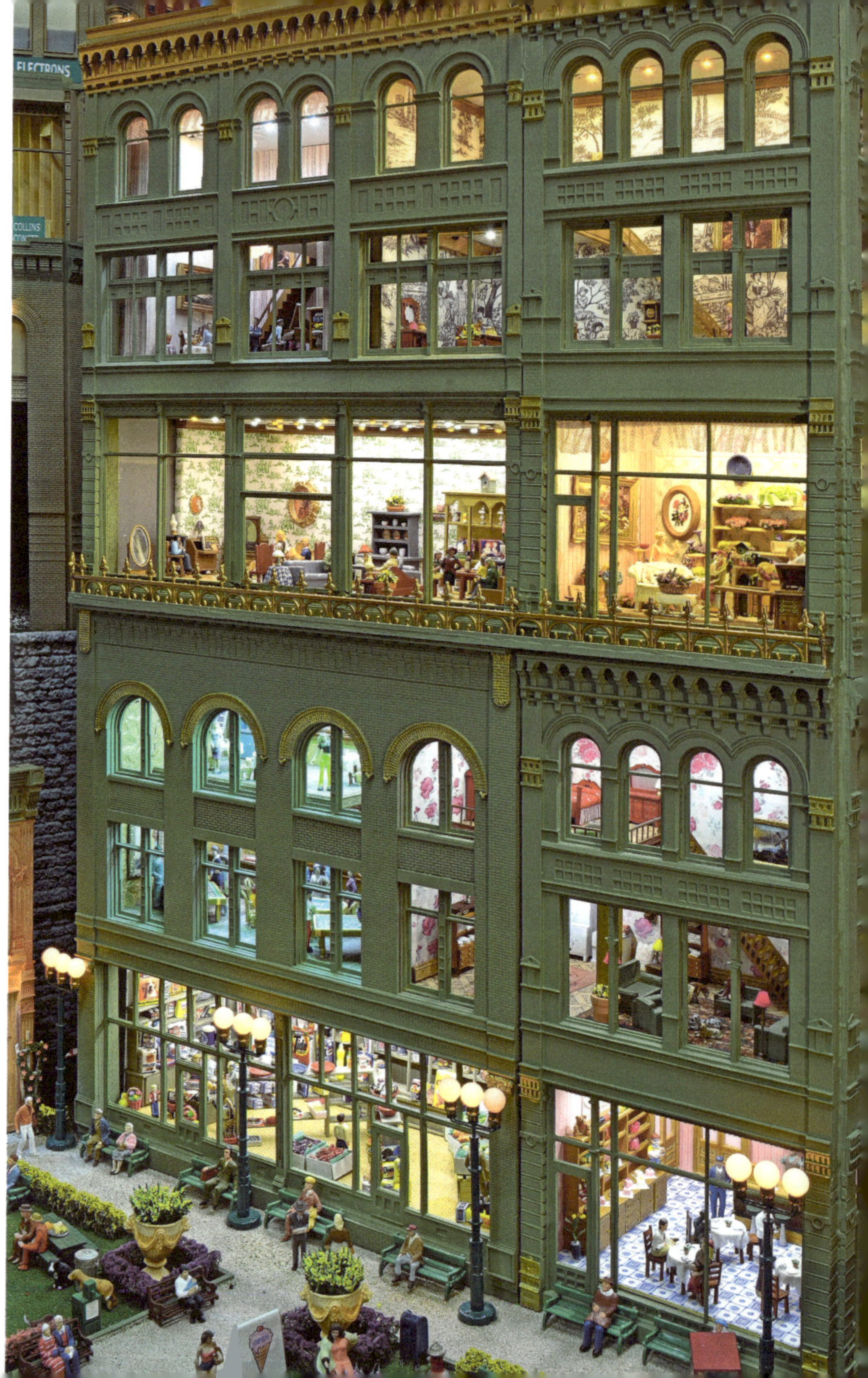

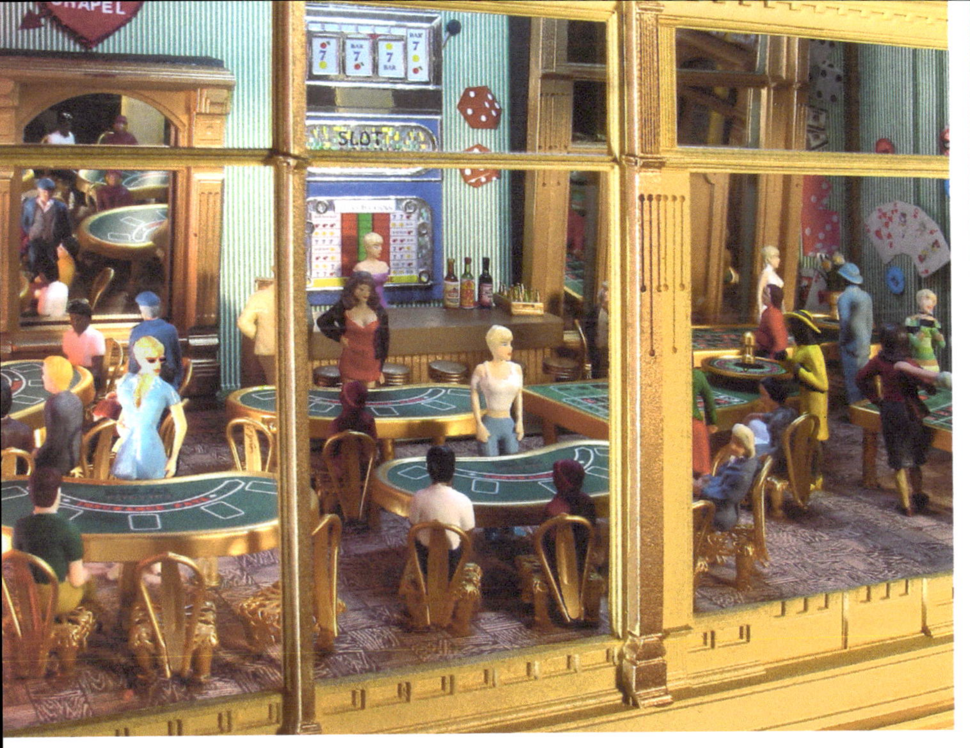

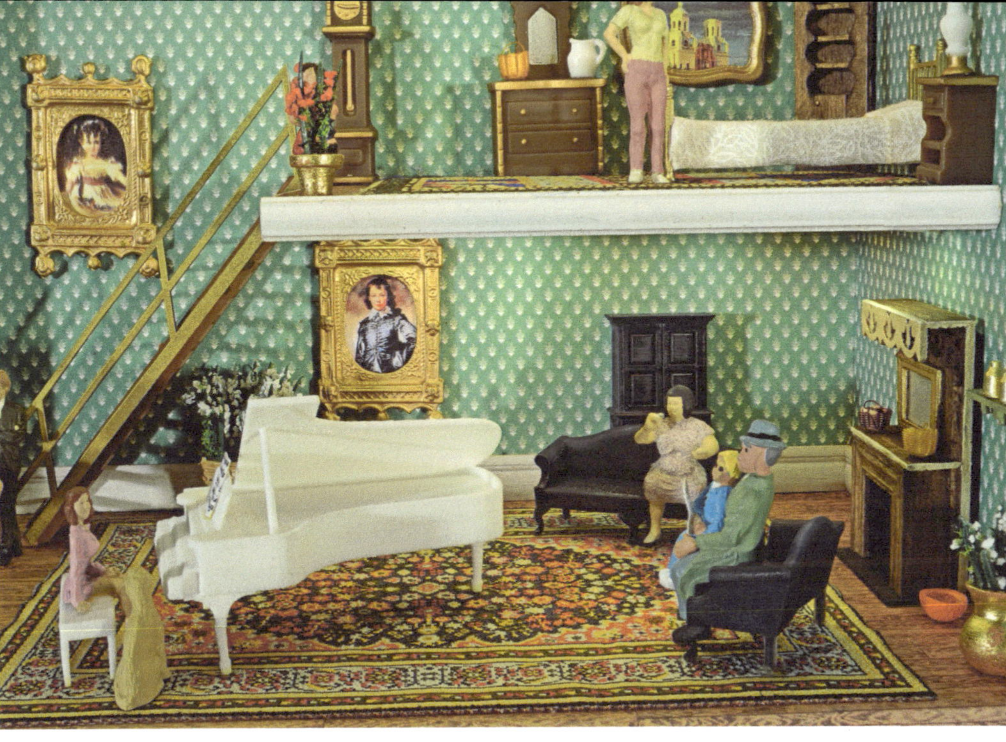

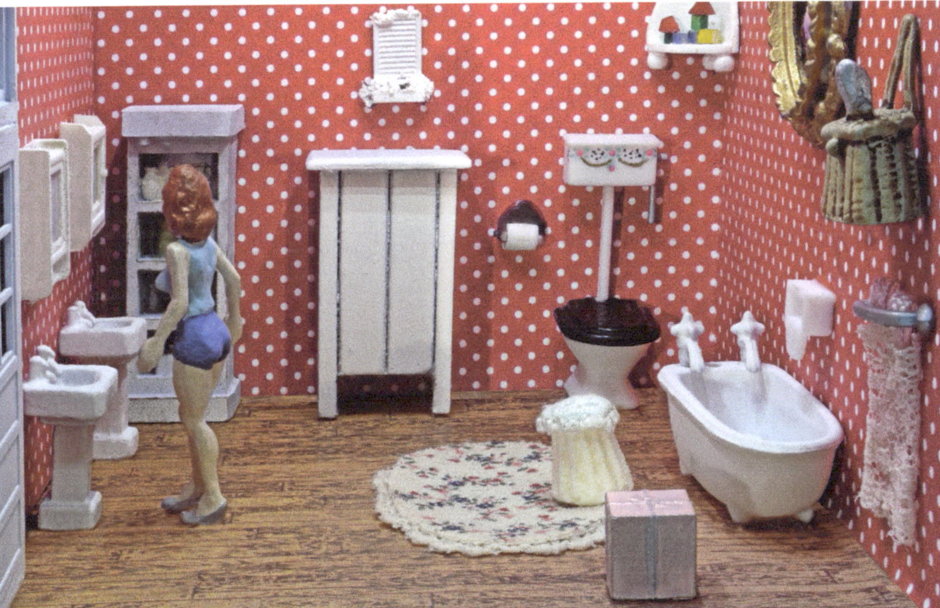

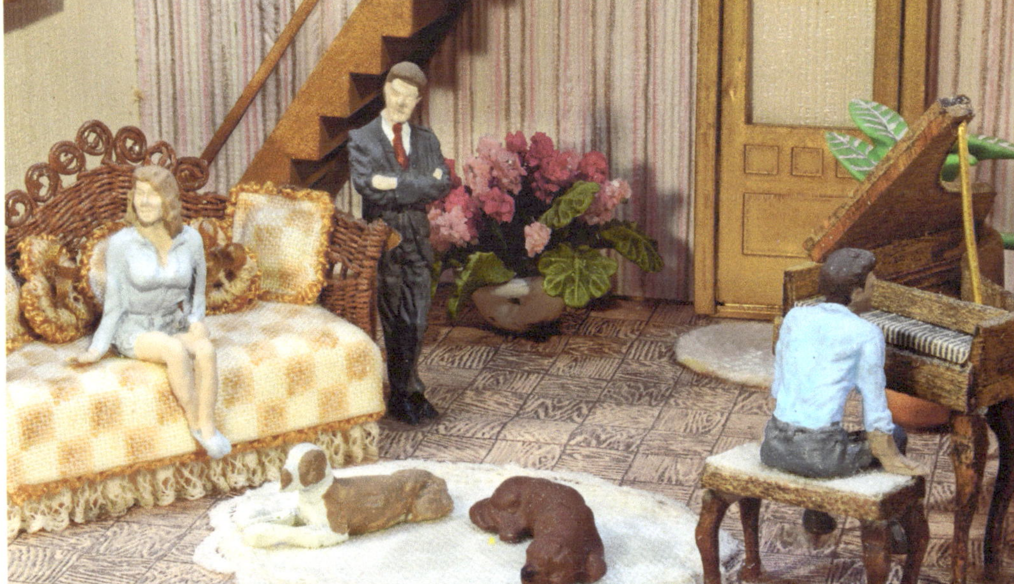

Detailed Interior Rooms

Shapeways 3D Printing company is a great source for O scale detail parts. The piano, sofas and highboy furniture in the Green Room are all Shapeways products.

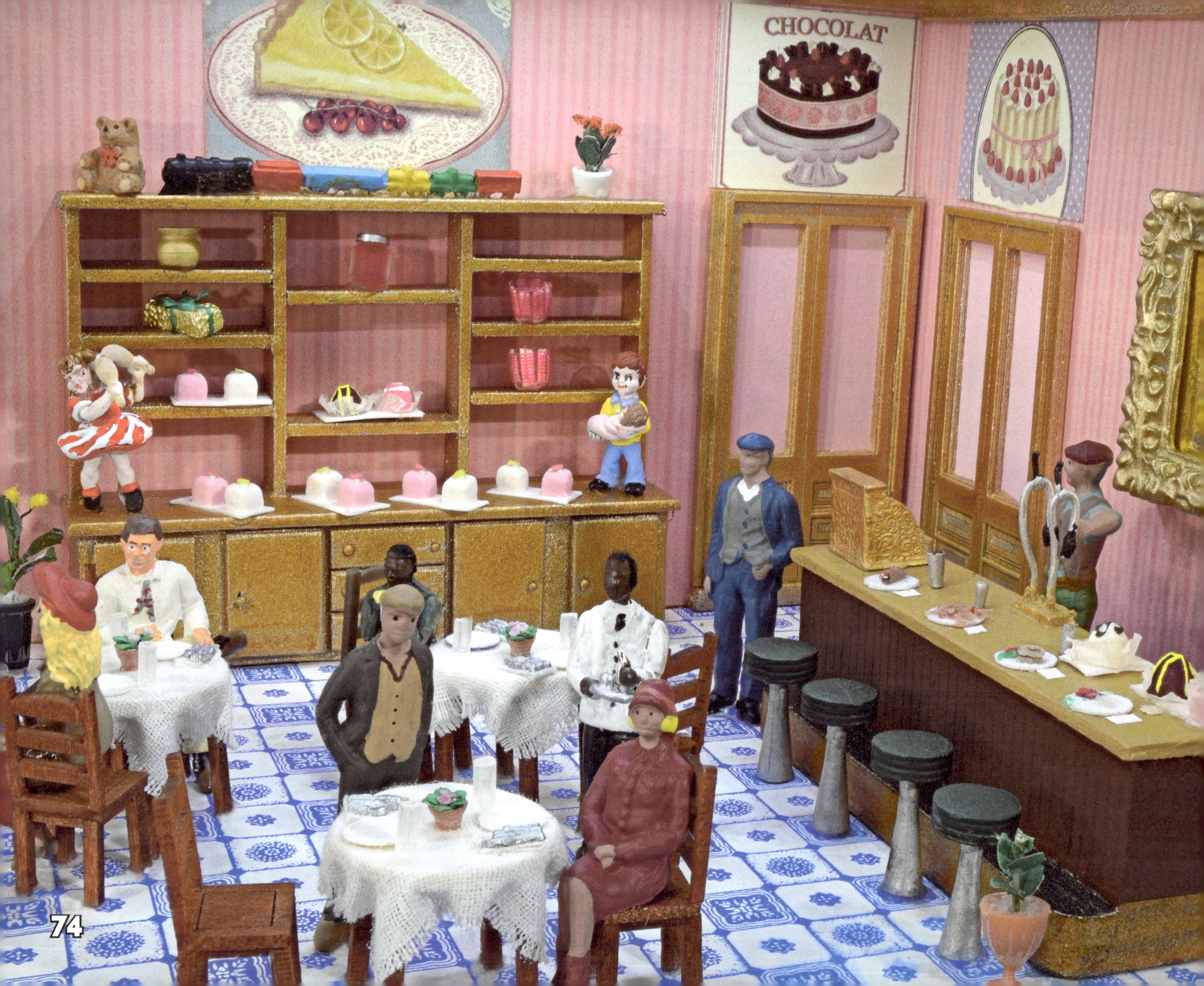
CHOCOLAT

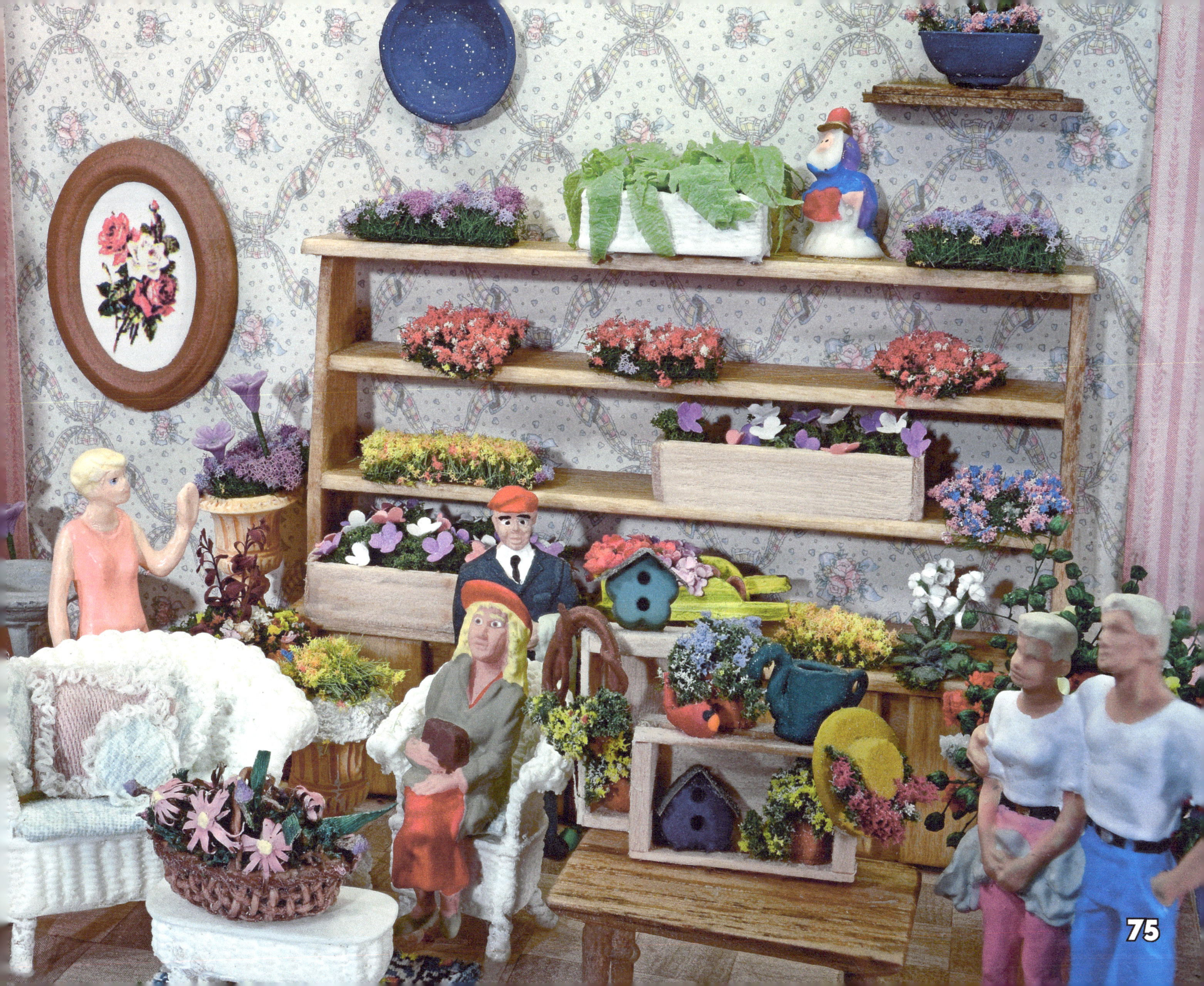

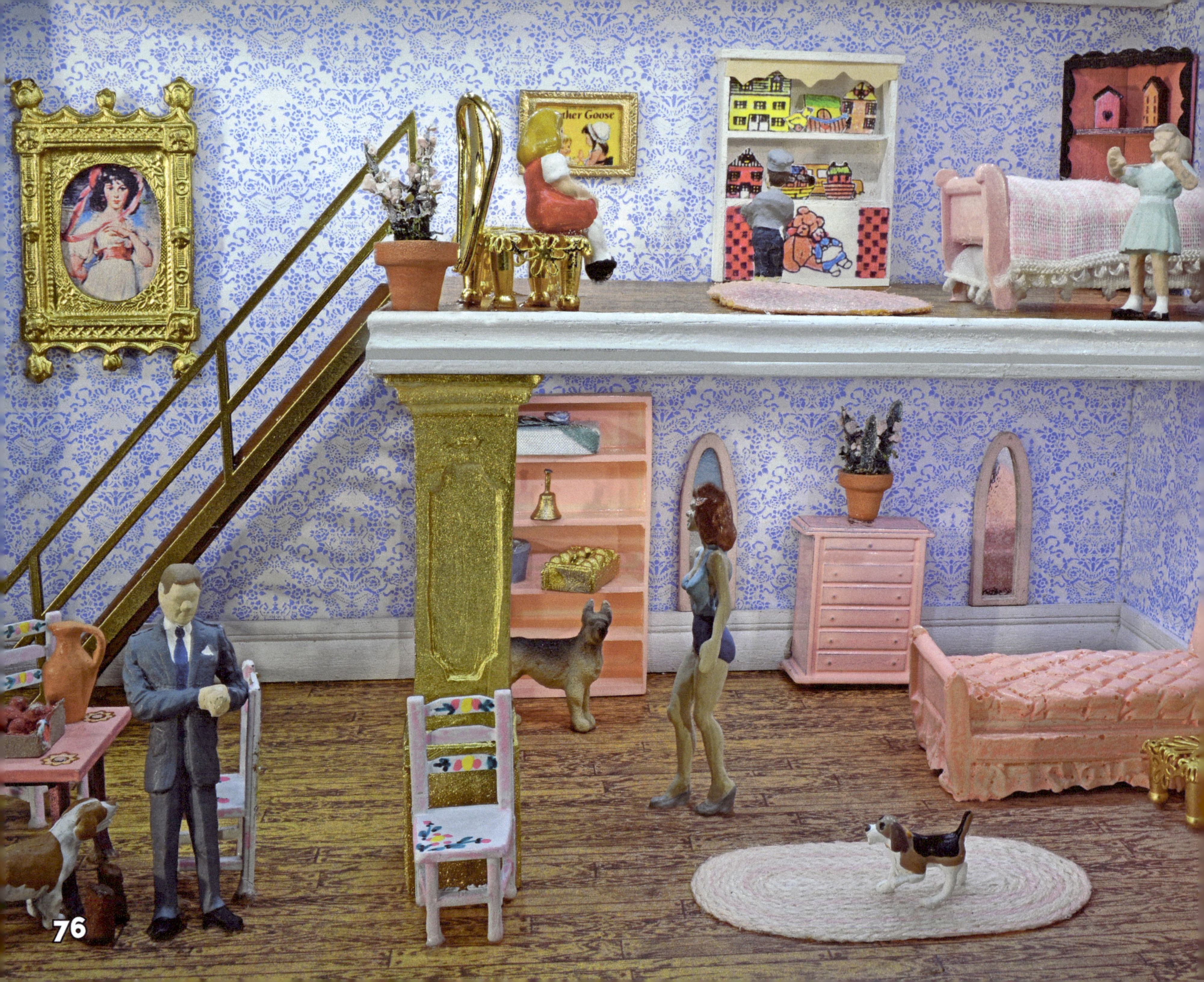

76

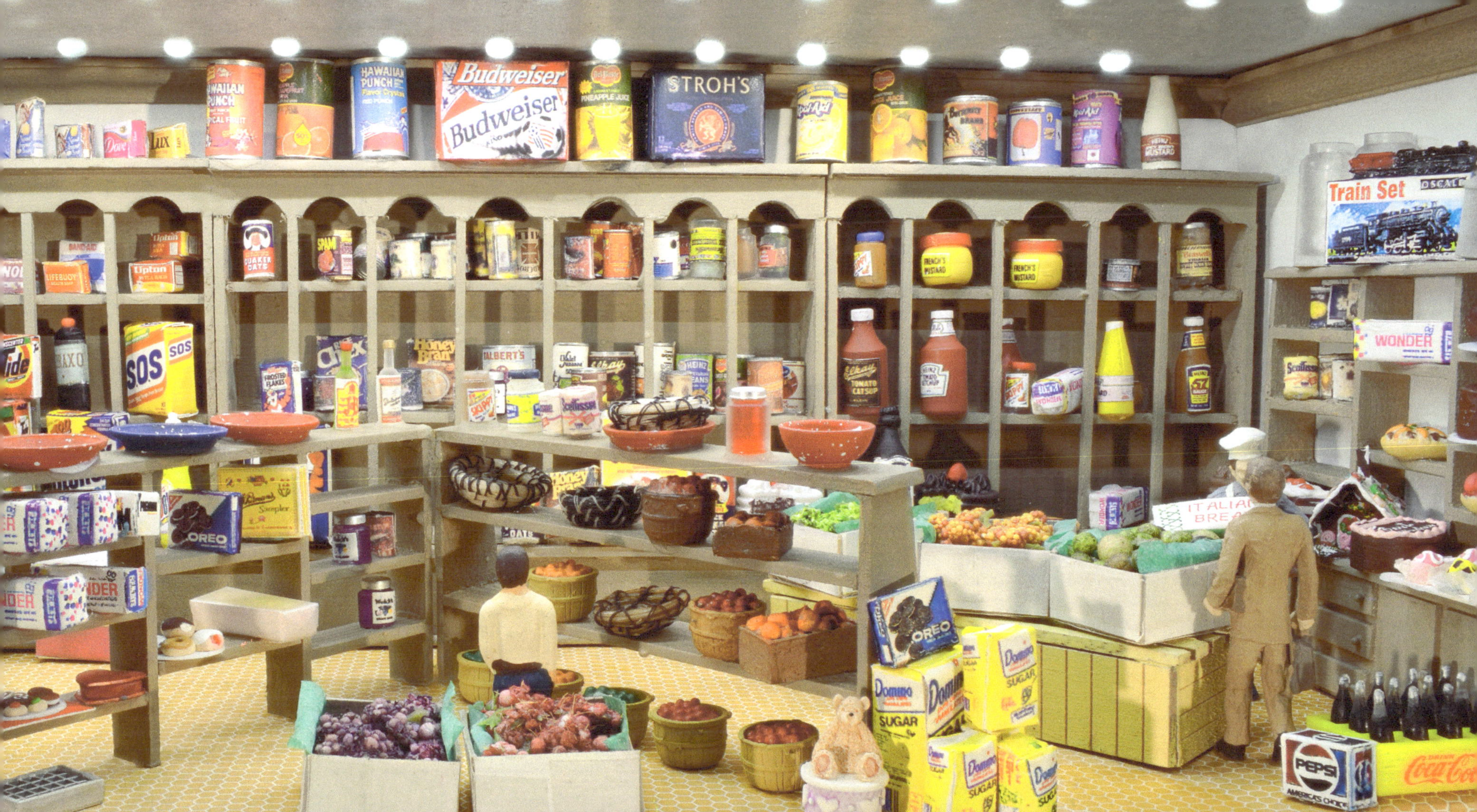

A *"Train Collector's Dream"* - Finding a Mint Train Set in An Old Store

This O scale model of an old general store presents a train collector's favorite dream. On the far right side of this photo, the man in the brown suit has found a new model train freight set high on a shelf next to the ceiling. Oh! It is his lucky day!

This general store is one of many interior furnished rooms on my O Scale Tower City train layout. The people, the cabinets, many of the produce items and boxes are O Scale or 1/4-inch to the foot. If I used only 1/4-inch O Scale items in my store scenes, you would not be able to identify the general theme of the scene because many quarter inch items are just too small. To fix that, I mix in 1/2-inch and 1-inch scale items with 1/4-inch O scale items. This makes many of the items easier to see. I have collected the items shown in this picture over the past 30 years. Scenic Express has many 1/4-inch scale items in their catalog and on their web site. I found the 1/2-inch and 1-inch scale items at dollhouse stores, miniature shows and by doing "Google" web searches. Good luck in your hunt!

TOWER CITY CONSTRUCTION REFERENCES

These model train manufacturers make the products which I used to build this model railroad.

MTH Electric Trains   mthtrains.com
Power source, operating system, engines and cars

GarGraves Track   gargraves.com

Ross Custom Switches   rossswitches.com

Scenic Express   sceneryexpress.com
Scenery, landscaping materials, miniature figures and furniture

Miller Engineering   microstru.com
Operating Neon signs, innovative lighting products

Innovative Train Technology   ittproducts.com
Sound modules

Korber Models   korbermodels.com
O Scale building supplies, kits and buildings

O Gauge Railroading   ogaugerr.com
O Gauge Railroading Magazine, AmeriTowne building kits

East Coast Enterprises   trainlayouts.com
Museum Quality Structures, bridges, trestles, and buildings

Walthers Model RR supply   walthers.com
General supply source for model railroad construction

Jack Pearce   jack_pearce4@sympatico.ca
Special lighting for autos, trucks, passenger cars

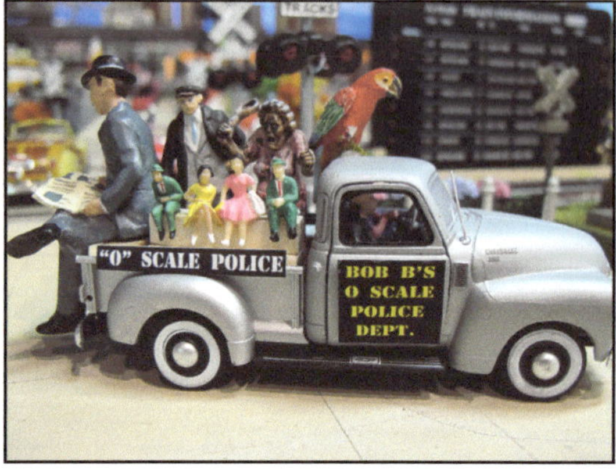

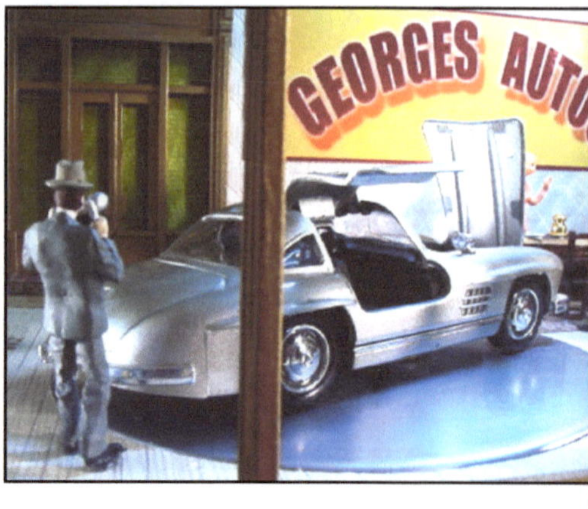

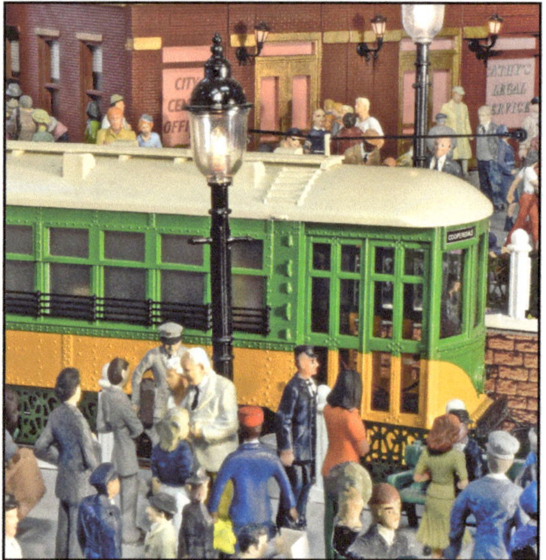

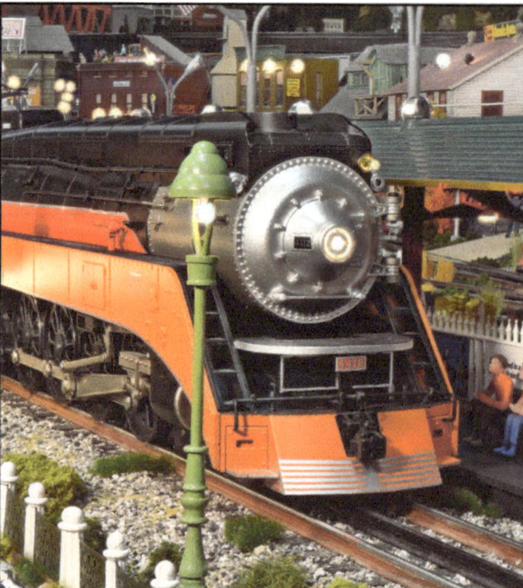

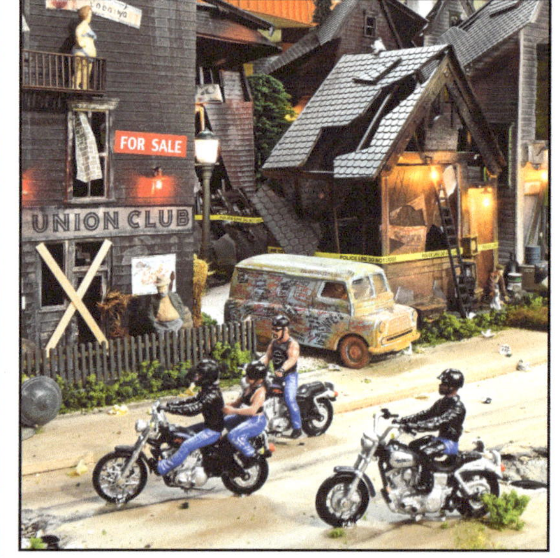

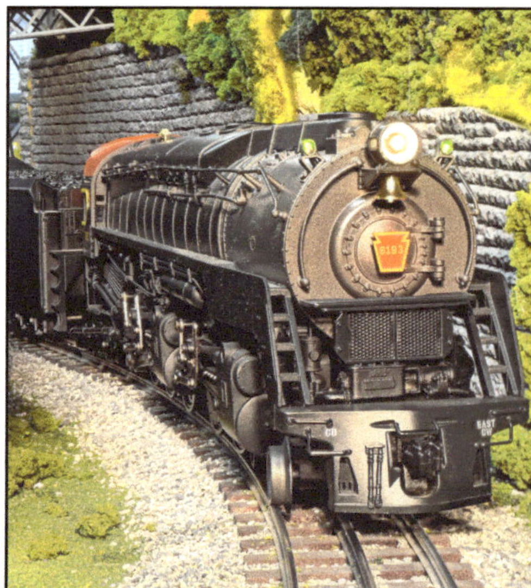

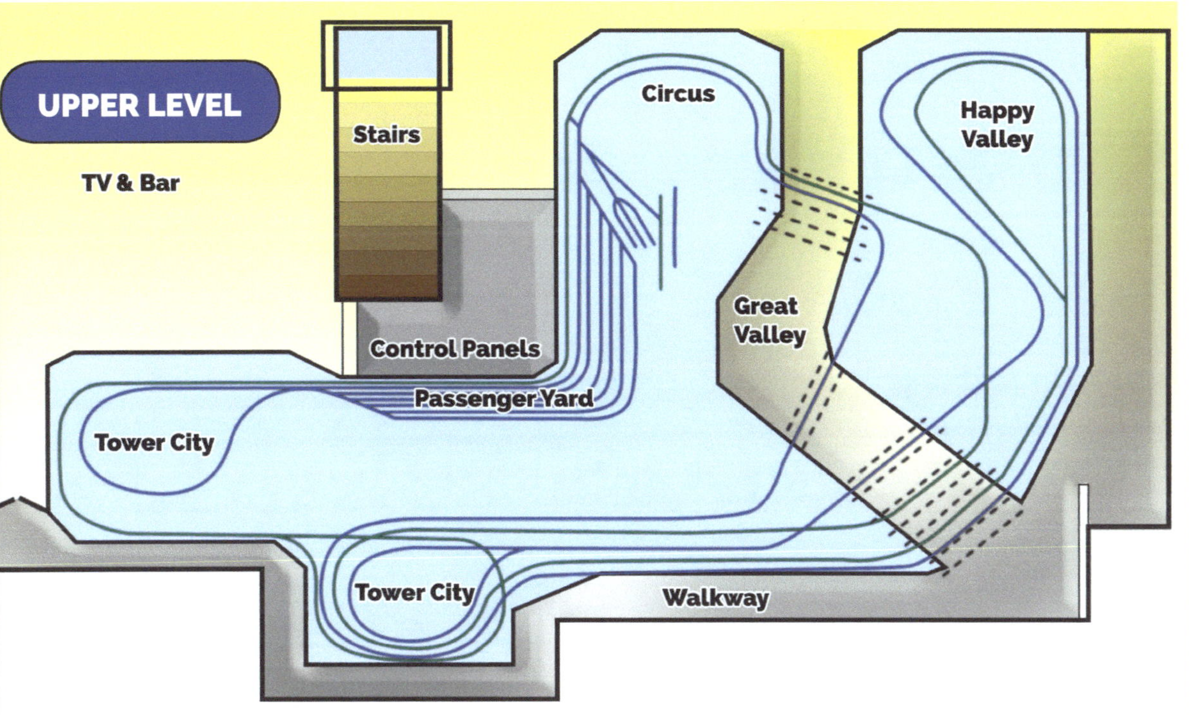

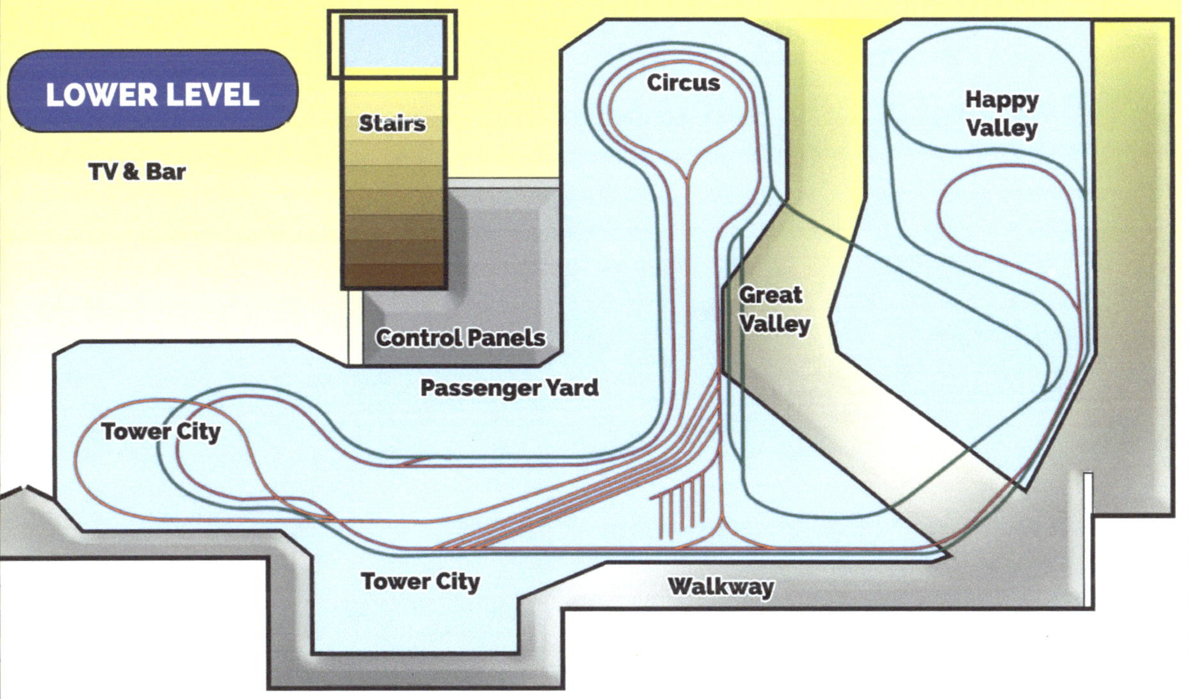

The Track Plan

My goal in designing this track plan was to make almost all the track visible from the operating platform. Unobstructed visibility of all the trains was priority number one in this design. I wanted kids and other visitors to be able to see <u>all</u> the action. I also wanted to mimic the multiple track levels you see in and around Chicago.

On my previous layout, tunnels and mountains dominated the scene. As the trains ran around the layout, they disappeared for long periods of time as they ran through the tunnels or behind the mountains. The kids lost interest or they cranked up the speed until the train was visible again. That resulted in problems from excessively high speeds.

I also wanted the bridges, trestles and elevated tracks to be an important and eye-catching attraction.

I built into the plan several passenger and freight sidings that are plainly visible from almost anywhere in the room.

I also took the advice of some of my friends who know and understand real railroading by building multiple engine sidings near the yards in order to switch out engines.

The end result is a very visually attractive, easy to run layout that kids of all ages enjoy!

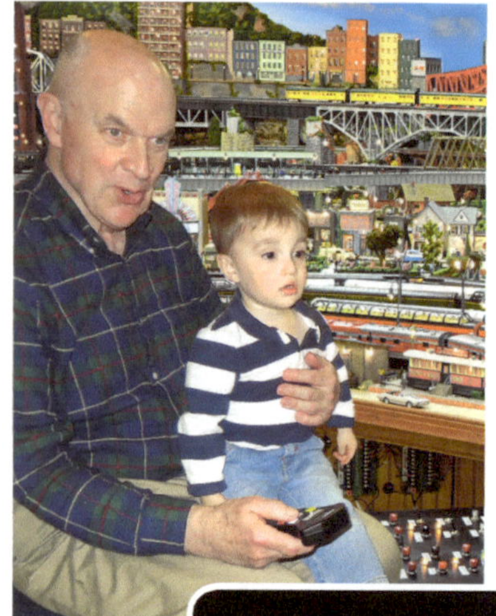
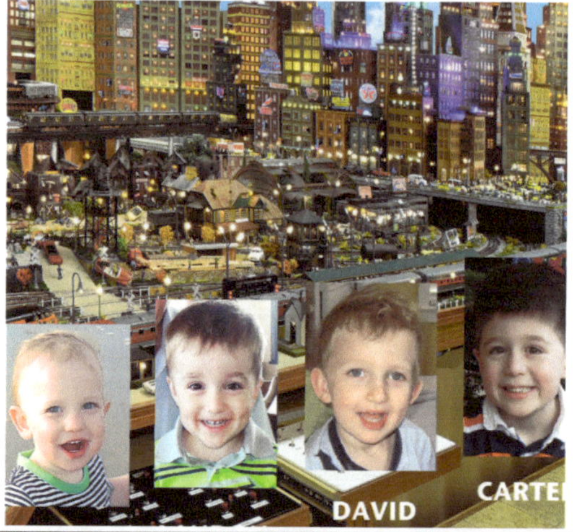

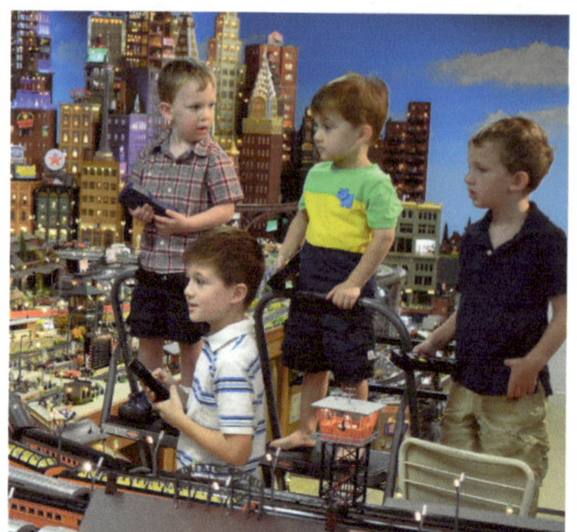
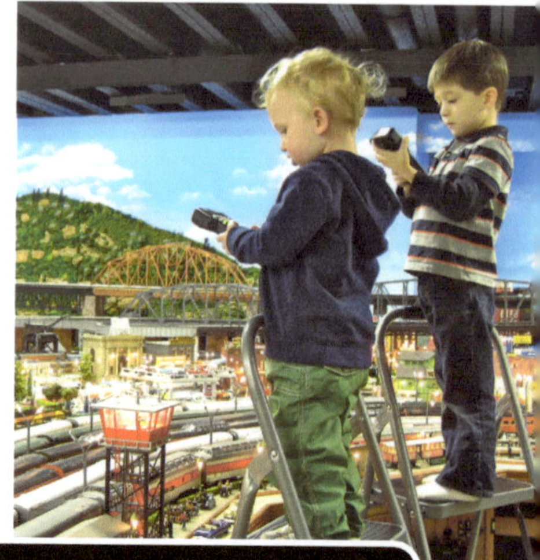

TOWER CITY TRAINS IS DEDICATED TO MY FOUR GRANDSONS

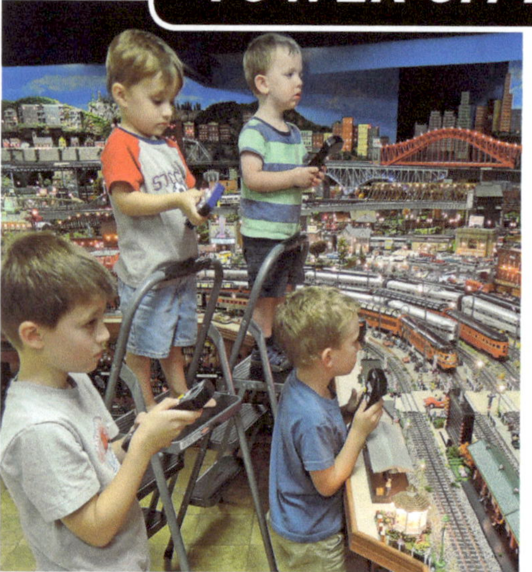
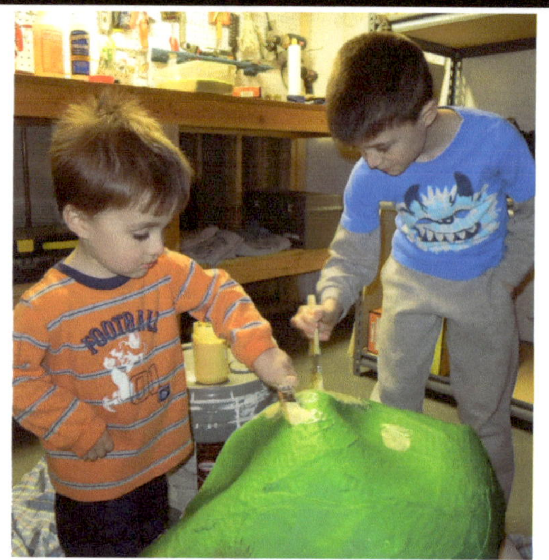
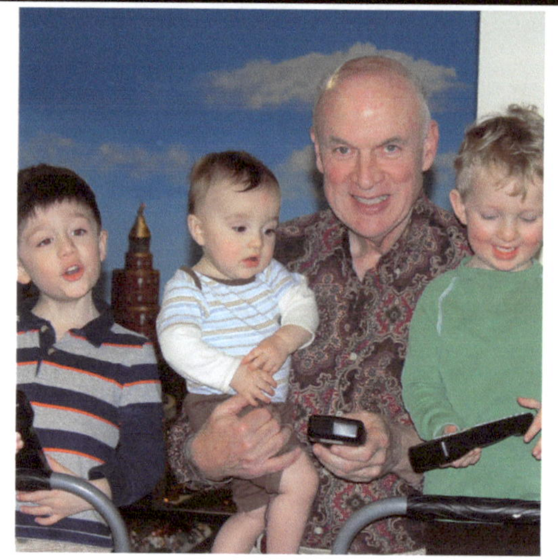
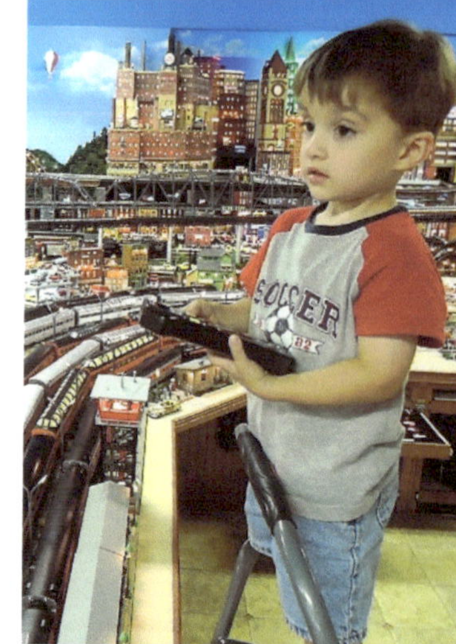

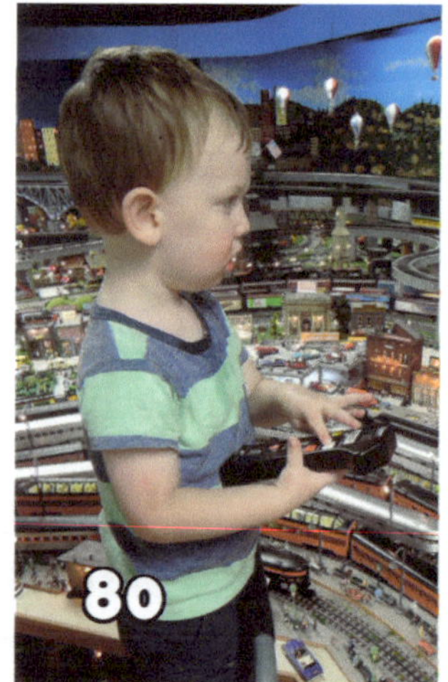

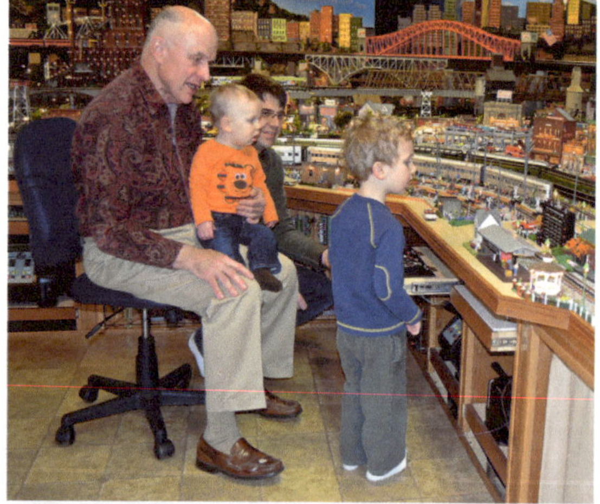
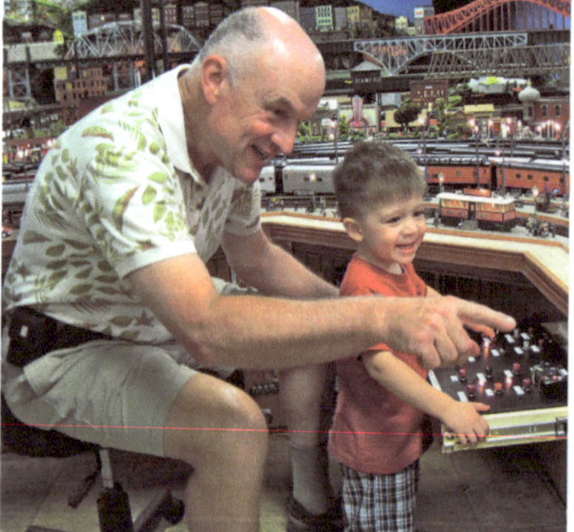
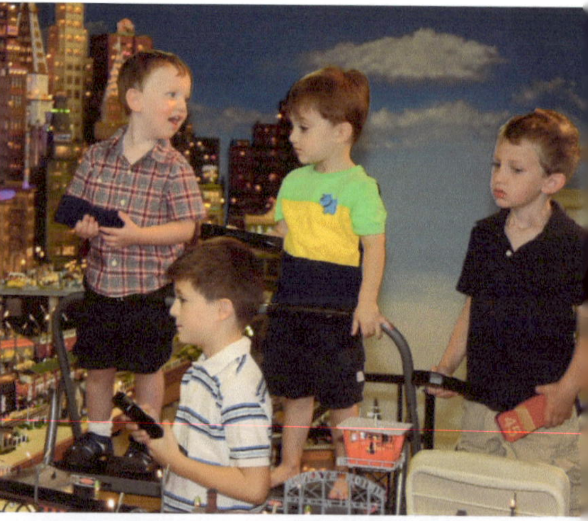